Nottingham

Uniform with this volume

SOUTHAMPTON *A. Temple Patterson*

In preparation

READING *Alan Wykes*

GUILDFORD *E. R. Chamberlin*

CHELTENHAM *Simona Pakenham*

NORWICH *A. P. Baggs*

NEWCASTLE *David Bean*

LEICESTER *Jack Simmons*

Nottingham

A BIOGRAPHY

Geoffrey Trease

Macmillan

© Geoffrey Trease 1970

First published in 1970 by
MACMILLAN AND CO LTD
Little Essex Street London WC2
and also at Bombay Calcutta and Madras
Macmillan South Africa (Publishers) Pty Ltd Johannesburg
The Macmillan Company of Australia Pty Ltd Melbourne
The Macmillan Company of Canada Ltd Toronto
St Martin's Press Inc New York
Gill and Macmillan Ltd Dublin

Printed in Great Britain by
WESTERN PRINTING SERVICES LTD
Bristol

Contents

For
Robert and Elizabeth
Leaney

List of Illustrations

List of Illustrations

The author and publishers wish to thank the following who have given permission for the photographs to be reproduced: British Holidays and Travel Association, 3b, 4a; J. Allan Cash, 2a; City Engineer, Nottingham, 1; Eagle Photos, Cheltenham, 16b; East Midlands Electricity Board, 15b; A. F. Kersting, 4b; Nottingham Castle Museum and Art Gallery, 3a, 11a; Nottingham City Publicity Department, 15a, 16a; Nottingham Historical Film Unit, 11b, 13a, 13b, 14a; Nottingham Public Libraries, 2b, 5, 6, 7a and b, 8a, 8b, 9a, 9b, 10, 12a, 12b; H. Tempest, 14b.

ACKNOWLEDGMENTS

My first debt is obviously to all those, whether professional historians or devoted amateurs, living or dead, without whose work there would be little material on which to base a book of this kind. My main obligations are indicated in the Select Bibliography, but many of the authorities there listed are themselves based on the efforts of countless forerunners to whom it is possible only to pay a general, but none the less grateful, gesture of homage.

My second debt is to all those who have given me help and encouragement, answering my questions and pointing out errors or omissions, for which (if any remain) I am of course solely responsible. I have to thank Mr Philip M. Vine, Town Clerk and Chief Executive Officer of Nottingham; the then City Librarian, Mr David E. Gerard, and Miss L. Edwards and Mr G. L. Roberts of the Department of Local History at the Central Library; Mr E. J. Laws, Art Director and Curator of the Castle Museum; Dr J. D. Chambers, Emeritus Professor of Economic History, University of Nottingham; Dr Malcolm I. Thomis, of the University of Stirling, who with a scholar's generosity allowed me a preview of his book, *Old Nottingham*; Mr M. W. Barley, Reader in Archaeology at the University of Nottingham, for a similarly kind preview of his article on Nottingham in M. D. Lobel's *Historic Towns*; Mr Emrys Bryson and Mr Gilbert Macklam, who have permitted me to quote liberally from their respective verses in *'Owd Yer Tight*; and finally – and most particularly – Mr K. S. S. Train, Honorary Secretary of the Thoroton Society, who read the manuscript and, through his comments, gave me the chance to tap his encyclopaedic knowledge of the town's past in all periods.

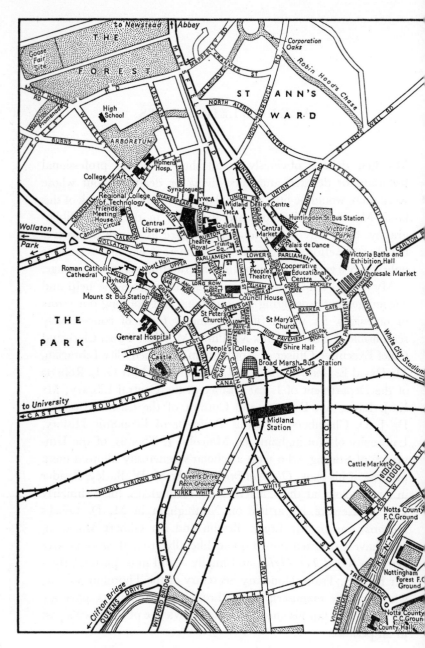

Nottingham Today

CHAPTER ONE

Personal Introduction

'You cannot conceive how beastly Nottingham is,' Hilaire Belloc wrote to Mrs Raymond Asquith in 1925. 'The town is like hell. I have known it for thirty-two years and it gets beastlier and beastlier.'

An odd quotation with which to open a frankly affectionate study of the place? But there is much to be said for getting the worst over, and though plenty of others have criticized my native city I doubt if any have been ruder than Belloc. He was a powerful writer but never an objective one, and God knows he had reason to lash out blindly just then. There he was, revered man of letters, named in one breath with Shaw and Wells, yet driven by financial need to produce publicity material for the new sugar-beet industry. Picture him stalking belligerently round the Colwick factory, bull-like head lowered, glowering at incomprehensible and detested machinery. What an employment for a man hailed by some as the greatest living master of English prose! All who have had to live by authorship will understand his eruption.

Everyone, in any case, has his personal view of a city. What brings people to Nottingham? For some it is a Test match at Trent Bridge, a cup-tie against Forest, or Colwick Races, for others a theatrical occasion at the Playhouse or a conference at the University. Others again come to choose rose-bushes, see a special Bonington exhibition in the Castle galleries, film a Lawrence story, follow up research on Byron, have fun at Goose Fair, or even, if they come from America, look for visible reminders of Robin Hood. Others again come upon their own affairs, the Assizes or a public inquiry or a private business negotiation. These probably have no view of the place, or time to think of anything outside their bulging brief-cases. To them Nottingham means simply a centre for regional boards and authorities, an area where bicycles, cigarettes, patent medicines, lace, hosiery and other eminently saleable goods are made.

Years ago I was talking to an old countrywoman in the Lake District. When she heard I came from Nottingham her eyes lit up at the memory of a visit paid at the turn of the century. 'What do you specially remember?' I asked, wondering if she would recall the shops or the crowds, Irving at the theatre or the electric trams. Without hesitation she said, 'All those bunches of prim-roses! Masses of them!' What had really delighted her Cumbrian eye was the display on the stalls of the vast open market, which survived until my own schooldays as the biggest in England.

So, to each of us his personal view – hell for Belloc, primroses for the old woman – and the same applies to the inhabitants, now close on a third of a million of them, but no two living, mentally and emotionally, in quite the same town. But that individual vision *can* be modified, widened, sharpened, by the lens of know-ledge. Otherwise there would be no point in books like this.

I have declared my interest: Nottingham born and bred. My first nineteen years were spent there. Not a year has passed since without my going back. I have seen a lot of other places, and acquired some standards of comparison to save me, I hope, from those hyperboles of parochial pride that so amuse the cosmo-politan. Yet I do not delude myself that I can be detached, even forty years on. Who ever saw his own mother with detachment? You either look back in anger or you write *con amore*. *Amore* always came more naturally to me.

Nevertheless, Whistler's portrait of his mother was not pre-sumably unrecognizable to other people. Subjectivity is no bar to fair representation. Only, it must be allowed for.

Nottingham lies just north of the Trent. Visitors were more aware of this when Trent Bridge provided the normal road-approach from London and the South. Now, if they use the M.1,

motorists enter from the west, as do most railway travellers, and
there is no dramatic awareness that they have crossed the broad
river which draws such a significant line across England. For, if
there is one particular place where you can say with any meaning,
'This is where the South ends and the North begins,' it is on Trent
Bridge.

Failing that symbolic and historical approach, there is much
to be said for the railway passenger's first view as he glides the
last mile from Derby, where he will inevitably have changed
whether he started from Edinburgh or Penzance. The motorist
who has just turned off the M.1 approaches from much the same
direction, but will see little but traffic-signs. From the train,
though, there is a panorama of the University with its slender
tower, the low green ridge of the Highfields campus rising from its
lake, and then another ridge densely covered with red brick and
blue slate, a first indication that this city is as hilly as Rome but
not as beautiful. Over there is the Nottingham of *Saturday Night
and Sunday Morning* with the drab box-shaped Castle on its
dramatic sandstone bluff, just as Alan Sillitoe described it: 'Castle
Rock, a crowned brownstone shaggy lion-head slouching its big
snout out of the city, poised as if to gobble up uncouth suburbs
hemmed in by an elbow of the turgid Trent.'

Sillitoe's hero, Arthur Seaton, was stirred to even more than his
usual cantankerousness by the mere sight of this landmark. He felt
it was 'sneering' at him. 'I hate that castle, he said to himself,
more than I've ever hated owt in my life before, and I'd like to
plant a thousand tons of bone-dry T.N.T. in the tunnel called
Mortimer's Hole, and send it to Kingdom Cum, so's nob'dy 'ud
ever see it again.' How far this resentment is shared by the citizens
is doubtful. Lawrence's characters in *The White Peacock* enjoyed
the castle. They 'stood on the high rock in the cool of the day, and
watched the sun sloping over the great river-flats', before turning
to explore the picture galleries and listen to the band playing in
the grounds. There is a similar passage in *Sons and Lovers*, where
Clara and Paul use their lunch-break to climb up and lean on the
parapet, listening to the cooing of the pigeons.

Today, something like six hundred thousand people pass

through the gate each year, so it is hard to see how Arthur Seaton's explosion would enhance the happiness of the masses. When the independent-minded citizens wanted to burn the Castle, they went and did so, after what they felt to be sufficient provocation. Then, in the fullness of time, they took over the blackened shell and turned it into the first municipal art museum in England. That was more truly the Nottingham way – a zigzag graph of violent protest followed by constructive progress – than Seaton's anarchic fantasy.

Ordinarily the man in the street takes a quiet, unsentimental pride in the town's past. I was prowling round the old Lace Market one morning, admiring the flaked façade of an eighteenth-century house now stranded among the Victorian warehouses: a car-park attendant materialised from nowhere and besought me not to miss the nearby stabling of a mansion that had stood there when this was a fashionable quarter. An hour later I was in the ancient Salutation Inn: it was a lorry-driver who pointed out the door leading down to the cave cellars, which can be visited if you ask the landlord.

Even when Nottingham really *was* hell for many of its inhabitants – in the Luddite town, for instance, of Byron's day – there was this affection for the past. John Blackner, the self-educated framework knitter and radical leader, with as much righteous indignation as the next man, still found time and heart in 1816 to write his *History of Nottingham*.

Any self-respecting topographical book should start with geology, which many of us find sadly deterrent.

Still, anyone can see that the city is founded on sandstone. There is the tawny precipice of the Castle Rock. Wherever the foundations of a new office-block are being gouged out, the same dry honey-coloured stone is revealed. Rock cellars, some developed from natural caves, underlie the city everywhere, admirable for the storage of strong liquor and other valuables. When in Victorian times the High School wished to enlarge its new buildings, it did not extend upwards or sideways but downwards, paring away its playground so that the cellars, when provided

with windows, became the classrooms of a fresh ground-floor. The
original blue-brick damp-course can still be seen, ten feet up the
walls.

Two of these little sandstone hills, rising from the small River
Leen and its adjacent marshes about a mile north of the Trent,
were the historical nucleus of the town. But there are other hills
and ridges behind, over which the suburbs have gradually extended. As Professor K. C. Edwards wrote, introducing the region
to the British Association assembled at Nottingham in 1966:
'Northwards from the city, the roads to Mansfield (A.60) and
Ollerton (A.614) lead over a sandstone formation known as the
Bunter Sandstone which presents a surface of broad undulations
which are reflected in the switchback nature of the roads themselves. . . .' Switchback, indeed – though nobody now can experience the full switchback sensation imparted by the electric trams
as they hurtled up and down those hills when I was a boy. Richard
Hoggart has splendidly described such trams as 'the gondolas of
the people', and in the Nottingham context his phrase acquires an
extra evocative quality. For the gondolas I knew in the nineteen
twenties were not the real ones gliding quietly over the Venetian
lagoon but the garish, rackety cars of the merry-go-rounds at
Goose Fair, surging and plunging to the ear-splitting blare of the
steam organ. The everyday Corporation trams were less flamboyant, but as they thundered down from the heights of Mapperley or took their undulating way to Arnold they were quite an
exciting form of transport, especially if you shut yourselves up in
the little curved-fronted alfresco compartment above the driver's
head.

Today, I suppose, those switchback roads mean little to the
average motorist. Only the local young, if they still ride bicycles,
can feel the alternative anguish and exhilaration of the gradients.

'The thin, poor soil,' went on Professor Edwards, 'so loose in
dry weather that strong winds carry it from the fields in dust
clouds (hence the term "blowing sands") does not encourage cultivation without special treatment. . . . These conditions provided
the ecological basis for the ancient forest of Sherwood. . . .'

That, too, chimes in with my early memories: the gritty dust storms that turned the playground into a little Sahara, the bald brown patches on the too-well-trodden slopes of the adjacent park, and a residential neighbourhood still known as 'Lenton Sands'.

This is not the whole story. There is 'the high ground called Mapperley Plains to the north-east', representing 'the escarpment of the Keuper Series', which the Professor defined as 'a considerable thickness of Red Marl underlain by sandstone called Waterstones. . . . The Marl itself assumes the character of a stiff reddish clay.' Now this much geology even I can grasp and relate to my own experience. For my father, a wine merchant by occupation but a countryman by instinct, lacking an adequate garden at our house in the middle of the town, rented one on the Hunger Hills. These Corporation gardens were steeply terraced plots, bowered in tall secretive hedges and entered by padlocked gates like doors. Historically they had been burgess parts, as medieval in origin, I suppose, as any strip of ploughland. Their heavy red clay produced the superb old-fashioned roses that were my father's joy. The clay I remember – my conscript journeys to The Garden were not always enthusiastically undertaken – but the wider significance was lost upon me. I had no idea then that the common lands had been known throughout history as 'the Clay Field' and 'the Sand Field', or that a saying had grown up in Stuart times, when the brickyards started and new houses began to replace the half-timbered sort, that 'Nottingham once stood on Mapperley Hills'.

Southwards lies a different landscape. 'The Trent valley', wrote Professor Edwards, 'has the form of a shallow trench . . . well over a mile wide, bordered by slopes of Keuper Marl, which are often steep enough to form cliffs, as at Radcliffe-on-Trent. These slopes are frequently clad with fine deciduous woods, as at Clifton Grove across the river from Nottingham.' Yet another geological area begins when the Trent is left behind, with the bus termini and the last houses which, if not within the city boundary, are in most practical senses part of Nottingham, and the roads climb over the Wolds into Leicestershire. This plateau 'is formed by a sheet of glacial boulder clay . . . a fragment of the great mantle of similar material which extends far across eastern England'.

There, then, is the setting with its geological basis: a broad river winding smoothly through a broad vale, and a nexus of little hills and ridges, the highest scarcely more than four hundred feet above sea-level, yet with enough steep ups and downs, and even a precipice, to produce an element of drama. It was a fine rolling landscape once, with the blue distances of Sherwood Forest fading away northwards. But now its natural contours are shrouded under the eighth largest city in England, and for the real geography, like the history, you have to grope and probe.

In the Castle art gallery you can see a watercolour done by Turner about 1830. It is a lively, picturesque scene, showing crowded sailing-boats on the River Leen. The Leen was – is – one hardly knows which to say – a tributary of the Trent, flowing west to east past the base of the Castle Rock, which is the background of the picture. Today, the Leen, which in 1883 was diverted into a canal and its original course filled in, would be as hard to follow as the lost rivers of London. And this is typical.

All your life you take a city for granted. Then you have to describe it to strangers, and you hesitate.

When I began to plan this book I had to go back to Nottingham and *look* at the place, as I suppose I had not looked at it since I was a boy. There were the things I remembered, and the things that had changed, and the things that had always been there but had been unknown and unregarded in the old days.

Much of the town and many of the changes are what you see everywhere else today. Giant packets of flats transform the skyline: not enough space now for those leafy council-house estates that were Nottingham's pride in the nineteen twenties, drawing respectful experts from afar. The multiple shops multiply. There are more and more shoe-shops. One has displaced the independent bookseller's where I chose my first books and learned to browse as well as buy. Books, alas, do not keep the till ringing continually as footwear does. The solid homely cafés, with their solid homely waitresses, have gone over increasingly to self-service. On the other hand, Chinese and Indian restaurants proliferate, and Italy contributes an elegant *trattoria*. All this you will see anywhere, like traffic wardens, pedestrian subways, launderettes and Jamaican bus-conductors. You could be in Birmingham or a dozen other provincial cities. This is the late twentieth century and it comes in a standardized wrapper. You have to look deeper for the differences.

I walked up Castle Gate and saw the ghost of what was fashionable Nottingham in the eighteenth century. Some fine Georgian houses survive, once the town residences of leading county families. At the top end, now preserved as a cobbled pedestrian-precinct, stands Newdigate House, where Marshal Tallard spent seven years of honourable captivity after surrendering to Marlborough at Blenheim: it is said that he taught the Nottingham bakers to make French rolls, introduced the cultivation of celery in his garden, and (if you can believe Defoe's sly innuendo) left other souvenirs of his stay in the town. Round the corner in St James's Street, I found the house where Byron lodged as a boy. Crossing the road towards the General Hospital, I read again the inscription on the wall which I had often pondered as a history-loving child: it indicates the spot where, on 22 August 1642, Charles I set up his standard and began the Civil War. All this in a five-minute stroll from the shopping-centre – and I had still to go through the Castle gateway, where three-quarters of our medieval kings had preceded me at one time or another.

History and business go ill together, except in small tourist-places. In Nottingham, as in London, the visible relics represent only a fraction of the events that have taken place. But there are enough old buildings and other vestiges to give the centre individuality. It is not all car-parks and cafeterias.

The Castle is the best viewpoint – the roof is not open to the public, but the gallery windows and the parapet of the grounds offer good prospects. I saw how the skyline had altered since I used to sit on the battlemented terrace of the school tower, outside the prefects' room, watching the dome of the new Council House rise slowly amid its scaffolding to dominate the city. Now, from the Castle, I saw how monstrous office-blocks were rising to challenge that domination. St Mary's fifteenth-century tower was still the prominent landmark it had always been, but Holy Trinity spire had gone, and the whole church with it, to make room for a multi-storey car-park. In the distance I was glad to see a dark, squat cone, which would surely puzzle a stranger: it was the stump of Sneinton windmill, still holding its hilltop in the eastern quarter of the city. There was a time when the windmills stood ranged along the skyline of Nottingham in an array that might have daunted Don Quixote himself. So, the skyline is not what it was, but at least the city *has* a skyline, thanks to the hills.

On the other side of the Castle lies the Park – once the King's Park, then the Duke of Newcastle's, and now simply The Park developed in Victorian times as an exclusive residential area. Here dwelt the carriage folk, building themselves pretentious *palazzi* of sometimes hideous elaboration. Cecil Roberts has recalled, in his autobiography *The Growing Boy*, how its splendours impressed him in the early nineteen hundreds, when its vast houses were kept up as they needed to be, by rich men like Jesse Boot the druggist, Bowden of Raleigh cycles, the Player brothers, Birkin and the tycoons of the lace trade. 'England has no lovelier residential quarter,' says Roberts, 'secluded, sylvan, yet built into the heart of the city.' That claim seems to me, having a poor appetite for Victoriana, almost as steep as the drives and crescents with which the hillside is laid out. I wish it had been developed in a better period, even thirty years before, when a line of more restrained villas did begin to creep along the adjacent ridge. But its proximity to the heart of the city *is* a wonderful thing. My private criterion for an ideal civilized life is that you should be able to walk, as in ancient Athens, from your home to the theatre. This you can do from the Park. When I stayed there recently with a friend we were able to walk down to the Playhouse in a quarter of an hour, dine agreeably in its restaurant, gay with red table-cloths and ancient playbills, and meander back in the moonlight by way of Park Steps.

The Park, as any old snob will tell you, is not what it was, what with nurses' hostels, houses divided up into manageable units, and the quite impossible mansions swept away in favour of flats with picture windows and sun balconies. But the trees, the silence and the dramatic declivities are unchanged. If I could live where I liked in Nottingham it would be in this 'splendid amphitheatre', as Roberts calls it, but in one of the smallest, gayest, most democratic of those new cliff-hanging flats, within a mile of theatres, concert-hall, bookshop, library, and everything that urban life can give.

That was how I grew up, not in the grandeur of the Park, admittedly, but just as centrally – ten minutes' walk 'down town' to queue for the gallery at the Theatre Royal or listen to the Sunday evening orators in the Market Place, and five minutes' breathless climb in the other direction, as the High School bell clanged its summons from the crest of the hill. Lawrence had climbed that hill, answered that summons, just twenty years before me, but as a 'train boy', whose tiresome daily journey from Eastwood probably did his health no good. 'The English are town-birds, through and through,' he was to write later. 'Yet they don't know how to build a city, how to think of one, or how to live in one.' I wonder if he would have softened his judgement if his schooldays had been more like mine?

I went recently to look at the house where I was born. It means little to me; I have no memories because we moved six months later, and I was not sure, till I found it, that it would still be standing. There has been radical rebuilding in that area and one adjacent street has vanished completely, for it is near the mountainous new Regional College of Technology, whose surmounting mast and aerial require an aircraft warning-light. But Chaucer Street was still there, quietly curving up the hillside, and Number Thirteen, now like me a little faded, still stood sideways to the street, looking across the garden at Numbers Fifteen and Seventeen. For the first time in my life I lifted the latch of the gate that served all three houses and stepped inside for a closer view, nerved to justify my intrusion if challenged. But I saw nobody, and to be honest I felt nothing.

Chaucer Street runs off Goldsmith Street, and Shakespeare Street is not far away. All this region, built over in the second half of the nineteenth century, is named like an outline of English Literature, with a few other worthies like Peel and Hampden thrown in. The inclusions and omissions may reflect the prejudices of the committee, or perhaps of one well-read and dominating member, who planned and christened the streets in the eighteen fifties. You can find Addison, Dryden, Southey and Tennyson, but not Byron or Shelley, though Burns slipped in, doubtless because the committee did not know enough about his private life. Scott is missing, but he is represented by the graceful sweep of Waverley Street, a rare case of a street named after a novel. Some of the lesser streets carry the appropriate Christian names, Oliver at right-angles to Cromwell Street, and Walter to Raleigh Street, where in a small workshop the famous bicycle was born.

Walking away from my own birthplace I was made curious by the sight of young men and women on every other street-corner, busy with sketching-blocks and drawing-boards. I fell into conversation with a heavily bearded youth who was drawing the old cinema which had also been the first home of the Playhouse. Yes, he said, they were all students. They were after architectural detail and lettering. I told him what *I* was doing and we made the obvious remarks about the changing face of the city. 'You've seen the big hole?' he asked, jerking his head towards the Victoria Station. 'I must,' I said. And I thought how 'the big hole' symbolized the whole process of change we had been speaking of. They were just then removing – wiping off the face of the earth – the great railway station from which, forty years before, I had caught the train to Oxford for my first term and in essence (I see now) left home for ever. Barely thirty years before that, they had been digging the original big hole, cutting into the sandstone to make the tunnels and cuttings and the handsome station below street level, opened with all the touching optimism of 1900. A million pounds it cost, a staggering sum then, and it had not lasted a full human lifetime. Now there would be only the clock-tower, preserved as a 'feature', but no late passengers for it to bring scurrying the length of Shakespeare Street. The last train had most irrevocably gone.

I did not go to see the big hole after all – would it have been too much like looking down into the grave of youth? Anyhow, I really wanted to visit the Arboretum, the park which was so much a part of my childhood because it faced the end of the road where we lived. In his novel, *Harris' Requiem*, Stanley Middleton makes his hero 'walk in the frowsty park, past the Victorian busts and the Chinese pagoda, and watch the ducks on the pond behind the low, lurching railing'. I did not find it 'frowsty' even on a bleak afternoon with hardly a flower showing in the brown borders: in fact, it had been opened up a lot since the old days, by the clearance of dingy shrubberies. But 'frowsty' was, in the context, legitimate novelist's atmosphere, and Middleton is never concerned to flatter the city in which he lives and writes.

The Chinese 'pagoda' is strictly just an Oriental canopy from which used to hang a bell, looted from a Canton temple by the 45th Regiment of Foot (later the Sherwood Foresters) in 1857. The bell had gone now – looted again, or for safer custody? The four Sebastopol cannon still glowered from the corners of the plinth, but the neat stacks of grey cannon balls had vanished. Even in the nineteen twenties, when young people are not supposed to have done all the dreadful things they do today, I remember that those cannon balls were sometimes found scattered among the flower-beds below. Now the temptation is no longer there.

But Feargus O'Connor's statue remained cleaned up and freed from the gloomy vegetation that once obscured it. I used to spell out its inscription without in the least understanding who he had been or the cause he had stood for. What a whiff of a bygone age it brings back – when a Member of Parliament could earn a statue 'erected by his admirers'!

That statue, for me, typifies the odd charm of Nottingham. Amid all the businesslike bustle and materialism of a modern city the history still peeps through in unexpected places. The fullness of that history surprises many strangers, and for that matter many of the natives. The best thing now seems to be to look at it, in straightforward sequence, from the earliest days.

CHAPTER TWO

The House of Caves

BRONZE AGE fishermen paddled canoes on the Trent where today white-vested oarsmen hold regattas. That is not romantic surmise. Two thirty-foot dug-out canoes, discovered after more than two thousand years in gravel-beds within a mile or so of Trent Bridge, formed the nucleus round which the attractive little archaeological section of the Castle Museum was reconstructed in 1968. No sooner was the work begun, making the best use of precious space, than three more of these prehistoric craft turned up at Holme Pierrepont, one excellently preserved, indisputably interesting, but also embarrassingly lengthy. It was like being offered a third alligator for a tank designed for a pair.

It was, however, an impressive reminder that human settlement in this area began early. Smaller finds from similar gravel-beds – fragmentary tools, weapons and such-like – prove that it began much earlier. Where Nottingham spreads its streets today there were men living, off and on, from the Palaeolithic period onwards. By Bronze Age times the district was well populated. By the Iron Age there were several little forts to the north-east of the modern city. There may even have been one on the Castle Rock itself, where the Museum now stands.

It is tempting to picture an early Nottingham that was a colony of cavemen. That temptation should be resisted. True, the caves are there, real as the canoes. Nobody knows the full ramifications of subterranean Nottingham, for the underlying sandstone is one gigantic honeycomb, in which men have continually improved upon Nature. Several inns and business houses declare their readiness to give visitors a glimpse of the twilight world beneath their premises, and those seriously interested can, by inquiring at the City Information Bureau for the current addresses and facilities. enjoy a more extensive exploration. But the Nottingham caves have never been developed as show-places, for they are not wonderlands of beauty and mystery – there are no glistening stalactites or underground rivers – and they have not yielded sensationally ancient traces of human occupation.

Alfred the Great's friend and biographer, Asser, refers to Nottingham 'which is called in the British tongue, Tigguocabauc, or "house of caves" '. That was in A.D. 868. No one can be sure how ancient the British name was by then, still less when the caves were first regularly occupied, but in all later periods people have used the caves for storehouses and dwellings, for the sandstone is clean, dry and easy to cut. John Evelyn, staying a night in Nottingham in the summer of 1654, 'observed divers to live in the rocks and caves, much after the manner as about Tours, in France', and there were Nottingham troglodytes at least as recently as Victoria's Diamond Jubilee, occupying caves at Sneinton with neat window-frames set in the rock face. Dame Laura Knight, as a girl, had a studio 'carved out of the Castle Rock itself'. During the air-raids of the Second World War thousands of people found shelter in the deeper caves. It seems reasonable to suppose that whenever primitive men settled in the neighbourhood they would have seen the convenience of such caves, set as they were in low cliffs rising dramatically from the swamps. But Tigguocabauc was no tribal centre even when the Romans arrived, although by that time there were towns like Colchester with a considerable native culture. The future Nottingham must have been an insignificant settlement, if indeed the 'house of caves' was permanently occupied at all.

The inhabitants of this region were then Coritani, one of the later invading tribes which had crossed the Channel from the Marne Valley a few generations before the Romans. As the legions fanned out in the first phases of their conquest of Britain, Ostorius Scapula recognized the Trent as the obvious half-way line it has always been. Halting to consolidate, he established a defensive zone along the Fosse Way, which his engineers built from Lincoln to Leicester, roughly parallel with the river, itself a useful moat protecting him from the untamed hill-country to the north-west. Leicester was the tribal capital of the Coritani, so the Romans sensibly adopted it as one of their own towns. The Coritani north of the Trent found themselves in a kind of No Man's Land, though doubtless, when things were quiet, they crossed freely into the occupied territory to visit their tribal centre. Those were days when, as even the blindest local patriot must admit, the Nottingham people had to do their shopping in Leicester.

Queen Boudicca's revolt flared up in A.D. 61, when the main Roman forces were far away in North Wales. Though the storm centre was in the south-east, where the massacres at London, Colchester and St Albans cost seventy thousand lives, Boudicca had help from the Brigantes in Yorkshire and other distant tribes, so it is not unlikely that the Coritani took a hand, especially when they heard that a large part of the Ninth Legion from Lincoln had been ambushed and wiped out. The nearest Roman fort to Nottingham was Margidunum on the Fosse Way, a seven- or eight-acre stronghold capable of holding a thousand troops. It may have been overrun at that time: the excavations have revealed charred timbers and fire-marks on the masonry, as well as human bones at the bottom of a well; but nothing is certain and the disaster may belong to some later period of the Roman occupation.

When the Romans recovered from this setback and pushed on with their conquest of the country, Nottinghamshire remained a backwater. Rome's engineers did not rise to the challenge of building the first Trent Bridge. They were content to cross the river elsewhere by paved ford or ferry, though there seems to have been a fort at Broxtowe, on the north-west edge of the modern city, by the end of the first century A.D. It is believed that about 1830 or 1840 some remains turned up in what is now the University Park at Highfields, and that these may have indicated the site of a villa. The find was not properly recorded and the spot has never again been identified. If there was a villa there, it was probably occupied by a romanized Briton, farming an estate on Roman lines. It would be an illusion to people Highfields with the ghosts of bygone Romans, sighing for the superior entertainments of the eternal city or chuckling over stale scandal from the imperial household. Nottinghamshire remained backward and British throughout those four centuries, with only a veneer of Mediterranean culture, scarcely noticed by the peasant guiding his plough. Christianity must have reached the district in the latter half of the period, for by 314 there was a Bishop of York at the Council of Arles; but how deep the faith went among the Trentside dwellers was as debatable then as now.

In the fifth century A.D. came the crumbling of the Roman Empire in the West. The Dark Ages began, most admirably typified in the history of the Nottingham region, since the darkness there is one of unsurpassed density, without so much as a glimmer of Arthurian armour to lighten it. It is rather like the interlude in a modern theatre when, though no curtain has been lowered between the scenes, the audience sits waiting in the black-out, sensing rather than seeing the scurry of urgent figures before the lights come up again to disclose a new but for the moment unpeopled set.

In this case the new scene is Anglo-Saxon Snotingaham. Snot, the founding father, was one of the vague shapes thumping about so breathlessly in the blackness. He has been and has gone, leaving no personal impression, only his regrettable name, under which the future Nottingham is now for the first time discernible in the strengthening light of recorded history.

Snot and his followers were probably Angles from Schleswig-Holstein, for these were the particular invaders who crossed the North Sea and took over the Trent Valley when the more famous Hengist and Horsa appeared in Kent. Thrusting their way up the valley, these Angles made their first settlement at Nottingham about A.D. 500. Like the Americans who pushed the frontier westwards in the nineteenth century, they wanted to farm in peace but were ready to fight for the land they needed. Their cultural standards were low. Ordinarily they lived in shacks, making a hole about two feet deep and stretching a roof of slanting poles overhead. The sandstone caves must have seemed comparatively luxurious. They burnt their dead – for which the nearby Forest

of Sherwood must have been invaluable, since a great deal of wood
is needed to consume a corpse. One of their cremation cemeteries
was discovered in 1842 at Holme Pierrepont, just across the river.

Gradually, over the next century or two, the tough primitive
invaders of the old Roman province evolved that quite high
Anglo-Saxon culture which modern historians are teaching us to
respect. Christian missionaries helped to develop links with the
Continent, with Rome and Byzantium. The faith must have
reached Snot's settlement about the year 630. Paulinus, a Roman
monk, was sent to England in 601 by Pope Gregory the Great, to
reinforce the efforts of Augustine who had arrived in Kent four
years previously. Paulinus soon established a headquarters in York,
and in 627, under the approving gaze of King Edwin of Northumbria, he conducted a mass baptism in the Trent at Littleborough.
That, of course, was a long way downstream from Nottingham,
almost at Gainsborough, but it seems a fair assumption that the
Gospel was preached to Snot's descendants not long afterwards.

This seed of Christianity had no chance to take root. In the
autumn of 632 the Northumbrian King (whose name survives in
the Sherwood Forest village of Edwinstowe) was defeated and
killed by a pagan Mercian chief, Penda, allied to Cadwallon King
of Gwynedd, whom the Venerable Bede stigmatized in his *History*
as 'crueller than a pagan'. Paulinus and his missionaries fled
south. Penda became King of Mercia and Nottingham fell under
his sway or, what was worse, lay in the zone he disputed with the
weakened rulers of Northumbria. Only when Penda himself was
killed in battle near Leeds in 654 did quieter conditions return.

It is small wonder that defence-considerations weighed heavily
with the first settlers in Nottingham, but they did not choose the
Castle Rock, preferring a less flamboyant outcrop of sandstone a
little to the east. Here they had a low but steep cliff looking across
the marshes to the river, and the other three sides in due time they
protected with a ditch and bank, doubtless topped with a palisade.
The oblong site measured about thirty-nine acres, today largely
covered by the sombre office-blocks and warehouses of the Victorian Lace Market. St Mary's, the beautiful mother-church of
Nottingham, stands in the middle where earlier churches have

preceded it since the beginnings of Christian worship in the town.

The boundaries of the original Snotingaham can be paced in a short stroll, starting behind the domed Council House. The north-west angle of the ramparts touched what is now Victoria Street. Treading in the footsteps of the bygone Anglo-Saxon watchman, you go along Warser Gate and Woolpack Lane, where the wide traffic-race of Lower Parliament Street overlies the eastern ramparts and noisily banishes all thought of the recent, never mind the ancient, past. Comparative quiet is regained at Hollow Stone, named from its passing through a cleft in the rock. As St Mary's tower looms on the crest of the hill, the road widens into High Pavement and descends again in a sweeping curve past the Shire Hall to Weekday Cross, where the markets were held.

This marks the westward limit of Snotingaham. The fourth side of the defences is lost under the buildings that lie between the roughly parallel streets of Fletcher Gate, named from the one-time 'fleshers' or butchers, and Bridlesmith Gate on the outer side of the ditch. Fletcher Gate leads to Warser Gate and Victoria Street, where this perambulation began.

All these 'Gates', and the others packed into the narrow confines of the old English borough – Pilcher Gate, Fisher Gate, Barker Gate, and so on – have nothing to do, needless to say, with exits and entrances. The word derives from the Danish *gade* or Norse *gata*, a 'street', and is a reminder of the Scandinavian influence that was to come, and to linger. There are just as many 'Gates' in the area built over after the Norman Conquest, including a Greyfriar Gate, though the Franciscans did not appear in Nottingham until about 1230.

The natural strength of the Anglo-Saxon site can be best appreciated from Cliff Road, formerly called Narrow Marsh, at the base of the hill. Here again the old name is eloquent, as is 'Broad Marsh' near by, and the fact that all the low ground stretching away towards the river is still known, despite its drab mantle of buildings, as 'the Meadows'. The names do a little, if not much, to blot out present ugliness and help the imagination reconstruct the scene as once it was.

The people living on this hill, sheltered within its embanked stockade, numbered well under a thousand. Like villagers the world over, before the invention of modern communications, they must have been largely self-supporting, though scholars now warn us not to exaggerate the self-sufficiency even of an Anglo-Saxon township. The meadows at the foot of their cliff provided grazing and a hay crop. In other directions stretched the forest, the fringe of which could be cleared for corn-growing. North and west lay the light sandy soil of Sherwood, of which it has been said that it needs a shower of rain every day and a shower of muck every night. To the north-east was the already-mentioned clay, heavier to plough but more rewarding. Leen and Trent provided fish. Sherwood furnished venison and smaller game, not yet preserved for the hunting of the few. In the main the Nottingham folk were farmers, or at least farmers part-time, with just as many smiths, carpenters, and other specialists as their small community could keep in work.

CHAPTER THREE

The Danish Borough

WE come to 'real' history, with dates and documents, in 868.

'At that time,' records the chronicler monk, Simeon of Durham, lifting his facts from Asser but polishing up the narrative, 'the heathen host left the Northumbrians and came with all dreadfulness to Snotingaham . . . and there did these false guests abide the winter; and their coming was unpleasing enough to the landfolk, each and all.'

These heathen were the Danish host led by Halfdan and Ivar the Boneless, sons of the notorious Viking chief, Ragnar Lothbrok. They had landed on the east coast in the autumn of 865, overrun Lincolnshire and occupied York. After terrorising the country as far north as the Tyne they switched their attention to the Midlands.

It is common, and tempting to both painters and pageant-masters, to represent the Danes sailing up the Trent in their long-ships. It was, however, their more usual practice to quit their galleys at the start of an invasion, round up all the horses in the vicinity, and operate thereafter in flying columns of mounted infantry. If they had limited themselves to the waterways they would have been easier to deal with. It is pretty sure that when they 'came with all dreadfulness to Snotingaham' they rode overland from York.

Though the boundaries of Anglo-Saxon England fluctuated, Nottingham lay normally in the big central kingdom of Mercia, stretching from the Welsh border to the Wash, so it was the King of Mercia, Burhred, who had to meet this threat. He appealed to his brothers-in-law, King Ethelred of Wessex and the nineteen-year-old Alfred. 'They, like lions stout of heart,' wrote Asser (who with the advantage of hindsight credited the younger brother, his future patron, with most of the initiative), 'shrank not ... and came unto Snotingaham ready to face the fray.' Thus the royal associations of the town get off to a spanking start with the youthful Alfred the Great.

Nottingham, however, was not to be numbered among his victories. The heathen were hard-headed folk, not given to running berserk at the first blast of a war-horn, never abandoning a strong position to fight at a disadvantage. They 'trusted to the walls of the fortress', not fancying the concentration of Mercian and Wessex men outside. The latter seem no more to have fancied an assault upon the stockaded hill. Peace was made, and the Danes retired – for the moment – to Yorkshire. Alfred and his brother rode home.

Within ten years Alfred was hiding at Athelney, Burhred a fugitive in Rome, and England so widely overrun that many a Wessex man was packing up to emigrate across the Channel. When the tide turned there had to be compromise. England was partitioned by a wavy line running from Mersey to Thames. Nottingham remained in the occupied half or Danelaw, becoming one of the five 'boroughs', or fortified towns, along with Derby, Leicester, Lincoln and Stamford.

'The Danes', says Sir Arthur Bryant in *Makers of the Realm*, 'were a vigorous, clear-headed folk: more alert and decisive than their English kinsmen.' Local patriots will be tempted to accept this generalization and think of Nottingham henceforth as a Danish town. Some may take equal pride in the fact that the character of the place was formed even at this early date as predominantly a centre for thrustful businessmen. For the Danes, Bryant continues, 'took to commerce as the next best thing to piracy, and proved as able with the scales as the battle-axe.... They loved, too, to build and sail ships. By doing so they brought wealth of a new kind to England. They made its first trading-towns – York, Leicester, Lincoln, Nottingham....' G. M. Trevelyan similarly mentions Nottingham as a combination of trading-centre and military garrison. 'Roads were scarce but rivers were deep, and commerce was borne in barges to the wharves of inland towns.' On the military side each of the Five Boroughs 'was protected by a palisaded mound and ditch; each had its own "law men", its own army and its own sovereign "Jarl" or Earl. From the borough, the Earl and his army ruled a wide surrounding district.' But big words like earl and army and town should not distort reality – the population was still well under a thousand, so the normal muster of fighting men was closer to an outsize gang than to a myriad host.

This small population was, of course, mixed. The Anglo-Saxon Nottinghamians had not been exterminated or driven away, and there were no great cultural or racial differences to keep the two groups apart. Guthrum accepted baptism after his defeat by Alfred, and in the course of time his fellow countrymen (who were in any case not much given to theological speculation) adopted at least the outward forms of Christianity with an equally easy-going good nature. Anglo-Saxon Christianity was not excessive in its demands. The Normans were later to profess themselves shocked by its slackness, and especially by its married clergy, while as early as 734 Bede complained of monasteries founded merely as devices for tax-evasion.

The more one studies this period, the less can one accept the old picture of our 'rude Anglo-Saxon forefathers', and the more is one struck by their affinities to our own society. Certainly, they must be visualised in their woollen cloaks and tunics, their crisscross leg-coverings and Phrygian caps, and the rooftops of Nottingham as steep and thatched, rising to a ridge-pole laid between two forks of forest timber, but the laws (and the literature) of the time are a warning against any tendency to underestimate the sophistication of the people. Divorce was easy, as Dorothy Whitelock points out in *The Beginnings of English Society*, and women held property with a freedom lost at the Norman Conquest and not fully recovered until modern times. Views on the upbringing of children compared favourably with those of some Victorians. Thus, 'one shall not rebuke a youth in his childhood, until he can reveal himself. He shall thrive among the people in that he is confident.'

Mortimer's Hole, traditionally the secret route used by young Edward III's sup-porters to surprise his mother's lover. More recently, the passage where the hero of Saturday Night and Sunday Morning *longed 'to plant a thousand tons of bone-dry T.N.T.' For visitors an easily accessible example of Nottingham's sandstone underworld.*

The Castle today: baroque mansion turned into museum. In D. H. Lawrence's Sons and Lovers *Paul and Clara looked down from its tree-clad precipice.*

Richard III's 'Castle of Care': reconstructed from the records. The river is the Leen. In the background the high tower and other royal apartments added by Edward IV and Richard III.

A generation after the establishment of the Danelaw, the counter-offensive of Wessex began. Alfred's son, Edward the Elder, pushed gradually up through Bedford, Northampton and Cambridge. To the west his sister, Ethelfleda, ruling the Anglo-Saxon half of Mercia from Tamworth, advanced eastwards and in 917 took Derby by storm and held it. Early the next year she added Leicester to her conquests. Stamford surrendered to King Edward, and the last two of the Five Boroughs, Nottingham and Lincoln, had no choice but to do the same. Edward was master of the country as far north as the Humber and as his sister died about this time he merged her West Midland kingdom with his own.

He visited Nottingham about 920, having already sent in a dependable garrison and ordered the repair of the defences. Studying the site himself, he decreed the building of a timber bridge, the first Trent Bridge, and of a fortification at its southern end. Once built, the bridge became a vital link between north and south and largely explains Nottingham's military importance throughout the next few centuries, when the great north road from London to York followed this line.

It was at Nottingham in 934 that Edward's son and successor, Athelstan, mustered his army to march against the Scots, when he won the famous (though unlocated) battle of Brunanburh and became the unchallengeable 'King of All Britain'. Within a year of his death, however, there was a dramatic reversal. 'What King of Dublin captured Nottingham, and when?' sounds like the teasing invention of a quiz-master, but there is a genuine answer. Olaf Guthfrithson, the Norse King of Dublin, was one of the coalition beaten at Brunanburh. When Athelstan was succeeded by his eighteen-year-old brother, Edmund, he sought revenge. The Irish-based Vikings landed and swept across England, occupying Nottingham and the rest of the Danelaw in 940. It was only an episode, if a disturbing one. Olaf died, and in 942 the *status quo* was restored. Perhaps it is best to say that Nottingham was under 'English' rule again, for the Danes and Anglo-Saxons were fast integrating.

The erstwhile pagans had now finally discarded the Wagnerian deities, but it must be confessed that Nottingham never shone as a centre of devout early Christianity. There was no monastery, no collegiate minster to rival the one established by the eleventh century at Southwell, destined to blossom later into glories of Norman architecture and to become the centre of a modern diocese. Nottingham produced neither poems nor chronicles nor exquisitely illuminated manuscripts. A ten-foot cross, carved but headless, standing near the western boundary of the modern city, at Stapleford, is about the only visible reminder of what was, in cultural history, a very considerable period. About all that can be said of Nottingham's ecclesiastical life at this date is that some church probably stood where St Mary's stands now, and that about 950 all this region was transferred from the diocese of Lichfield to that of York, presumably to bolster the power of the northern archbishops after the successive blows they had suffered since the first Danish invasions.

Even now, peace was uneasy, and the threat of fresh Scandinavian attacks had to be reckoned with. Nottingham shared the same recurrent crises as the rest of the North. Thus, in 1013, King Sweyn of Denmark led a mighty fleet of longships up the Humber to Gainsborough, and all the old Danelaw, whether from sentiment or prudence, acknowledged him as their lord. But, like Olaf Guthfrithson before him, he died within a year of his triumph, and there were two more years of conflict before his son Canute established himself as unchallenged king of all England.

Now opened the last chapter, the final fifty years, before the Norman Conquest. Canute's reign was a good period for trade – he was for a time king also of both Denmark and Norway – and doubtless the Nottingham men shared in the benefits of the firm régime he established. More and more of them lived by trade and manufacture. Only a minority were now full-time farmers, holding allotments in the common lands outside the ramparts. Nottingham even had a mint, though the distinction is not as grand as it sounds, for most towns had 'moneyers', authorised to strike coins.

Government was simply organized. Nottingham was a royal borough, with a headman or 'reeve' to collect taxes and tolls and to see that the laws were observed. There were, in point of fact, quite a surprising number of trade restrictions, fixing prices, prohibiting exports and in other ways giving the early Englishman a foretaste of pleasures to come. The men of Nottingham had to accept the reeve appointed by the King and had strictly speaking no democratic rights, but it was usual (and prudent) for a reeve to consult with the older and more influential inhabitants, the 'law men', and try to run things smoothly according to precedent. Such time-honoured phrases as 'what we've always done in the past' were now hammered out, to be used gratefully by a million committee-members yet unborn.

In the early days of the Danelaw the fortified boroughs had served as military centres for whatever area of countryside they could effectively dominate. About the year 1000 these areas were permanently demarcated as 'shires', so permanently indeed that the boundaries of Nottinghamshire have remained almost un-altered since then. A shire reeve, or sheriff, was appointed to these areas. The power of the earls now tended to be concentrated in the hands of a few great lords. In the south there was Godwin, Earl of Wessex, and in Mercia Leofric, husband of the well-remembered Godiva. Nottinghamshire thus came within the sphere of Leofric, whose young grandson Edwin became earl just before the Norman Conquest.

Whatever clear-headedness the Nottingham men had inherited from the Danish side must have been severely tested by the events of 1066, a confusing year at best, and to none more so than to the dwellers by the Trent.

In the previous year, called out with other Midlanders by their earl, they had had to march as far as Northampton in an effective demonstration which persuaded Edward the Confessor to give the earldom of Northumbria to Edwin's brother, Morcar, in place of the tyrannical Tostig who had been driven abroad. No sooner was this achieved than news came, in January 1066, of the King's death and his succession by Tostig's brother, Harold, Earl of Wessex. This relationship did not in itself worry them, for Harold and Tostig were by no means devoted to each other, but they were both Godwins, a family always at odds with the earls of Mercia, and Nottingham probably drank the new king's health without particular enthusiasm.

The first half of the year was uneasy with rumours of invasion. In September, while Harold was concentrating on the danger from Normandy, his exiled brother returned with Harald Hardrada and a Norwegian army and sailed up the Humber to attack York. Again the Nottingham men had to arm and march with their earl. Edwin and Morcar were badly defeated at Fulford, and it is likely that there were more Nottingham casualties in this battle than in any of the other fighting that year. Doubtless the survivors of the Nottingham contingent rallied enough to join Harold when he hurried north a few days later and avenged their defeat by the tremendous victory of Stamford Bridge. But when he turned and thundered south again to meet his own doom at Hastings, Edwin and Morcar and their badly mauled troops were unable to keep up with him, and played no significant part, so far as is known, in resisting William the Conqueror.

CHAPTER FOUR

The Coming of the Normans

In Nottingham, as the old year went out, perhaps nobody grasped what has since been impressed upon every schoolboy: that 1066 was a watershed in English history and that the view ahead was completely changed.

Men knew, of course, about the slaughter at Hastings in October. They had heard, too, of their own Earl Edwin's submission to the Duke of Normandy at Berkhamsted, along with other leaders who saw the futility of fighting on. They had heard, or would certainly hear in a day or two, of William's Christmas coronation at Westminster. But how far would it affect their own lives? Wars had rolled over the country before, invading kings had triumphed briefly and then died, and things had gone on much the same. So, calmly, taking their cue from their earl, they accepted the situation. There was not much choice, with Harold, Tostig, Harald Hardrada and most of the other principal actors stiff in their graves. The Norman survived unchallenged, but surely he would make little difference to Nottingham?

There they were wrong, as Edwin and his brother were wrong. 'Cold heart and bloody hand now rule the English land,' a Norwegian scald declared. William brought new ideas and disciplines, and imposed them with ferocity. In 1068 there was rebellion in the West. That summer it spread to the North. Edwin and Morcar joined the rebels there: they knew now that the old Anglo-Saxon nobility had no hope of keeping their positions under this terrible new overlord. William came north to deal with them. He paused briefly in Nottingham, noticed the sandstone crag to the west of the town, assessed its strategic value, and ordered the building of a castle there. Like the other fortresses with which he dotted his new kingdom, it followed the 'motte-and-bailey' pattern, that is to say a wooden tower where the Museum stands today, on the highest part of the rock (which made an artificial mound or motte unnecessary), and then a large enclosure or bailey where the grounds now extend. The tower was in an impregnable position. The almost sheer cliff fell a hundred and thirty feet to the Leen. Later, probably this had two channels, one close to the base of the rock and cut by the Normans, to create yet another defence and to provide power for the Castle's corn-mills. On the inner side, a slope like a house-roof and a dry moat at its foot protected the tower from any force that might penetrate the bailey from the direction of the town.

Architectural splendours came later, when earth and timber were replaced with masonry, but as a construction work the original fortress must have been impressive. That work presumably fell mainly on the townsmen, with a handful of Norman supervisors experienced in such projects. More than one hundred motte-and-bailey castles were put up in the generation following the Conquest. Few were so large, or played so continuous and vital a role in medieval history, as this one.

From the beginning William made it a 'royal' castle. The responsibility for building it, and then holding it as constable in the King's name, he gave to one of his followers, William Peverel, together with a fief known as 'the Honour of Nottingham', including lands in six shires, to support him. Nothing is known about Peverel. There is no reason to believe the story that he was the Conqueror's bastard son.

William revisited Nottingham in the following year, 1069, when there was another northern rebellion, backed by King Sweyn of Denmark. The town took no part, unless some loyal individuals slipped away to join their former lord, Edwin. He had been disappointed by the poor reward for his submission (he had hoped to marry the Conqueror's daughter) and now like his brother Morcar decided on belated resistance. This revolt was put down with systematic terrorism. Much of the North was turned into a depopulated wilderness. Morcar soon afterwards linked up with Hereward in the Fens, but ended his days in one of William's dungeons. Edwin, fleeing towards Scotland, was treacherously murdered. There was then no Earl of Mercia to stir nostalgic loyalties in Nottingham. Henry de Ferrers became the chief land-owner in that part of the Midlands. His principal seat was Tutbury Castle. He and his successors were Earls of Derby but sometimes called themselves Earls of Nottingham as well. The two shires were linked under a common sheriff until Tudor times.

Peverel's castle remained outside the town boundaries until the nineteenth century, when this historical anomaly produced some unjust penalties for the county ratepayers after the Reform Bill riots. There naturally grew up, however, a settlement of Normans, their dependents and camp-followers, outside the main gate on the gentle slope that fell away eastwards to the modern city centre and the English borough rising on its own hill beyond. The old town clung to its identity, and the newly developing area (which was two or three times as extensive but not so densely built-over) became a separate Norman Borough. The distinction was slow to disappear. The terms 'French Borough' and 'English Borough' were used until the mid-fifteenth century, separate juries were called for the Quarter Sessions until the late seventeenth, two sheriffs and two coroners were elected until 1835, and to this day two maces are borne before the Sheriff of Nottingham in proces-sions. This dual arrangement was not peculiar to the town – it grew up in Norwich, Northampton, Stamford and elsewhere – nor was the use of the legal term, 'Borough English', which acknowledged the different inheritance customs of the two com-munities, but in the records of Edward III's reign the term is specially associated with Nottingham.

The enlarged town formed a rough oval, with the original borough occupying the south-eastern quarter, while the Castle stood at the south-western edge. An idea of its length is easily gained by standing in the Castle grounds and looking eastwards towards St Mary's tower. From north to south the distance is barely half that, but harder to measure by skyline indications. It can be walked briskly in five or ten minutes, starting from the Theatre Royal, and going down Market Street, across the great square, and down Wheeler Gate and Lister Gate as far as Wool-worth's. The long northern boundary of medieval Nottingham is marked by the busy thoroughfare of Parliament Street, which runs past the columned portico of the Victorian theatre and exactly follows the line of the town wall and ditch built in the thirteenth century. The Playhouse and the Albert Hall offer two more useful points of reference, for they also stand just outside the medieval boundary, which continued from the end of Parliament Street (where the very name 'Chapel Bar' is significant) up Park Row to the Castle, now obscured from this side by the massive blocks of the General Hospital.

It is worth taking this amount of trouble to get orientated and to form a clear mental picture of the scale and layout. For this relatively small area, staked out in Norman times, *was* Nottingham as late as 1845. Nearly everything happened within these narrow confines – and the final breaking of the bonds was to form one of the classic stories of Victorian social and industrial history. The area, or more correctly the once-Norman part of it, is still quite accurately described as 'the city centre', for most of the big shops, restaurants and places of amusement lie either in it or just outside its perimeter.

It would be quite a mistake to suppose that the increased area after the coming of the Normans was matched by a growth in population. Twenty years after Hastings, when the Domesday survey was made, the sheriff reported sixteen fewer householders than there had been in the reign of Edward the Confessor. This did not deter the Conqueror from putting up the town's tax assessment from eighteen pounds a year to thirty. Making the usual kind of estimate of the average household, we must picture a town still of no more than eight hundred inhabitants, slowly increasing to about three thousand at the end of the Middle Ages. As no doubt some newcomers did arrive with Peverel, and form the nucleus of the French Borough, it is obvious that the English community diminished in those years – a natural enough decline, for there must have been some local young men who fell at Fulford, Stamford Bridge or in the rebellions against William, or who fled overseas. So, to begin with, if the garrison is excluded, the Norman-French immigrants barely made up for the reduced numbers of the English.

Still, population figures can be a misleading index of importance. Thanks to the royal castle, Nottingham now attained a position it had never enjoyed as a mere trading-town. Almost all the medieval kings were visitors at some time or other. They mobilized armies there, kept court, summoned councils and parliaments, or simply rode forth to enjoy the hunting in Sherwood. Nottingham, in its smaller way, served as the Windsor of the Midlands. And just as the Castle stood outside the borough, enhancing its importance and affecting its life in countless indirect ways, soon there was the great Cluniac priory of Lenton, just beyond the Castle Park, founded either by the first William Peverel or his successor and namesake about 1109. This grew into the richest of the Nottinghamshire monasteries and held its own famous fair outside the town. Though never as magnificent as Fountains or Glastonbury, it was a great house in its heyday, with thirty monks and all the lay staff that went with them. Several kings, notably Henry III and the first three Edwards, slept in its guest-chambers. The priory stood beside the Leen, about midway between the Castle and the site of the modern university. Today not a single ivy-grown cloister-arch survives, though excavation has revealed foundations.

But the splendours of Lenton lay in the Plantagenet future. Norman Nottingham was a rough place. Culturally, England had slipped back. For a while the townsmen had a grimmer time than under their Saxon and Danish kings.

It was in these years that Sherwood, the 'Shire Wood', became a forest in the strict sense understood by Norman law. This legendary region (surely, with Arden, the most famous forest in literature?) stretched twenty miles to the north and about eight miles from east to west, a small area, when you come to think of it, to offer so rich a variety of adventures. The greenwood came to the edge of the common fields bordering the town. Those fields sloped up to the skyline ridge where Forest Road now runs, and fell as steeply on the far side to meet the 'waste'. On that far side a vast recreation-ground preserves the name, 'the Forest', though it is mainly open turf, a kind of Hyde Park tilted at an angle, a green island round which the tide of brick-and-mortar crept a century ago. Because of the ridge the forest was invisible to the Norman town, but it was very near, a beast lurking behind the hill. The Robin Hood episodes that involve Nottingham fit acceptably into this picture. Although it was distinctly more than a bow-shot from the gates to the greenwood, an athletic outlaw could have covered the intervening space very quickly. And just beyond the skyline, in the Rock Cemetery which neighbours the recreation-ground, there are little caves inevitably associated, if without historical evidence, with Robin and his band. But the whole question of historical evidence for Robin Hood is better looked at in a separate chapter, for the outlaw's shadow falls across a broad period of time and he fits no convenient slot in a chronological order.

William Rufus came to Nottingham, but probably his successor, Henry I, did not. The Norman kings spent much of their time in France, fighting in defence of their family's earlier possessions and quarrelling with their jealous brothers or disloyal offspring. The Conqueror's sons and grandchildren were a passionate and perverse brood, and though they seldom showed their flushed faces in Nottingham the town more than once suffered the calamitous backwash of their upheavals.

This was particularly so in the years of anarchy following Henry's death. He had previously lost his only legitimate son through the sinking of the White Ship and had tried to arrange for the crown to pass to his daughter, Matilda. This was contested by his sister's son, Stephen, and by the numerous barons who could not at that date stomach the idea of a woman on the throne. As to the rights of the matter, is seemed a fine distinction. Matilda and Stephen were both grandchildren of the Conqueror: one was his son's daughter, the other his daughter's son. William Peverel (either the son or the grandson of the first Peverel) declared in favour of Stephen and held the Castle in his name. This led to a surprise attack upon Nottingham in 1140 by Matilda's half-brother, Robert, Earl of Gloucester, one of King Henry's plentiful bastard children. On this Robert fell the main task of leading Matilda's forces in England while her husband, Henry of Anjou, fought for her claims in Normandy. Robert's men were unable to break into the Castle, so they fired the town and rode away.

No sooner had the unfortunate people rebuilt their homes than they faced new troubles. The Earl of Gloucester beat Stephen at the Battle of Lincoln. Peverel was captured there, whereupon Nottingham Castle was handed over to one of Matilda's local supporters, William Pagenel of Bingham. Within a year the tables were turned. Peverel was freed and came storming back to claim his own. This time, thanks perhaps to his knowledge of the defences and the sympathies of the citizens, the surprise attack was successful. Matilda's partisans fled and Peverel resumed possession.

The struggle dragged on. Matilda had the arrogant temper of her family and would not let go. Her son, the future Henry II, destined to loom large in Nottingham history, made his first appearance in 1153 and laid siege to the Castle. Peverel drove him away by setting fire to the town and depriving his forces of shelter. The prince retired, muttering emphatic promises of revenge. The citizens, philosophically rebuilding their charred cottages once more, reflected that, whatever the function of Nottingham Castle, it was obviously not the protection of Nottingham. It was probably soon after this that the town built itself a strong west gate with a massive portcullis slung between two drum-towers. The gateway remained until 1743. The name, Chapel Bar, still survives.

Peverel's loyalty to King Stephen was poorly rewarded, for Stephen died in the year following the siege, having agreed with Matilda that her son should succeed him. Peverel had now to acknowledge as his undisputed king the hot-tempered twenty-one-year-old he had so recently defied. Soon came peremptory orders under his new master's seal: he was to surrender the Castle, and all the lands comprising the Honour of Nottingham, to Ranulf, Earl of Chester. Before Peverel could hand over, however, Ranulf died suddenly. On such occasions the limited medical knowledge of those days encouraged a good deal of guesswork, and poison was a favourite guess. Ranulf may easily have succumbed to some internal affliction that did not get into the textbooks until centuries later, but even if Peverel's conscience was clear he could not wait until then for his innocence to be established. Henry, fresh from his coronation, was on his way to Nottingham. Peverel sensibly vanished. Probably he went no further than Lenton Priory, had his head shaved, put on a monk's habit and lived out the rest of his days undisturbed. There was nothing unusual in a layman's thus retiring to a religious house. Elderly people, even without Peverel's urgent motive, regularly arranged the matter by purchasing a 'corrody' or annuity, guaranteeing them board and lodging for life. It may have been embarrassing for the Prior, to shelter a fugitive from the new king's displeasure, but it would have been difficult for him to refuse Peverel sanctuary in the house he had himself endowed.

It was in February 1155 that Henry II rode into Nottingham, opening a new era in the history of both castle and town.

CHAPTER FIVE

The Early Charters

THE first of the Plantagenet kings brought a demonic energy to everything he did. It was appropriate that Henry preferred the short cloak fashionable in Anjou to the cumbrous trailing garment favoured by the English barons. 'Curtmantle', as he was nicknamed, dashed hither and thither through his dominions (which included half France as well as all England), rapping out orders without the waste of a minute. He rose early, ate sparingly, hardly sat down except at table, and doodled restlessly in chapel. It is sad that most people remember him, if at all, for his connection with Becket's martyrdom. Whatever his responsibility for the 'murder in the cathedral', Henry was one of the most brilliant administrators ever to run the affairs of this country.

Nottingham shared in the general prosperity and order he brought after the 'nineteen long winters' of the struggle between his mother and Stephen. 'Merchants went out safe to the markets,' testified a chronicler of his reign. In thirty-five years as king, Henry more than doubled his revenue, but it was not by extortion. Indeed, he began by halving the taxes of Nottingham, so that the town could recover from its recent burning.

Soon after Henry's accession, in 1155 or thereabouts, he gave the place its first royal charter. It was a modest enough grant, conferring no kind of self-government, but at least it defined the cherished privileges of the people. Any man who had lived in Nottingham unchallenged for a year and a day earned thereby the 'freedom of the borough', and even if he were a runaway serf he could not be hauled back to his master. All had to contribute their share of the tax-assessment, which was collected by two bailiffs and handed over to the King's representative, the Sheriff of Nottinghamshire and Derbyshire. That famous character, the Sheriff of Nottingham, had as yet no separate existence. To lessen the tax burden of the individual, the borough was allowed to levy tolls on river-traffic between Thrumpton and Newark and similarly on the north-to-south road-traffic between Retford and Rempston.

There was, further, the right to hold a market on Fridays and Saturdays, and a monopoly of manufacturing dyed cloth within a radius of ten miles. The long history of Nottingham as a textile centre had obviously begun, for there were enough weavers in 1155 to form a guild and pay forty shillings a year for the privilege. The street-name, Lister Gate, indicates where the 'listers' or cloth-dyers once spread out their gaily dripping handiwork, where the houses ended and the 'broad marsh' began. Cloth was sent to Nottingham to be dyed red, blue, green, and 'murrey' or mulberry. Medieval dyers had no wide range of colours at their disposal – hence the tendency for some towns to be known for a single hue, such as Stamford scarlet, Beverley blue and Lincoln green.

Yellow was the colour specially associated with Jews, and it was about this time that they appeared in Nottingham. There had been none in England before the Conquest. Now, for two centuries, they played a vital part in economic life. Being unable to take a Christian oath, they were automatically barred from most activities. They could not hold land or do military service as knights, nor could they enter any of the 'closed-shop' trades that involved membership of a guild. What they *could* do was lend money at interest, which Christians were forbidden to do, the Church teaching that usury was a sin. Naturally enough, the number of Christians prepared to lend money interest-free was not equal to the demand for credit, and not only the kings and barons but even the Church itself found the Jewish money-lender a convenient solution of the difficulty. Many a Cistercian abbey was based on Jewish loans. Aaron of Lincoln boasted that he had done more than any other man alive to build St Albans.

The Jews were drawn to Nottingham by the increasing importance of the Castle as a royal residence and the consequent
comings and goings of the great ones. They had a synagogue near
Lister Gate, but seem to have lived in various streets: if there was
a ghetto, it probably developed when restrictions were placed
upon them. There is no record of any strong anti-semitic feeling
in the town, and Nottingham knew none of the savage pogroms
that occurred elsewhere.

Henry was a great castle-builder on his own account and a keen
dismantler of other people's strongholds that could serve as a focus
of rebellion. He had already found from painful experience that
Nottingham was a key position he must keep in his own control.
He spent lavishly on the transformation of the fortress, sub-
stituting massive stone walls and towers for the original earth-and-
timber defences.

Exactly what the Castle looked like, either then or after the
improvements by the Yorkist kings, nobody can say. Of the
medieval buildings little remains but the formidable gatehouse,
itself much restored. To picture it, we must blot out everything
else we see today – the 'Castle', doubtless a fine mansion when the
Duke of Newcastle built it in Charles II's reign, but now suggest-
ing from a distance a brace of giant, grimy, balustraded biscuit-
tins set side by side; and the leafy slope below it, the lawns and
paths, bandstand and memorial statue, seats and sandwiches, shrill
children and pensive pensioners and unhurried Corporation gardeners. We must visualize a complex of buildings, with at least
two courtyards – the inner bailey and the vast outer bailey – and
a great number of lean-to wooden shanties lining the base of the
walls inside, providing storehouses and kitchens and workshops for
the smiths, farriers, carpenters and other craftsmen essential to the
daily life of the place.

There was noise. Medieval man pitched his voice for outdoor
communication, and Henry's own was harsh and cracked. There
was colour. And, needless to say, there was smell: new bread and
meat sizzling on the spit, hot metal, fresh wood-shavings, stale fish,
and unfailing in the background the stink of man and horse and
hound. Yet it was the smoke of the coal fires that drove away

Eleanor of Castile in 1257, when she had come prepared for a long visit.

Perhaps a distant prospect is fairer? What did the Castle look like to the townsman who seldom if ever had cause to pass its gates? To picture what he saw we must again blot out not only the modern view but every holiday memory of Chepstow, Conway and the rest of the romantic ruins that stand crumbling like old cheeses up and down the country. There was no ivy, needless to say, on Henry's ramparts. The walls were not even venerably grey. They were probably white-washed. The towers were not the roof-less shells a tourist normally clambers up. To imagine Nottingham Castle as it really looked from outside it is better to think of the castles pictured in illuminated manuscripts – clean cut, dazzling white, with a cluster of roofs and timber galleries above neat-notched battlements.

To this stronghold Henry came often on his tireless progresses through the kingdom, each bustling advent shattering the customary quiet of the little town with a mighty rumble of wagons and chatter of courtiers and chalking of doors by marshals who had to billet the overflow in private houses. Though the modest foundations of a central government were being laid at Westminster, the effective capital of England was still wherever the King happened to be that day. So, from time to time, it was at Nottingham. There Henry, scribbling, shouting, listening, never forgetting a name or a face, kept secretaries and messengers continually on the hop. And when the mood seized him he waved away the interminable parchment-rolls, bellowed for his horse, and rode out to hunt in Sherwood. He loved his sport and would always make up the time by working far into the night.

Soon after Becket's assassination in 1170 the King endowed Newstead Priory, most likely as part of his elaborate penitence. There had been for some years a little Augustinian community, the Canons of Sherwood, and Henry must often have passed their house as he rode north through the forest to the hunting-lodge he built himself at Clipstone. Now he chose them as the beneficiaries of his uneasy conscience. Newstead is nine miles away, and still well outside the modern city-boundary, but it belongs to the Corporation, which maintains it as a historic monument, a shrine of Byronic relics, and a pleasant objective for a country drive. It can hardly be omitted from any study of Nottingham.

It was not, of course, all firm government and good order even under Henry. He had an unmanageable family. Richard Lionheart and John were but two of his four highly individual sons, who were continually plotting and fighting against him and each other. And there were always dissident barons ready to back them and take a sporting chance on which brother would be the next king. One such baron was William de Ferrers, Earl of Derby. In June 1174 he raided Nottingham while Henry was in France. The horrors of Stephen's reign were repeated. The town was overrun at the first onslaught, some of the people cut down, others taken prisoner. Then the rebels ransacked the houses, fired them, and rode away. The Castle garrison took no recorded action.

This was just one episode in an uprising that affected much of the Midlands and East Anglia. Henry reacted with his usual speed, a speed truly remarkable under the conditions of travel and communication in that century. On 8 July he landed at Portsmouth. Thence he rode to Canterbury and did conspicuous penance at Becket's tomb. Back in the saddle, he led his forces northwards to put down the rebellion. By the last day of July he was accepting the submission of Ferrers and the other ringleaders at Northampton. He let them off lightly, and Ferrers lived on to meet a Crusader's death at the seige of Acre fourteen years afterwards. Henry did not linger to inspect the damage at Nottingham or elsewhere. On 8 August he embarked again at Portsmouth, having settled the business in exactly a month. Back in France he tried to satisfy his sons with a redistribution of estates. Prince John received an increased share, being granted the castles of Nottingham and Marlborough, together with the then substantial allowance of a thousand pounds a year.

Less than twelve months later, Henry was again in England, making an overdue tour of his realm. 1 August 1175 found him riding into Nottingham and turning an ill-tempered eye upon the local nobility and gentry. He accused them roundly of breaking the forest laws. His Chief Justiciar, Richard de Lucy, spoke up

manfully in their defence, and, like a good civil servant, produced
the official instructions which should have covered them, nothing
less than Henry's own letters telling him to throw open the royal
forests and fishponds while the King was away campaigning, and
to allow any who wished to take game and fish there. Henry's
temper was not improved by being shown the files and he ignored
them. It was not a royal visit, probably, that gave widespread
pleasure.

When the King moved on, he seems to have left his tame bear
(a not inappropriate pet) at the Castle. Early the next year, when
the Court was preparing to celebrate Easter in great state at
Winchester, word came that the animal was to be taken down
there. Christmas, however, was spent at Nottingham. Two of the
princes, Geoffrey and John, kept their father company, and so,
one would imagine, did the bear.

The importance of the Castle is underlined by the disputes
over its possession during the next reign. When Henry died at
Chinon in 1189, both his surviving sons were also on the Continent. Richard was committed to the Crusade, was determined
to go, but had natural suspicions of what John might get up to
during his absence. To square his brother, he gave him a great
slice of lands and honours, including the former Peverel Honour
of Nottingham, but with two significant qualifications: the Honour
was not to include control of the Castle it was designed to sustain,
and John had to swear that he would not set foot in England for
at least three years. It was about this time that Nottingham
received its second charter, granted by John and confirmed by
him when he became king, giving the townsmen the right to
choose their own reeve (subject to John's approval) and providing
for the said reeve to pay the taxes direct to the Exchequer, by-
passing the County Sheriff. This seed of democracy was not sown
by John out of any sympathy for local self-government. Like the
charters granted by many a more lovable monarch, it had to be
paid for.

John did not long keep his oath to stay in France. He knew
that Lionheart might not return from the Holy Land and that a
new king might be required at any time. He learned also that

Richard had named their nephew, Arthur of Brittany, as heir. John felt justified in breaking his oath and taking steps to safeguard his interests. He crossed the Channel and began an acrimonious dispute with Richard's representative, William Longchamp, the Chancellor. In particular, John tried to get possession of Nottingham Castle. Three times it was handed over, twice he was induced to give it up again, but it was once more in his hands when the news came that Richard was in an Austrian dungeon and might never be set free. When Richard did get back to England in March 1194, he made a bee-line for Nottingham, arriving there on the twenty-fifth. John was by then in France again, but his two constables, Ralph Murdoc and William de Wendeval, were stoutly holding the fortress in his name. Siege operations had begun when Richard arrived. Furious at being defied, he headed an assault which carried the outer defences. The garrison wilted when they realized that he was there in person, for, besides being undeniably the King, he had a terrifying record as an overthrower of strong places. On the twenty-eighth they opened the gates and let him in.

Richard immediately summoned a royal council. He sat between the two archbishops in the Castle hall. The Queen Mother was there to hear her sons' quarrel debated as a high matter of state. The Council called upon John to appear within forty days and answer the charge of treason. Richard then rode off into the forest to enjoy two days at the Clipstone hunting-lodge. He went on to Southwell to meet the Scottish king, William the Lion, and the two monarchs travelled to London together. John met his brother in Normandy a month later and made his apologies. In the following year he was back in Nottingham, dispensing lavish hospitality. Thereafter he behaved himself, more or less, until 1199, so that Richard, on his death-bed, reversed the succession arrangements and nominated him the next king.

Nottingham saw a good deal of the new monarch. John found reassurance in the Castle's strength during the seventeen years of his uneasy reign. Indeed, the frequency of royal visits often served as a rough barometer of political pressures. Down to the time of Charles I the town saw most of its sovereign when there was trouble in the air. John was there in 1210, preparing to march against the Welsh rebels, when he heard the disturbing rumour that his barons were plotting to depose him in favour of the elder Simon de Montfort. It was false, and it was left to their sons to fight for power more than fifty years later, but the mere existence of such a rumour indicated John's unpopularity.

Two years later, in September 1212, Nottingham was again the mobilization-centre for an expedition against Wales. The town hummed with the gathering of the feudal levies and the grumbling of their reluctant leaders. John arrived in a fury and ordered the hanging of the eight Welsh hostages before he would sit down to his meal – probably the most horrible incident recorded in the long history of the Castle, which is pleasantly free from atrocities. John's fury was due partly to the unhelpful attitude of his own great barons, who made it plain that if John marched against Wales he would march alone: they would all remember the Pope's pronouncement, so far conveniently ignored, which absolved them from their allegiance. So, after a few days, the King took the London road, and the various detachments went their homeward ways.

Runnymede and Magna Carta came three years later. The agreement was immediately broken, fighting started, and the barons called in the King of France. John spent his last Christmas in Nottingham Castle, which he had prepared for a possible siege. The region was hostile to him, but by holding its two key fortresses, Nottingham and Newark, he counted on dominating it. It was at Newark, in the following October, that he died.

CHAPTER SIX

Robin Hood

THIS seems as good a moment as any to pause and consider Robin Hood.

He is usually depicted as the contemporary of Richard I and John. This is the period of *Ivanhoe*, in which Robin is introduced as 'Locksley' (the name of the Nottinghamshire village tradition-ally regarded as his birthplace) and Friar Tuck also appears. Here, as in countless other ways, Scott has influenced the fiction-writers who have followed him. The difficulties in accepting that date will be dealt with shortly.

Whatever the head-scratching of the scholars, it might as well be admitted at once that, true, false, or non-proven, the Robin Hood story is more important to the world at large than anything else to do with Nottingham. In lands where Test cricket arouses no quiver of interest and where the origins of a bicycle matter nothing so long as it goes, Robin Hood is recognized as an old friend. The Russians know him as Robin 'Good', just as they know Hamlet as 'Gamlet'. To the Icelanders he is Hróa Hött, while to the Poles his lieutenant is Maly John, and to the Romanians the whole shadowy band of outlaws has appeared in print under the delight-ful title of *Umbrele din Pădurea Sherwood*. Even in the steaming jungle of Brazil the young reader escapes in fancy, and in Portu-guese, to the cooler forest north of Nottingham. Robin and his men are loved by far-off nations who do not care a button for Arthur and all his Round Table.

Only an extreme optimist would come to Nottingham expecting authentic relics, and the citizens are too honest (or a cynic might say too unenterprising) to manufacture them. Even in the Trip to

Jerusalem no one points to a genuine alehorn that once brushed the outlaw's russet beard. There is no tomb, for every schoolboy knows that Robin died in Yorkshire, bled to death by a treacherous nun of Kirklees. Long ago there was a grave *there*, and an epitaph copied by an antiquary giving the date as 1247, but the evidence has long vanished and the epitaph sounds like a fake. Little John, for his part, is said to lie in the churchyard of his reputed birthplace, Hathersage in Derbyshire, where an outsize skeleton was exhumed in 1782. The long grave is still marked, and Hathersage is worth a visit for the incidental Peakland scenery, though hardly for any evidence it offers of the outlaw's authenticity. The same might be said of all the places, some much closer to Nottingham, whose names suggest an association – Robin Hood's Well or Stable or Larder, Friar Tuck's Well, and so forth. Such place-names are generously scattered over Nottinghamshire, Lincolnshire and Yorkshire.

Within the city Robin and his band are loyally commemorated. 'Little John' is the name of the great clock in the Council House: his mellow boom is said to carry seven miles with a favouring wind but is mercifully silenced during the night hours. Under the dome, in the shopping-arcade, Robin is one of the four historical themes treated by Denholm Davis in his frescoes. Friar Lane, leading up to the Castle, takes its ancient name from the Carmelites who established themselves there about 1272, and it has nothing to do with Friar Tuck, but Maid Marian Way, which meets it at right-angles, is a purely modern exercise in demolition and road-widening. 'An insult to Maid Marian,' declared the local Professor of Architecture when it was under construction in 1965, 'and one of the ugliest streets in Europe.' This seems to me an exaggerated claim.

At the top of Friar Lane, with the outer wall of the Castle as effective background, James Woodford's seven-foot bronze statue of Robin dominates a group composed of Will Scarlet, Alan-à-Dale, Little John, Tuck and other famous outlaws. Unfortunately, as Eros long ago discovered in Piccadilly Circus, bows and arrows present an irresistible temptation to vandals. Replacements and repairs have proved expensive. Neither floodlighting nor a prickly

hedge has deterred the offenders. It has been suggested that a siren
be fitted, to wail when a finger is laid on the sculpture, or that the
bow be electrified, or that a moat be excavated and filled with
dye. The artist himself was driven to propose, philosophically,
'Let Robin hold his bow, and leave the arrow to the imagination.'

Inside the Castle the outlaw is commemorated only obliquely,
in the regimental museum of the Sherwood Foresters, whose
associated volunteers, the old 'Territorials', were known as the
Robin Hoods.

So there are no ancient relics, only names and modern representations. A stranger inquiring for 'the Forest' will be directed to
the public park with its games pitches and bowling-green, its skir-
mishing dogs and entwined lovers. 'Sherwood', similarly, is the
pleasant residential suburb just beyond. The romantically named
'Robin Hood's Chase' is a pedestrian way, the thinnest possible
ribbon of green (though none the less welcome) running through
one of the drabber Victorian quarters to St Ann's Well Road,
another name that no longer lives up to its promise. The real
Sherwood, the hunting-ground of kings, survives only in isolated
tracts of woodland, interspersed with farms, collieries and the
stately homes that have earned this area the alternative title of
'the Dukeries'. Little remains of the true forest save the oaks
in Bilhagh, the birches in Birkland, and the wooded stretch of
Budby.

But was there such a person as Robin Hood? If so, when?

The problem bristles with difficulties to delight the specialist
scholar and weary the common reader.

Take, for instance, the traditional encounter with Richard I.
How neatly it would fit into those two April days in 1194 when
the returned Crusader is known to have sought relaxation at his
hunting-lodge!

Alas, Robin's famous longbow was not then an Englishman's
weapon. The Welsh used it, but the English swore by the cross-
bow. The six-foot bow and its clothyard shaft drawn to the ear
belong to the English archer of a later period.

Likewise, it is too early for Friar Tuck. There were no friars in

England until 1221. There were no friars anywhere in Richard's lifetime.

Strictly speaking, there was no 'Sheriff of Nottingham' until 1449, when the town's two bailiffs changed their title – but that really is splitting hairs, for Robin's traditional antagonist would not have been the town's officer but the Sheriff of Nottingham-shire and Derbyshire, whose responsibilities included Sherwood Forest. So that is not a real difficulty. The other two are.

They have led some people to argue that Robin must belong to a later period. In *The Truth about Robin Hood* P. Valentine Harris connects him with a Robert Hood of Wakefield who may have been involved in the Earl of Lancaster's rising in 1322, but his evidence does not convince Maurice Keen, whose more recent book, *The Outlaws of Medieval Legend*, is probably the best study of the whole subject. There was quite a different Robert Hood described in 1230 as 'a fugitive from justice', and as far back as 1450 Walter Bower placed him in the time of Simon de Montfort and the Barons' War, that is, 1265 – a war, incidentally, in which the longbow was still an undervalued instrument of homicide.

'It is surely beginning to look', says Maurice Keen, 'as though in this quest for a historical Robin Hood we are pursuing a will o' the wisp.'

There must, however, have been *somebody*.

Robin was a well-known, well-beloved character by 1377, when Langland, in his revised version of *Piers Plowman*, makes the chaplain Sloth admit:

I can not perfitly my pater-noster as the prest it syngeth:
But I can rymes of Robyn Hood and Randolf Erle of Chestre.

In the same strain one of Langland's contemporaries, the author of *Dives and Pauper*, unknown but thought to have been a Fran-ciscan, wrote acidly of reluctant churchgoers: 'Late they come and soon they go away. If they be there a little while, them thinketh full long. They have liever go to the tavern than to Holy Church. Liever to hear a song of Robin Hood or of some ribaldry, than for to hear Mass or Matins. ...'

These 'rymes of Robyn Hood', as they have come down to us,

belong to the late Middle Ages. 'Robin Hood and the Monk' may go back to Edward II's reign, but, says Maurice Keen, 'most of our early ballads seem to bear a date between about 1450 and 1500', though 'the world of which they sing sounds older'.

In those last words lies the explanation of some of the bothersome inconsistencies. We know, we have documentary evidence in Langland and elsewhere, that still earlier ballads were going the rounds long before those that bear the linguistic stamp of '1450 and 1500'. We know from other literary examples how poems, handed down orally over many generations, not only change their wording but add fresh incidents and characters, and (what can be most deceptive) introduce material that would be an anachronism, unthinkable in the old version. The *Iliad* has gathered such excrescences as a boat collects barnacles: hence the 'Homeric Question'. In the same way it is easy to understand why Friar Tuck (like Maid Marian) appears in some ballads and not others, and how the details of the archery could have been changed when the longbow became the accepted weapon.

As well as the ballads there were, of course, the mummers' plays, in which by the end of the Middle Ages Robin Hood and Maid Marian were leading characters. The item, 'liveries for Robin Hood', figures in household accounts. The *Paston Letters* contain Sir John's lament in 1473 for the departure of his keeper, 'W. Woode, which promised he would never go from me, and thereupon I have kept him this three year to play Saint George and Robin Hood and the Sheriff of Nottingham.'

So by then, indeed long before then, Robin was an established hero, and men thought of him as a character in the remote past. Writing in 1420, the Scottish chronicler Andrew of Wyntoun thought that he and Little John were operating in 1283, but John Major, in his *History* published in 1521 (about ten years after the printing of *A Lytell Geste of Robyn Hode*, based on the ballads), dates the outlaw 'about the time of King Richard I, according to my estimate', and adds, 'His deeds are sung all over England. . . . He was the prince of robbers, and the most humane.'

This brings us back to square one, the reign of Lionheart or soon afterwards; and if friar and longbow can be explained as later additions there is no reason to disbelieve in a real outlaw leader as the root of the legend. After all, Charlemagne existed and probably had a follower named Roland, even if there was no magic horn and it was local Basques rather than Saracens who laid the ambush at Roncesvalles. We can accept Arthur as a Romano-British chief in the Dark Ages without having to believe in Excalibur or the trimmings added by Tennyson. It is far easier to understand how a few inconsistencies crept into the ballads, and why in that largely illiterate era there is no documentation, than to explain how a completely fictitious hero could have been conjured out of nothing and firmly established, without help of television or comic strip, in the hearts of a whole people.

There is no doubt whatever that the outlaws and their doings, as we know them from the stories, had their close counterparts in such records as do exist, even though the names do not match. Maurice Keen thinks that one Roger Godberd 'deserves special notice', seeing that 'the scene of his activities was Robin Hood's own forest of Sherwood' and 'much of his career is reminiscent of that of the ballad hero'.

This Roger and his brother were seeking pardon in the autumn of 1265 after the Battle of Evesham (was Bower thinking of them when he made Robin a follower of Simon de Montfort?) but they seem to have been outlawed and to have become a serious threat to the peace. An Exchequer Account of 1266–7 refers to the counter-measures taken by Reynold de Grey, who had been appointed Constable of Nottingham Castle after the royalist victory. He was given a considerable force to 'suppress the enemies of our lord the King' – two knights with their men-at arms, twenty mounted crossbowmen under a captain, and twenty archers and ten crossbowmen on foot. Led by Reynold de Grey's lieutenant, Roger de Leyburn, this little army fought two battles with the outlaws, one in the heart of the forest, without any satisfactory result. In fact, they lost horses to the value of £63.

Roger Godberd and his brother were still enjoying their freedom in 1270, and were largely responsible for the complaints pouring in to the King that 'through outlaws, robbers, thieves and malefactors, mounted or on foot, wandering by day and night, in the counties of Nottingham, Leicester and Derby, so many and great homicides were done that no one with a small company could pass through most parts without being taken and killed or spoiled of his goods'. Henry's reply to this was to levy 100 marks from the three afflicted shires and hand over the money to Reynold de Grey for a further effort. This time the Constable had more luck. Roger was caught and, rather surprisingly, not hanged on the spot but ordered by the King to be detained until further notice. His fate is not recorded. Perhaps it can be assumed, or perhaps not. Henry III was a kindly, indecisive man – not for nothing was he nicknamed 'Heart of Wax' – and there may have been political considerations in the case. His son Edward had a more forthright approach to outlaws. When Adam Gurdon, a knight who had taken to the road, was terrorising travellers between London and Winchester, the prince sought him out and defeated him in personal combat.

It was a great age of outlaws, in Sherwood and elsewhere, and when Edward came to the throne he sensibly ordered the clearance of thickets on both sides of the highway to make ambushes more difficult. Only six years after the capture of Roger Godberd there was still plenty of lawless activity in the Nottingham neighbourhood. The Steward of Sherwood, John de Lascelles – the officer, that is, commanding the King's foresters and specifically responsible for the hunting-grounds – caught two men carrying bows and arrows in the prohibited area. He locked them up for the night in a house at Blidworth, the village where, incidentally, Will Scarlet is said to be buried. During that night the house was raided by twenty armed men and the prisoners spirited away, an incident quite in the vein of the Robin Hood stories.

What was the secret of this character's immense popularity and what makes him comprehensible to modern men throughout the world?

He was, says Maurice Keen, 'essentially the people's hero'. The theme of the ballads 'is the righting of wrongs inflicted by a harsh system and unjust men'.

The ballads are sometimes tough and unsqueamish. Though

Robin's famous chivalry to women and championship of the poor are early features of the story, there is a crude flavour of reality about them very different from the false sentimentalism introduced in later centuries. Robin has been progressively reduced to a character fit for the toddlers, a pantomime figure to be played by a strutting principal boy. Sherwood has been overgrown by Hollywood. Any hint of Robin's radical sympathies has been resented as an intrusion of modern political propaganda. Yet in earlier ages his revolutionary significance was taken for granted. Ralegh, defending himself against a charge of high treason in 1603, cried out indignantly: 'For me, at this time, to make myself a Robin Hood, a Wat Tyler, a Kett, or a Jack Cade – I was not so mad!' His bracketing of Robin with those three is interesting, for all were leaders of actual rebellions.

Is it so fanciful, then, to see in the Sherwood outlaw the first of a long line running through Nottingham history as a continuous thread of protest – Roundheads, dissenters, Luddites, Reformers, Chartists and many more, ever varied in their views but consistent in their challenge to the established order? Byron, speaking up for the frame-breakers in the House of Lords, was another. So was William Booth, the Salvationist. In our own century writers as different as D. H. Lawrence and Alan Sillitoe have been at least alike in their fidelity to this tradition.

Robin Hood, voicing an exultant cry as he bestrode the Sheriff's body in the market place, defied an unacceptable social system on the very spot where, century by century, those later rebels were constantly to renew the struggle. The ballad tells how

> All the people of Notyngham
> They stode and behelde;
> They saw nothing but mantels of grene
> That covered all the Felde.

It was a portent of countless mass conflicts the same square would witness down the ages.

CHAPTER SEVEN

The Growing Town

NOTTINGHAM CASTLE became a pleasanter residence under John's successor, Henry III, who believed in comfort. He took a personal interest in decoration, and was specially fond of delicate green backgrounds for the painted cloths with which he hung his walls. The Queen's apartments here were adorned with a sequence depicting the exploits of Alexander the Great, and quite likely the scheme reflected Henry's own taste, for it is known what close attention he gave to such details. The records show that, however feeble he may have been in handling his barons, he was tireless in harrying builders and decorators at his various castles. The chapel at Windsor, we read, was to be painted 'as the King enjoined by word of mouth'. He had an almost modern concern for sanitation, and a constable was apt to receive abrupt instructions to improve matters 'as he values his life and liberty'. At the Tower of London Henry was emphatic: 'Since the privy chamber of our wardrobe is situated in an undue and improper place, wherefore it smells badly, we command you on the faith and love by which you are bounden unto us, that you in no wise omit to cause another privy chamber to be made in the same wardrobe in such more fitting and proper place as you may select there, even though it should cost a hundred pounds.' At Nottingham he ordered new windows, a louvre and a dais for the great hall, a new altar, sedilia and murals for the Queen's Chapel, and wainscoting for her chamber and his own.

These improvements did not, of course, come at once. Henry was only nine when his father died, and though he reigned for fifty-six years thereafter he was not at first in a position to impose

his tastes and standards. His conflict with his barons, who had a
very different set of priorities, did not come to a head until almost
half a century after his father's humiliation at Runnymede. In this
conflict Nottingham was, as usual, too important to escape in-
volvement.

When, in 1258, Henry had to agree to the Provisions of Oxford,
drawn up by twelve representatives of the disaffected barons, he
was forced to appoint one of the twelve, William Bardolf, as
Constable. Within a year or two, however, he felt safe enough
again to dismiss Bardolf and put John de Baliol into his place,
that same Baliol whose widow founded the Oxford college. Early
in 1264 the two factions prepared for civil war. Bardolf seized the
Castle again in the interests of Simon de Montfort. Baliol was with
the royalist forces, which now moved north and took Nottingham.
The old violent days seemed to have returned. As the chronicler,
Matthew of Westminster, wrote, 'There was no peace in the realm.
All things were wiped out with slaughter, burnings, rapine and
plunder. Everywhere there was wild crying and lamentation and
horror.' It is not surprising that a year or two later Nottingham
began building a town wall as an insurance against such misfortunes in the future.

Meanwhile, Bardolf surrendered the Castle to Henry, made his
peace, and enrolled under the royal banner. Henry did not restore
Baliol but appointed a new constable, a local knight, Sir John de
Grey. Having kept Easter with proper solemnity, the King led
his army south to relieve Rochester, which de Montfort was
besieging. Henry covered the hundred and fifty miles in five
days, good going for a king better at colour schemes than at
campaigning. Afterwards, he may have wished that he had not
hurried: within a month he had lost the Battle of Lewes and was
de Montfort's prisoner, along with Baliol, Bardolf and many
others.

At Nottingham the immediate sequel was another change in
the custody of the Castle: John de Grey, the royalist, was ejected
in favour of a prominent de Montfort man, Hugh le Despenser,
who also held the high office of Justiciar of England. The inhabitants who suffered most from the shift of power were the Jews,

who were closely identified with the lavish expenditure which had made Henry unpopular. The barons tended to be anti-Jewish in sentiment. There were disturbances in London, Lincoln and even in Nottingham, where the Jewish community was relatively small. Some Jews, alert to the scent of further trouble, left for more tolerant kingdoms on the Continent.

They were wise, because they had lived out their usefulness in the eyes of those who had previously been glad to borrow from them. The Church's doctrine on usury was yielding to pressure, and excuses were being found to justify good Catholics in charging interest. Banking families such as the Medici would soon be the powers behind the medieval thrones. Why borrow from a Jew, it was now argued, when you could do business with an Italian Christian? This was the time when the name 'Lombard' acquired its special flavour of finance. The Nottingham Jews included 'David the Lombard' and 'Amyot the Lombard', so called either because they actually came from Italy or found it a good protective label. During the quarter-century following Lewes the position of the Jews worsened steadily, especially when Edward I succeeded Henry, and imposed one disability after another upon them, as Hitler did in his early years. Finally, when Edward was in Nottingham in 1290, the order was issued expelling all Jews from England. Not until Cromwell's time were they allowed to re-enter the country. In Nottingham they did not reappear noticeably until the early Victorian era when they contributed valuably to the expansion of the lace trade.

Meanwhile, apart from this demonstration of hostility to the local Jews, the second half of the Barons' War had little effect on Nottingham. When the Lord Edward escaped from captivity and resumed the struggle on his father's behalf, all the marching and counter-marching were in the West Midlands. Despenser quitted the Castle to join de Montfort and perished with him in the slaughter at Evesham. The liberated King Henry installed yet another constable. It was that Reynold de Grey who had so much trouble with the outlaws of Sherwood.

These national excitements, though they take up much space in history-books, represent only a few months out of two long reigns

which between them covered nearly a century after the death of
John. In that century Nottingham men were born, lived and died,
and were most of the time free to mind their own business. Henry
granted them a new charter in 1230, and extended their privileges
in later years. When Edward came to the throne he seems to have
been displeased with the burgesses for some reason. He suspended
these privileges for several years because of 'certain transgressions
which the burgesses and community of our town of Nottingham
had committed out of confidence in their liberties'. Whatever their
misdeeds, the townsmen received a new charter from him (and an
increased tax-assessment) in 1284. Henceforth they were allowed
to elect a mayor of the town and a bailiff (later to be called a
sheriff) for each of the two boroughs.

How the system worked cannot now be exactly determined,
owing to the loss of the ancient municipal records and in particular
a volume referred to as 'the Old Red Book', which seems to have
enshrined the details of civic rights and privileges and to have been
appealed to by the disgruntled lower sort in times of controversy.
In the Nottingham chapter of her *Town Life in the Fifteenth
Century* Alice Stopford Green points out that even the definition
of a 'burgess' is uncertain, and she quotes some of the ambiguous
phrases used in surviving documents, such as 'the Mayor, burgesses and community' and 'the Mayor and his brethren and the
commonalty of Nottingham'. In theory all the townsmen probably
had a share in local government, but in practice they left it to a
small group of the more influential, and these in course of time
developed into an oligarchy of leading families, extremely hard
to shift.

The Castle and Lenton Priory, both outside the town's
boundary and jurisdiction, were potential sources of irritation.
The Priory controlled all the three parish churches and appointed
their priests, and its annual fair was a thorn in the flesh of the
town's traders, but it did not provoke the hostility seen in other
places where the local monasteries wielded really oppressive
powers. Similarly, relations between town and castle seem to have
been reasonably cordial, except for a stormy spell in the reign of
Edward II. In that period, 1313 to 1315, the Constable was John

The old sculpture and the new

'The Resurrection', English alabaster, 1400–30, now in Castle Museum. Some experts regard the battlement motif as proof of local manufacture.

James Woodford's bronze Robin Hood, beneath the Castle's outer walls. Second only to Eros as a temptation to vandals.

Newstead Abbey: successively an Augustinian priory, family seat of the Byrons, and literary shrine.

Wollaton Hall: flamboyant conceit of an Elizabethan tycoon, standing in its well-stocked deer-park two or three miles from the city centre. Now houses Natural History and Industrial museums.

Segrave, who was on very bad terms with the population in general though he enjoyed the support of the Mayor. The latter so infuriated the townsmen that a group got together and killed him, at the same time assaulting some of the officials and staff from the Castle. The actual killer of the Mayor was seized, however, and was about to be dragged off to the Castle when his sympathisers set all the church-bells ringing by way of a general alarm and a crowd rushed to his rescue. A year or two later the Constable experienced an even more violent demonstration of Nottingham 'protest'. One Robert Ingram and his supporters rang the tocsin, assembled the people with arms and banners and attacked the Castle, battering at the gates and blockading the fortress for more than a week, during which time neither Segrave nor any of his men dared venture out for fear of their lives.

These were exceptional disturbances. Mostly the town went its humdrum way, growing slowly and enlarging its contacts with the wider world.

Many men remained at least part-time farmers, trudging home at dusk with shouldered implements, their livestock pattering and lurching down the narrow streets in front of them. The town lands, the Sand Field and the Clay Field, still stretched up to and over the northern skyline, patterned with the stripes of medieval cultivation. Once the harvest was gathered, the unfenced plots became common grazing. The two 'Fields' were vast and had their own natural features with subdividing place-names. They fell into little valleys – Larkdale (today, the General Cemetery) and Wrendale (the Arboretum) and Lingdale where Waverley Street now runs. Sandcliff was the modern Wollaton Street. The Coppice and the Hunger Hills still retain their names.

The crafts and trades were increasing in diversity and importance. There were pottery kilns and smithies burning Sherwood charcoal. The surname 'le Spicer', in the list of mayors and bailiffs, shows that there was a livelihood for such specialists as the apothecary. Other surnames are equally informative. John le Fleming, one of the two Members of Parliament in 1295, is a reminder of the commercial link that was being forged with Flanders, as more and more Derbyshire wool began to be shipped

down the Trent from Nottingham and transferred to sea-going
vessels in the Humber for export to the Low Countries. Thomas
Mapperley's name shows that he came from the Derbyshire
village so called. He settled in Nottingham and transmitted the
name to what is now one of the pleasanter residential quarters,
built over the highest of the hills.

Wool was important. The Nottingham wool merchants were
among those summoned to York in 1322 to fix the 'staple' regu-
lating the market. There were lead ingots also from the Peak,
brought down by packhorse trains and transferred to river-craft at
Nottingham, and there was coal from the shallow workings of
Wollaton, near Lenton Priory. Such traffic meant extra business
and toll charges for the town's benefit.

Some of these tolls were specially authorized by the King for
limited periods under 'murage' grants to meet the cost of the new
wall. This was a formidable construction of white sandstone, thirty
feet high, six or seven feet thick, and reinforced at intervals with
even more massive buttresses. Sections come to light, from time to
time, when foundations are being excavated for new buildings,
but the archaeologist fights an unequal battle against the jugger-
naut of commercial development.

Like many more modern defence schemes the wall was terribly
costly and obsolete before it was finished, or rather given up. For
two generations the townsmen watched this white elephant creep
yard by yard along the line of the existing ditch (now Parliament
Street and Park Row) sometimes making no progress whatever
until another grant of murage was decreed. They must have
known that it would be no protection in their own lifetime but
perhaps they did not grumble unduly. After all, it was providing
employment and was being financed by the tolls levied on strangers. Within a few generations people had begun to steal stone
from it, and by Charles I's time there was nothing left above
ground-level.

It was during the thirteenth century that the friars arrived.
The Franciscans appeared about 1230. Henry, always a charitable
monarch, gave them a house at the foot of the Castle Rock. Later
he granted them timber from Sherwood, so that they could build

themselves a proper convent with a chapel, which they replaced in stone in 1303. Grey Friar Gate still indicates the general location. These friars were outward-looking, practical men whose contribution was not exclusively religious. They made a wharf on the River Leen just at their doors, which enabled goods to be embarked and unloaded at the very entrance to the town. The White Friars, or Carmelites, arrived about the time of Edward I's accession. They established themselves on the west side of the great market place at the corner of what became Friar Lane.

There were now two or three thousand people in Nottingham, with three parish churches, St Mary's, St Peter's and St Nicholas's, and several small 'hospitals', which were sometimes as much almshouses as places for the sick. Originally two of these were for lepers, but when the disease diminished they were converted to other charitable purposes.

There was some kind of grammar school well before 1289, when the first documentary evidence appears. We do not know what it was like, but we know that literacy was steadily growing throughout the country, for Langland was complaining, in the next century, though perhaps with his usual dyspeptic exaggeration, that 'every cobbler's son and beggar's brat goes to school nowadays'. Probably the Nottingham school was closely linked with St Mary's Church. Certainly, when a piece of property on 'The Pavement' was conveyed in 1382 to William de Adbolton, Master of Nottingham Grammar School, the name of the then Vicar, Robert de Retford, was coupled with his. All the historic schools of Nottingham were to begin in one of two streets bordering the churchyard, either Stoney Street or High Pavement.

Edward II plays no great part in Nottingham history, though he certainly came there. He was on his way in August 1318, when he met the rebel Earl of Lancaster outside Loughborough and made a short-lived agreement with him. In the following year, when the Scots tried to kidnap the Queen in Yorkshire, she was sent hurriedly to safety in Nottingham Castle. And it was there eleven years later that she figured in the melodramatic affair of 'Mortimer's Hole'.

Visitors are taken down the Hole today. It is a relatively salubrious affair, as 'secret passages' go, descending through the dry sandstone. It is advisable to go after lunch, not for digestive reasons, but because school parties enjoy preference in the morning.

Isabella in 1330 was not more than thirty-eight. A daughter of the French King, she had married Edward II when she was sixteen. She was described then as 'the rose among the fairest', but later, when an unsatisfactory married life had embittered her, as 'the she-wolf of France'. Edward, whose tastes lay elsewhere and otherwise, started tactlessly by passing on her father's wedding-gifts to his friend, Piers Gaveston. Although, in the fullness of time, he did give her four children and his rebellious barons liquidated Gaveston, the royal marriage was never a happy one. In due course Isabella went back to France, taking the future Edward III with her. There, at the French Court, she started her affair with the fugitive Roger Mortimer, one of the great Marcher Lords who, after serving Edward II with distinction in Ireland and elsewhere, had quarrelled with him and fled abroad. By March 1326 his relationship with Isabella was common talk in England. In September, using the fourteen-year-old prince as a figurehead, they landed in Essex and headed the revolt which deposed Edward II and proclaimed Edward III. The bestial murder of Edward II at Berkeley Castle a few months later was arranged by Mortimer and certainly neither obstructed nor denounced by Isabella, who continued for the next three and a half years to live openly with her lover, to the growing disgust of the people. Mortimer, though he took no official post, was the real master of England. Surrounded by a bodyguard of wild Welsh mercenaries, who spread terror wherever they went, he went on progress through the kingdom with his mistress, handing out favours and key appointments to his followers.

This, then, was the situation in October 1330, when Mortimer and Isabella arrived in Nottingham for the parliament they had summoned there. The gossip in the taverns is not difficult to imagine.

The boy King was in the Castle too. It is not quite true to say, as guidebooks sometimes do, that 'Edward III and his followers obtained entrance to the stronghold', an inaccuracy repeated by the notice-board above the spot. Edward himself was inside all the time. He had to be: he was nominally King of England and the gathering parliament was summoned in his name. Also, he was under Mortimer's eye. Isabella's lover was not blind to his own unpopularity. He knew there were plots against him. Those same Welsh mercenaries who protected his own life, and now commanded all the Castle entrances, were equally effective in seeing that none of Mortimer's opponents could gain control of the King.

Edward was now within a month of his eighteenth birthday, when a young English sovereign traditionally came of age. He had become a father some months earlier, when young Queen Philippa bore him the future Black Prince. Edward knew all about his mother's goings-on with Mortimer – who did not? – and quite enough about his father's murder. And he himself was no indecisive Hamlet.

The Court took up residence in the Castle on 7 September and during the next six weeks the air must have been thick with conspiracy. Mortimer felt he had the situation in hand. His Welshmen could deal with any open show of force. At night the Castle keys were kept in Isabella's bedchamber. So confident was he that in a stormy scene on 19 October not only his chief opponents but the King himself was interrogated in front of the Council. All naturally denied knowledge of any plot. William de Montacute (later the first Earl of Salisbury) defended himself with hauteur, declaring somewhat ambiguously that he would return a sharp answer to any accusing him of connection with any conspiracy 'inconsistent with his duty'. After the council meeting broke up, he said to Edward, with much less ambiguity: 'It would be better to eat the dog than that the dog should eat us.' Edward agreed to act that very night.

But how? Montacute and his friends had to be off the premises before lock-up time and Edward himself was virtually a prisoner in a fortress patrolled by Mortimer's followers. It was arranged that Edward should speak to the Deputy Constable, William d'Eland, of Basford, who was in charge while the Constable himself, Lord Grey of Codnor, was absent. Eland was ordered, on his allegiance to the King and on pain of being hanged later if he would not co-operate, to leave unlocked the postern gate opening upon the Castle Park. Eland needed no persuading. He explained at once that he had a better idea. There was a secret passage leading from the base of the rock and emerging in one of the Castle courtyards. He would show them this.

That evening he kept a rendezvous with Montacute and the other conspirators, about two dozen of them, all fully armed. They met in a thicket in the Park – there would have been more of them, had not some missed their way in the darkness. But there were enough.

They moved quietly to the base of the precipitous crag, passed through the hidden entrance and climbed the sandstone passage. Edward joined them in the courtyard. They went straight to where Mortimer was – he was not actually, at that moment, in the arms of his mistress, but in the next room to hers, still anxiously conferring with the Chancellor and his other satellites.

Only now was the alarm sounded. A steward of the royal household suddenly appeared, dagger in hand, shouting something about 'traitors'. He was instantly cut down. Another knight tried to defend the door. He too was killed. Whatever happened then was soon over: some say that Mortimer accounted for one of his attackers before he was overpowered, others that he tried to conceal himself behind a curtain. It is not certain whether Isabella was there all the time or whether she rushed in from the next room in a vain effort to save him.

When morning came it was proclaimed that the King had taken over the government himself. Parliament was prorogued and would reassemble at Westminster. In the town there was a quiet round-up of Mortimer's followers, or such as had not made themselves scarce. Mortimer was taken to London, tried by his peers and executed like a common criminal at Tyburn. Isabella did not, as is sometimes suggested, spend the rest of her days in captivity, but for another twenty-seven years travelled freely from one of her various estates to another, enjoying honourable treatment and the full use of her property. She and Edward remained on good terms. Each had plenty to forgive, and in a medieval royal family murder and conspiracy were occupational hazards one had to live with.

During his fifty-year reign Edward III made further additions to the Castle and more than once summoned Parliament to Nottingham, when the little town must have been bursting at the seams with the mustering of bishops and barons, burgesses and knights of the shire, from all over the kingdom, together with their often considerable retinues. Luckily, in those days, proceedings were relatively brief.

Nottingham people could be excused if they took more interest in their own local affairs, in which they had some say. The Town Council or Corporation had not yet fully evolved, but leading townsmen served on a body called the Mickletorn Jury. They kept a continual eye open for public nuisances and individual misbehaviour, and once or twice a year brought their list of 'presentments' before the Mayor, sitting in a judicial capacity with the support of the coroners and bailiffs.

The Mayor had considerable powers. He could fine offenders, punishing an 'affray of blood' (such as a punch on the nose) with a penalty of sixpence, when that sum might be a day's wages. He could walk through the market and order the instant seizure of unwholesome foodstuffs. He was the accepted arbitrator in numerous disputes. By 1354 he needed a clerk, the humble forerunner of the modern Town Clerk. By 1360 he was allowed the expenses that his multifarious duties involved.

This was a few years after the Black Death, which, striking Dorset in August 1348, had crept up into the Midlands by the following spring. There are no accounts of what happened when it hit Nottingham: the imagination can only work from the general facts, few but stark. It is reckoned that a million and a half people in England were wiped out, between a third and a half of the entire population. The only exact figures for this district are the records of dead clergy kept by the Church. For the priests in the Nottingham deanery the mortality that year was over thirty-five per cent, or one in three. There is no reason to suppose that the laymen fared better. Yet life went on, a fact which may bring comfort to those who regard our own century as uniquely doom-laden. The 1377 poll-tax figures suggest that the population of the town had risen again to about three thousand.

One local record tells its own story. Just before the Black Death there had been serious flood damage to Trent Bridge, which then comprised nineteen low arches, the various town wards being normally responsible for maintaining one or more of them. To help with the abnormal expenditure the town was granted tolls for five years, on payment of ten shillings annually to the Exchequer. But in the year of the plague it proved impossible to collect even that modest sum.

An indirect consequence of the Black Death was the stimulus given to the local trade in alabaster. This stone is soft and easy to work. The acute labour-shortage (which had so many other effects in English economic history after the plague) made it an ideal material for the altarpieces and other stone carvings that were in continual demand.

The extraordinary thing is that these alabasters, which can be admired in places as far apart as the National Museum of Iceland, Santiago de Compostela in Spain, and the Dalmatian island of Korčula (as well as, more conveniently, the Victoria and Albert or the Castle Museum itself) were not recognized as English work at all until about 1890. Once on the trail, however, the art historians found ample evidence that English alabaster had been exported all over medieval Europe both as unworked stone and as finished carving. Nottingham, being near the sources of the material, was the chief though not the only centre of the trade.

Some of these artists are known to us by name, though surviving work cannot be attributed to individuals or even with absolute certainty to the town. One well-known figure was Peter the Mason, who lived in St Mary's Gate, and in 1367 received a commission from Edward III for an altarpiece for St George's, Windsor. This massive work (now vanished, alas) cost two hundred pounds and was in sections. The Sheriff had the task of finding the ten carts needed to transport it. The journey took seventeen days.

Orders like that did not often come the way of Peter and his fellow 'arblasterers', as they were called. Small panels, images and occasionally secular items such as salt cellars were the basis of the industry. Triptychs were popular as altarpieces, for the hinged panels could be delivered separately and could be folded during Lent to conceal the carved and brightly coloured scenes. It was not only in churches that these alabasters were set up. Many a private house had, if not its chapel, at least a corner treated as a shrine, with a small image of the Virgin or a plaque of the Head of John the Baptist. The latter was a Nottingham speciality and was a good selling line even in London.

The truth is, the Nottingham arblasterers were not among the world's greatest sculptors and, though their handiwork is well worth looking at, it was at best folk art with a considerable element of mass-production.

The alabaster was quarried first near Tutbury, rather more than twenty miles away, and later at Chellaston Hill near Derby. The stone is a form of gypsum and is used now for countless workaday purposes involving plaster. Newly quarried, it responds easily to the carver. The harder, polished-marble effect we normally associate with it comes from exposure to the air. The Nottingham craftsmen thus started with the great advantage of getting their material new and soft, but it was quite common for distant customers to buy blocks to be carved by their own artists. Thus, in 1414, the Abbot of Fécamp sent his agents all the way from Normandy to Hull by sea, after which they travelled on horseback to Nottingham, where they signed a contract with Thomas Prentis for a quantity of Chellaston alabaster to be shipped to France.

That again, like the Windsor altarpiece, was a specially important transaction, the Abbot doubtless wishing to have some outstanding work of art created under his own supervision. More typically, the alabasters were produced in the workshops round St Mary's Church by merely competent craftsmen who followed stock designs or just slightly varied them to order. In the case of the panels the scene was first drawn, or rather cut into the soft stone in outline – a Crucifixion or an Entombment, the Entry into

Jerusalem or St Giles shoeing a horse possessed by the Devil, or whatever well-known subject was required. The surrounding stone was pared away until the figures stood out in bold relief. They were then richly painted and gilded by another craftsman known as a 'stainer'. In the case of distant orders, like the one for Windsor, this might be done afterwards, when the carving had survived the journey, but the smaller and cheaper work would be coloured in the Nottingham workshops. Nicolas Hill was famous for his painting and gilding.

Why was this famous trade forgotten? How was it that until late Victorian times it was almost impossible to see an English alabaster without going to France or further? The answer in a word is, of course, the Reformation.

The trade flourished exceedingly in the fifteenth century and right on into the Tudor period. Then, under Edward VI, it ceased abruptly. An Act of Parliament in 1550 ordered the destruction or defacement of all religious 'images of stone, timber, alabaster, or earth, graven, carved or painted' under pain of fines and imprisonment. Needless to say, the law was not literally obeyed in every case. Certain enterprising gentlemen cashed in on the resulting panic and created a black market for export. As the English Ambassador in France complained to the Privy Council eight months later, 'Three or four ships have lately arrived from England laden with images, which have been sold at Paris, Rouen and other places . . . and eagerly purchased . . . which needed not had their Lordships' command for defacing of them been observed.'

Countless other carvings were lost for ever. It was all too easy to convert them by fire into plaster of Paris. Some, however, were hidden. One altarpiece turned up in York in 1957. Nottingham's own collection in the Castle Museum includes a beautiful Virgin and Child, a St Peter and an unknown bishop, all found beneath the floor of a derelict church in the county as long ago as 1779. These figures were carved about 1400 and stand three feet high. In the south chancel aisle of St Mary's is a small panel of much the same period, which someone hid beneath the floor when news of the government ban arrived from London.

The trade Nottingham lost then was eagerly snapped up by the craftsmen of Malines. They began where the English arblasterers left off, still importing the stone from the Derbyshire and Staffordshire quarries, carving it for the undiminished market in Catholic Europe, and, it must be admitted, advancing from the stylized medievalism of the Nottingham artists to something livelier and more experimental. In 1967 this Nottingham–Malines connection was underlined by a notable exhibition in Brussels, which brought together the work of both schools and opened the eyes of many art-lovers to a hitherto rather undervalued form.

CHAPTER EIGHT

The Castle of Care

RICHARD II was in Nottingham for most of the summer of 1392. He was then conducting an acrimonious dispute with the Londoners, who had refused him a loan. In punishment he had suspended their civic liberties and removed the Court of Chancery to Nottingham. Twenty-four London burgesses, including the renowned architect, Henry Yevele, made the long trek north to crave his pardon, which they finally gained at the intercession of the Queen, Anne of Bohemia.

It was during this visit that the young King signed, on 8 July, a licence authorizing John Plumptre, a local wool merchant or 'stapler', to found the charity which still flourishes under his name, and – what is considerably more remarkable after close on six centuries – under the direction of his namesake and descendant. The original John Plumptre lived on the spot now occupied by the Flying Horse. When he died in 1416, he bequeathed the house to swell the endowment already provided for the 'hospital'. The Plumptre Hospital was in fact an almshouse for 'thirteen widows, broken down with age and depressed by poverty', and two chaplains were to take care of their spiritual comfort. The Hospital was more than once rebuilt in later centuries, and, its endowments having appreciated, today accommodates more residents than ever it did, and in conditions fitting for the twentieth century. The founder's family continued prominent in Nottingham until the death of John Plumptre, M.P., in 1791, and, though long since removed to Kent, they still manage the affairs of the Hospital and provide housing which is as badly needed as ever it was. Other names occur in the roll of its bygone masters, but a Plumptre has now held the position in unbroken sequence since 1703. Many a noble house with a cluster of sonorous titles might envy the continuity, and the social contribution, of all those plain Mr Plumptres stretching down the ages from 1392.

Richard II was in Nottingham again in 1397. He summoned a council there to denounce the treason of his chief opponents: his uncle the Duke of Gloucester, soon afterwards murdered by his order, the Earl of Arundel (beheaded), the Earl of Warwick (banished) and the Archbishop of Canterbury, also exiled. Parliament now 'was as a catspaw in the King's hands'. As noted earlier, Nottingham saw most of the sovereign when political troubles were brewing.

Richard himself was deposed and murdered two years afterwards, but for some time there were rumours that he was still alive and in Scotland. This talk circulated in Nottingham. The Warden of the Grey Friars, John Gounfrey, was arrested with another Franciscan, Robert Leycestre, for spreading the story. They were sent bound to London and imprisoned in the Tower. Leycestre was one of eight friars hanged at Tyburn for preaching sedition against the new king, Henry IV.

Nottingham did not see much of the three Lancastrian Henrys, though they remembered the Castle when they wanted a safe place for prisoners. The future James I of Scotland spent several years there from 1407 onwards, and in 1422, when Henry V was distributing his French captives, mainly to Welsh fortresses, he sent two dozen to winter in Nottingham. In the March of the previous year he had visited the town with his bride, Shakespeare's engaging Katharine of France, on the triumphal tour following her coronation. The Prior of Lenton, Thomas Elmham, had been the royal chaplain at Agincourt. His history, *Gesta Henrici Quinti*, is the most important contemporary account of the period.

But it was Henry VI's reign that was to contain events of more local significance, for it saw the new town charter of 1449. This was the most momentous of all the charters, and was properly celebrated by the city in 1949. The then City Librarian, the late Duncan Gray, contributed an admirable souvenir volume,

Nottingham through 500 Years: a Short History of Town Government.

Henry VI made the town a county in itself, 'separate, distinct, divided' from the shire. Only the royal fortress and 'the King's Hall', later the Shire Hall, kept their extra-territorial status. The bailiffs were promoted to the dignity of sheriffs and tried civil disputes in a county court. Seven aldermen were to be elected for life from the ranks of the burgesses. They were to act as justices of the peace and wear crimson gowns like their London counterparts. Nottingham thus at last attained full civic independence, under the King, with a full complement of dignitaries supported by small fry such as the unpaid 'decennaries' or petty constables in each of the seven wards, the watchmen, and the Mickletorn jurors, the prototypes of Dogberry, Verges and their colleagues in *Much Ado*.

Civic business was transacted in the stately Guildhall at Weekday Cross, part of which served as a jail for debtors and other offenders. It would be a mistake to picture fifteenth-century Nottingham as a new-born democracy. True, it was not too difficult to become a burgess, whatever that meant, and in the early days strangers could be enrolled on payment of half a mark, or six shillings and eightpence. But the average burgess, even if born and bred in the town, had in practice little say in its affairs. The Corporation was a tightly knit, self-perpetuating clique of a few leading families – as in London, Venice, Florence and the other great cities of the period. The Mayor had to be an alderman, and the aldermen were elected for life, and they had to be chosen from an oddly termed category of leading townsmen known as 'the Clothing', comprising forty or fifty who had already proved their reliability by holding minor office. It is easy to understand, in such circumstances, how a few names like Plumptre and Willoughby recur over and over again in the records, and how Thomas Thurland, an enormously rich wool stapler and local benefactor, came to serve nine or ten times as mayor. Part of Thurland's tomb remains in St Mary's Church, where he endowed a charitable Guild of the Holy Trinity. His name lives on also in Thurland Street, site of the mansion he built, which in after-days was to provide hospitality for the Stuart kings.

One of Thurland's outstanding contemporaries was Geoffrey
Knyveton, who held office for life as clerk of the works to Nottingham Castle and a number of other royal castles and manors in the
Midlands. Mayor in 1446, Knyveton must have been closely concerned with the obtaining of the charter which the King signed
in 1449. An experienced administrator, with a good deal of legal
experience in land disputes, Knyveton was probably intolerant of
too much interference by the humbler ratepayers, and an order
made during his year of office, on 25 November 1446, indicates
his recipe for good local government, 'that xii and the Mayor be
chosen to order and dispose of as they think meet of all things
belonging to the Commonalty of the town without interruption or
contradiction of any person within the town'. The twelve were to
be the aldermen with enough other substantial men to make up
the number, and this body, the town's executive committee, so to
speak, evolved into the Common Council. But it was still not
unknown for a much larger gathering to be convened; and seventeen years later, when Thurland had to pass by-laws 'against light
women' and 'against keeping of bawdy houses', he mustered one
hundred and thirty burgesses to give him moral support.

For the most part, however, the man in the street was firmly
excluded from the council chamber, and the town records, right
through the fifteenth and sixteenth centuries, abound in his lusty
but unavailing protests. The rank and file clamoured for an
annual reading of the Red Book detailing their rights and
privileges. In vain, presumably, because sometimes their petitions
were shakily supported by the words, 'according to the Red Book
as we do think'. As ratepayers they agitated to know 'how the
residue of our money is bestowed, for our money is therein as well
as yours was, and it is convenient that we know'. Like many a
ratepayer in later ages, they were left wondering. For some people
it might not have been at all 'convenient' for them to know. Alice
Stopford Green, an early student of these records, contrasted the
'apathy' of another famous city, Southampton, with the independent spirit of medieval Nottingham, 'the belief of its people in an
ideal liberty, steeped as it is in strong emotion'. The Mickletorn
Jury provided one safety-valve, and its regular 'presentations'

offered a means of checking or at least criticizing the misdeeds of the ruling clique. The records of the year 1511/1512 include complaints against the Mayor himself for selling unfit herrings in the market, the Mayor and the chamberlains for their neglect to repair the town gates, and one of the ex-mayors for his encroachment on the common lands.

If the 1449 Charter was, for Nottingham, the main event of Henry VI's reign, the outstanding and still visible landmark of that time was St Mary's Church, which was rebuilding between 1450 and 1470 with its splendid prodigality of windows and the central tower, battlemented and pinnacled, so prominent a feature on even the modern skyline.

The church must have been just about finished when the hapless Henry VI was murdered and at once began to acquire, among his more superstitious sympathizers, the unofficial status of a saint. One miracle credited to him is worth mentioning because it concerns the Nottinghamshire village of Caunton and a pastime destined later to win many supporters in the town itself.

William Bartram, wrote a monkish chronicler, had been playing what 'is called by some the foot-ball-game . . . a game, I say, abominable enough, and, in my judgement at least, more common, undignified, and worthless than any other kind of game, rarely ending but with some loss, accident, or disadvantage to the players themselves'. So it certainly proved for William Bartram, who 'being struck in his most sensitive parts by the foot of one who played with him, sustained long and intolerable pains, but,' concludes the monk triumphantly, 'having seen in a dream the glorious King Henry, suddenly received the benefit of health'. Encouraged no doubt by this miracle, the local youths must have continued to practise their abominable sport, for nearly four centuries later Notts. County was founded, today the oldest of the world's professional clubs.

Worse fouls than any seen in football mar the closing decades of the Middle Ages. In the Wars of the Roses Nottingham could not avoid its usual embarrassingly strategic role, though this time the town escaped damage and there was no fighting in the immediate vicinity. Nottingham men had to be found, however, to serve and die on distant fields. Such a troop was sent off in red jackets with white letters sewn on them to join the King at York in 1464.

Though never fought over at this time, the town was the setting for some tense dramatic episodes, offering material for splendid scenes which Shakespeare unfortunately neglected to write.

Both the Yorkist sovereigns, Edward IV and his brother Richard III, were frequently at the Castle and carried out extensive repairs. It was, along with Windsor and Warwick, one of the few major fortresses they troubled to maintain, for by the late fifteenth century artillery was becoming too good and there was a general feeling that castles had had their day.

Edward IV made for Nottingham in July 1469, hoping to block the southward drive of the northern rebels which (he suspected) was instigated by his former ally, the Earl of Warwick, though that formidable 'King-maker' was himself far away at Calais. Edward called a council to discuss the crisis. Richard of Gloucester was there – it was one of several occasions when the famous brothers met under that roof and wrestled with the life-and-death problems besetting them. But they had no forces at their command beyond a mere couple of hundred archers. The northern rebels swung west through Derby and then took Leicester, so that it was now Edward who was cut off from the south. The news came that Warwick had crossed the Channel and was in London. Henry VI was still alive, a prisoner in the Tower, and could easily be restored as Warwick's puppet.

Edward could not stay idle. He took a chance and rode off to meet Warwick and negotiate. A few days later he was Warwick's prisoner. After another year of political vicissitudes he was an exile at The Hague. When he returned in the spring of 1471, landing in Yorkshire ostensibly only to claim his family inheritance, he again made for Nottingham. By the time he got there he had gathered the support he needed, and it was at Nottingham that he reasserted his claim to the crown. The question was settled in his favour by the battles of Barnet and Tewkesbury, and the murder of Henry VI, which followed in a matter of weeks.

The tall blond Plantagenet was at Nottingham twice in 1473, and knowing his tastes we may imagine both castle and town alive with gaiety on the arrival of the Court. Edward was on progress round the Midlands. On the first occasion, in May, the Queen was expecting a child, born in June when they had passed on to Fotheringay: this was Richard, younger of the two 'Princes in the Tower' and doubtless named in compliment to his Uncle Gloucester, who had certainly been at Nottingham with them, for he appeared at the Council meeting held by Edward on 12 May. In September the Court was back again.

Apart from other business and pleasures, Edward must have been keeping an eye on his building-schemes, now in full swing. He was adding a massive octagonal tower at the north-western corner of the inner bailey, today the Castle Green. Though it was probably finished well before his death it was attributed by later generations to his brother and known as 'King Richard's Tower'. What Richard III *did* complete was the splendid range of state apartments adjoining it. With their mullioned bay-windows facing across the vast courtyard to catch the morning sun, these new quarters must have greatly enhanced the comfort of the visitors. With all this expenditure and activity, and with the constant come-and-go of a court which belonged rather to the Renaissance than to the Middle Ages, Nottingham was a lively place. The records of the Borough Court speak of gambling dens, light women and bawdy houses, and of the attempt to impose a closing-time at nine o'clock. The town's equivocal reputation for gaiety goes back a long way.

Edward and Richard probably met there in October 1481, when Edward was considering an expedition against Scotland (Nottingham was always a favoured mobilization-centre) and Richard may have come down from the northern counties where he was so genuinely popular. Edward was not too sure of his own popularity just then, and after staying three weeks he gave up his Scottish project and turned south again.

Eighteen months later he was dead, and Richard, as soon as he heard the news in Yorkshire, took the road to Nottingham, an ideal place from which to consider the tricky situation facing him. Edward's son, the Prince of Wales, now Edward V, was twelve. Richard was to be Protector during his nephew's minority.

This is no place to go over the controversies that still divide historians, but the dramatic associations of Richard and Nottingham cannot be appreciated unless some salient events are remembered.

Edward V was at Ludlow, the Yorkist family seat on the Welsh Marches. Richard meant to meet him at Northampton so that they could travel to London together. But at Nottingham he learnt that the widowed Queen and her much-mistrusted relatives, the Woodvilles, were planning to disregard his appointment as Protector so that they could govern the country themselves. Richard hurried to Northampton, to find that the boy King had been taken on to Stony Stratford and that excuses were being made to keep them at a distance. Richard knew he was outnumbered if it came to an open fight, but he never lacked courage. By a bold coup he outfaced his hesitant opponents and secured control simultaneously of the boy's person and the whole political situation. How thereafter he was able to persuade himself that his brother's marriage had been invalid and that neither of the princes was legitimate, so that he could take the crown as Richard III, must be studied elsewhere by those interested.

Traditionally, Richard called Nottingham 'the castle of his care' (some associate the phrase more particularly with that octagonal tower his brother had added), and in view of all that happened it was not an unfair description. The special reason for it was personal, though not without political overtones: it was here in April 1484 that a messenger from the North brought the news that his ten-year-old son, Edward, had died. 'You might have seen his father and mother in a state bordering almost on madness,' wrote the Croyland chronicler, 'by reason of their sudden grief.' Not only had they lost their son but they knew they would never have another. Anne, to whom Richard was devoted, was chronically ill and died in the following March, probably of the tuberculosis, which had already carried off her sister. Richard certainly knew care as he paced the high ramparts of Nottingham and pondered all the questions, small and great, that were brought to him for decision.

Among the lesser problems was the completion of the new state apartments, only one storey high at the late King's death. Richard decreed that they should be finished with an upper storey of timber instead of stone. The result – a foretaste of the coming era in which comfort would replace defence – was a range of half-timbered buildings with well-lit rooms, wainscotted and tapestried, with moulded ceilings, carved beams, and cheerful open hearths in front of great stone chimneypieces.

The Court was back in Nottingham for two months that autumn. On Friday afternoon, 11 September, the town was all agog for the arrival of the ambassadors from James III of Scotland, seeking peace. The Earl of Argyll, Chancellor of Scotland, together with the Bishop of Aberdeen and other notables, led a coruscating cavalcade through the Castle gates. The following morning, before High Mass, Richard received them in the great hall, enthroned under an emblazoned canopy. It was a scene in the best traditions of the Elizabethan drama. One can almost hear the sweet shiver of off-stage trumpets and some actor rolling off the sonorous titles:

My lords of Norfolk and Northumberland . . .

and proceeding to catalogue the Earls of Shrewsbury and Nottingham, the Chancellor, the Bishops of Worcester and St Asaphs, and all the other notables who were present, and whom any hack playwright would have found it child's play to arrange in blank verse. This eminent throng fell back so that the Scottish emissaries could advance to the dais and make obeisance. Archibald Whitelaw, King James' secretary, then delivered a Latin eulogy of Richard and presented the mission's credentials on bended knee. There could have been few moments in his short reign when Richard looked so splendidly and unchallengeably the master of his kingdom.

That flash of sunshine did not last. By the following June (the fatal year of 1485) he was back in his well-named Castle of Care, knowing that Henry Tudor was about to land in arms but uncertain where. Past contestants for the crown had come by way of the south coast and the east, but Tudor might appropriately land in Wales. From Nottingham Richard could turn quickly in any direction. By the same cool process of thought he did not start useless troop-movements. He had a small force with him. For the rest, he warned the commissioners of array in all the shires to prepare for mobilisation. He sent to London for the Great Seal: it must not fall into the hands of his enemy. On the evening of 1 August a travel-weary Master of the Rolls, Thomas Barowe, slid from the saddle in the courtyard and was conducted to the chapel, where he knelt before the King and delivered the Great Seal in its white leather bag.

That same day Henry Tudor sailed from Harfleur. On 7 August he landed at Milford Haven. Richard received the news four days later: with Drake-like aplomb he was enjoying some sport at his Bestwood hunting-lodge, some miles from the town. He took no panic action. He must know which way Henry was going. He sent off mounted scouts to get news. He issued orders that his main supporters should rendezvous at Leicester.

That was Thursday. It must have seemed a long week-end in the Castle of Care. Richard was eager to get moving. He was a brave enough soldier but he was also a skilful general. It was no use marching until he had reports on Henry's progress. Monday was the Feast of the Assumption. Whether from genuine religious feeling, or as a convenient excuse for waiting another twenty-four hours, Richard declared that he would not start until Tuesday.

It was as well. That Monday brought a stream of messengers. Lord Stanley sent word he was sick and could not ride to join Richard. His son, Lord Strange, who was in attendance at Court as hostage for his father's loyalty, tried to make an unobtrusive departure from Nottingham. Brought back and interrogated, he protested his father's innocence but confessed that he himself and his uncles were involved in a plot.

Another messenger rode in with the news that Henry had reached Shrewsbury – and that nobody had struck a blow against him. For the first time Richard's calm cracked briefly. He shouted: 'Treason!' Soon came a fresh report: Henry was advancing eastwards through Shropshire and had arrived at Newport. It looked as though he were making straight for Nottingham. Richard recovered his uncanny calm. Was it fatalism or confidence? At this point it was more likely still confidence. He cancelled the order to march next morning. He slept at Bestwood on Tuesday night and hunted on Wednesday. Riding back to the lodge that afternoon he found a messenger waiting with bad news from the North: the Earl of Northumberland, by what looked like sabotage, had delayed the mobilisation of the East Riding. And it was the North on whose love and loyalty Richard had always been able to depend.

He remounted and returned hastily to the Castle. More messengers. Henry's army had veered south-eastwards. Was he making for London now? He must be stopped. The time for action had arrived. Early next morning came news that Henry had camped near Lichfield. Richard gave his men their marching orders. To-morrow he would leave for Leicester as originally planned.

So, on Friday morning, he rode out from his Castle of Care for the last time, 'with a frowning countenance and truculent aspect, mounted on a great white courser', and the townspeople watched the long column uncoil across the meadows, over Trent Bridge and down behind the crest of Wilford Hill. Bosworth was fought on the following Monday, and Richard, crown on head, battle-axe in hand, met a valiant end amid a mêlée of false friends and enemies. The enigma of his character remains, but he had scarcely lived long enough to pack in all the calculated villainies that Shakespeare and the Tudor propagandists attributed to him. He was thirty-two.

CHAPTER NINE

The Tudor Peace

BOSWORTH makes a neat break in history-books but at the time its finality was not so obvious. Within two years Nottingham was to see the new king in arms again, and every prospect of a bloody conflict uncomfortably near.

The Yorkists had rallied behind Lambert Simnel, a pretender in a double sense, since his claim to be Richard's nephew was untrue. But he had the support, oddly enough, of a genuine nephew, that Earl of Lincoln whom Richard had made his heir after the death of his own child. After a coronation in Dublin, Simnel crossed to Lancashire with a force including two thousand hard-bitten German mercenaries and a horde of Irishmen armed only with long knives, who made up in ferocity what they lacked in equipment. As these moved south the people of Nottingham must have quaked in their shoes, and whatever their party sympathies viewed Henry VII's approach with considerable satisfaction. Henry, needless to say, was less concerned with the protection of local lives, property and virtue, than with the seizure of the strategic bridge.

On Tuesday evening, 12 June 1487, he pitched his camp among the trees on Bunny Hill about six miles south of the town. Next morning, his advance guard pushed forward into Nottingham, but he moved his main camp only a little nearer, into the beanfields of Barton-in-Fabis, quartering himself in a house at Clifton. The next day was Corpus Christi. He heard Mass, probably in St Mary's. Then he passed on through the town to welcome the reinforcements led in by Lord Strange, who had confessed his disloyalty to Richard in this same place two years before, but had survived to flourish under the new régime.

Henry's forces now closed in upon the town, camping in the meadows and at the base of the Castle Rock, while Lord Strange's contingent spread out towards Lenton Priory. In the morning, probably to the town's politely disguised relief, they were off again, the shining caterpillar winding its way back across Trent Bridge and disappearing along the road to Radcliffe. It was rumoured that the Yorkists were heading for the other river-crossing at Newark, and that if Henry did not stop them they would race him for the possession of London.

That night Henry camped at Radcliffe – the mileage covered by medieval armies seems singularly unimpressive now – but very early the next morning, the Saturday that ended this short but suspense-full week, he got his men onto the better marching-surface of the old Roman Fosse Way. By nine o'clock he faced the enemy array somewhere between Elston and East Stoke, from which latter village the battle takes its name. In this battle, which few teachers trouble their pupils with, since it is a tag-end from a period it is neater to close with Bosworth, seven thousand wretched lives were thrown away.

Thereafter Nottingham, and England, really did enjoy a century and a half of freedom from full-scale civil war. There were of course alarms and excursions. In 1513, when the Scots exploited Henry VIII's absence in France by launching an invasion. Nottingham was the mobilization-centre for Lord Lovell's reserve army of fifteen thousand men, but the news from Flodden soon removed that anxiety. There was more pressing danger in 1536 from the Pilgrimage of Grace, a rising touched off by agrarian unrest as well as Catholic zeal. York fell to a rebel force of thirty thousand, who moved south on Doncaster. The King, resolved to confine the trouble north of the Trent, put the Earl of Rutland in command of Nottingham Castle and bade him prepare for a siege. Guns and provisions were taken in, the defences strengthened and a garrison of four or five hundred men mustered, including the local gentry, but the revolt died away and not a shot was fired from the batteries.

In these and many other crises the town had to furnish its quota
of fighting-men, and though Nottingham itself might be undisturbed the individual citizens often saw service, and sometimes
died, in distant places. The quota in 1559, for service against the
Scots, was ten archers and thirty-one bill-men or halberdiers. On
other occasions the draft was required for operations in Ireland,
or to aid Henry of Navarre, or to prepare for a Spanish invasion.
The conscription of Englishmen was not, as some have imagined,
an innovation of 1916. But in medieval and Tudor times there
was no central bureaucracy to organize the call-up of individuals,
and the local authority was given the unwelcome task of finding
the requisite number of men.

Apart from the demands of foreign service, and occasional
alarms nearer home, it is true to say that the land enjoyed peace
for a hundred and fifty years. When that peace at last came to
be broken, by the hoisting of King Charles I's standard in 1642,
it is interesting to note that the scene was Nottingham.

What was the town like in the Tudor era?

Little survives from those days except two of the three parish
churches: the third, St Nicholas', was demolished in the Civil War
and afterwards rebuilt. The Trip to Jerusalem Inn, wedged into
the base of the Castle Rock, claims to be the oldest in England,
with Crusader connections as early as 1189, but the claim (to
speak charitably) is regrettably lacking in documentation. The
picturesque name appears late in the records, and it seems likely
that the present public-house evolved from the Castle brewhouse.
The Salutation Inn, with its overhanging gable and deep rock-
cellars, is more convincingly Tudor or late medieval. The Flying
Horse bears the date 1483, which seems based on no stronger
authority than most of the other dates displayed by Nottingham's
older licensed houses. Otherwise, most of the buildings are gone.
Shopping-centres cannot afford history. Thurland Hall – once the
home of Nottingham's own Dick Whittington, a mansion the
Stuarts were to prefer to their own dilapidated castle – survives
only in the name of a short and unimpressive street, where
businessmen spring from their cars to visit bank or stockbroker,

and women shoppers cut through to keep a coffee date. And
the rest of Tudor Nottingham has gone the way of Thurland
Hall.

The documents, however, become more plentiful from this
period. We can at least imagine Tudor Nottingham, people its
streets, and put names if not faces to some of its citizens.

Men like Thurland had created a prosperous town in which
fine chimneyed and glass-windowed mansions stood cheek-by-jowl
with thatched cottages and cowsheds. John Leland, Chaplain and
King's Antiquary to Henry VIII, recorded his impressions in
1540:

> Nottingham is both a large town and well builded for timber
> and plaster, and standeth stately on a climbing hill. The Market
> Place and street, both for the building on the side of it, for the
> very wideness of the street, and the clean paving of it, is the
> most fairest without exception in all England.

The Market Place which so pleased Leland was the site of the
Saturday market and the famous Goose Fair, continuing so until
the nineteen twenties. The still older but much smaller daily
market flourished at Weekday Cross until 1800.

The great five-and-a-half-acre expanse of this Market Place,
now sometimes disparagingly referred to as 'Slab Square', was
already in Tudor times paved with boulders taken from the bed
of the Trent. The quadrilateral space was enclosed by 'Rows' of
gabled half-timbered buildings. Unlike the famous and still extant
'Rows' of Chester, these did not possess the upper tier of sidewalks
which evolved in the more confined area of the former Roman
city, but they did have projecting upper storeys, a feature copied
in the Victorian and later buildings that have replaced them, so
that Long Row still has a more or less continuous colonnade to
provide meagre shelter from the rain. Angel Row, Smithy Row,
Beastmarket Hill and Chapel Bar are all names still in use, and
help to conjure up the scene as Leland saw it, but the southern
side, originally Timber Row, has been refined into South Parade.
The Spice Chamber, the Drapery and the Shoebooths are long
forgotten, but older people still remember the Shambles, a gory

and malodorous passage occupied by the butchers, where today's shopping-arcade runs beneath the Council House.

These various 'Rows' were broken only by the narrowest gaps giving access to the square. The wide modern streets, through which the green double-decker buses roll ceaselessly in and out of the 'City Centre', date only from the improvement schemes of Victorian times. Market Street was Sheep Lane until 1865. Clumber Street, still narrow enough in all conscience, was Cow Lane, renamed after one of the Duke of Newcastle's estates in compliment to His Grace for giving sixteen feet of land for its widening.

It was not only on market day that these lanes echoed with the bleating and lowing of livestock. Many citizens kept their own cows as well as their own horses. Indeed, in 1588 the question most urgently exercising the minds of residents in Barker Gate was not 'When is the Armada coming?' but 'Who is going round in the middle of the night and milking our cows?' The culprit was identified as the wife of a drunken ne'er-do-well, driven to this form of theft by sheer necessity.

A wall ran the length of the Market Place from east to west. The old story was that its function was to prevent fighting between the 'English' and 'French' sections. This seems improbable, because the wall was only breast-high and had gaps for convenient passage, and if it had been necessary to separate the two boroughs a much shorter north-to-south wall would have been more effective. Finally, although the Market Place has been the scene of innumerable riots down the ages, there is no history of violent animosity between the Anglo-Danish residents and the Normans who came in after the Conquest. A more likely explanation is that the wall was a sensible subdivision, separating the livestock on the south side from the malt, corn, oatmeal and other commodities laid out to the north. The wall remained until the eighteenth century, by which time any resentment against the Normans would have worn rather thin, but a runaway bullock would still have been unwelcome among the pottery stalls.

A well was sunk in the Market Place for the use of traders and their beasts. There were other common wells at the far end

(Chapel Bar) and elsewhere in the town. There were crosses, besides Weekday Cross, indicating the various departmental trading-centres – the Hen Cross (in Cuckstool Row, later the Poultry), the Butter Cross not far away, and the Malt Cross at the western end of Long Row. Less happy landmarks were the stocks, the pillory and the ducking-stool, a feminine punishment appropriately located where trade was largely in the hands of the women. For serious crime there was a dungeon under the Guild-hall not far away.

The daily business and manufactures were, of course, carried on in the surrounding streets as they always had been, usually at the dwelling-house of the trader, who, apart from his own family and a servant or two, might accommodate apprentices serving for seven years and trained workers, or journeymen, who had not set up on their own. These skilled tradesmen included weavers, tailors, glovers, 'corvisers' (shoemakers), saddlers, 'lorrimers' (bridle-smiths), and many more, not forgetting the renowned 'arblasterers', until their craft was ruined by the Reformation. There was pot-tery, though the making of the best-known brown salt-glaze ware began only with James Morley in late Stuart times. Nor was the hosiery trade yet born, destined to play so important a part sub-sequently, but as William Lee's invention of the stocking-frame belongs to the Tudor period it is worth mentioning here.

In medieval days hose were made by stitching together shaped pieces of cloth. The first knitted stockings entered England from Spain in 1547, a present to Henry VIII who died that year. It took the English a little while to unravel the mystery of their manufacture, but soon many hands were knitting busily, and the old seamed cloth leg-covering was driven out of fashion by worsted and then by silk stockings for those who could afford them. Both sexes wore them but the men could display them more – the Elizabethan dramatists seem to have had an obsession about the shapeliness of the male leg. By 1589, if we may believe a pleasant old tradition, the Reverend William Lee of Calverton, just outside Nottingham, found his courting seriously obstructed because his sweetheart had half her mind and both her hands perpetually engaged upon her knitting. Not content with the normal male reaction of irritation, Lee applied his own mind to a constructive solution, and spent seven years inventing the stocking-frame, which would knit a thousand loops a minute against the mere hundred of his beloved's busy fingers. Lee tried to get a patent from Queen Elizabeth, but could not win her support. After years of frustration he went to France, confident of more encouragement from Henry of Navarre, but the assassination of that enterprising monarch dashed his hopes for the second time. Lee died soon afterwards in Paris, but his brother James returned to England with most of his machines and the workers he had trained. So, belatedly, framework knitting did establish itself, and was taken up in due course in the Nottingham area, but at first only in a small way in comparison with London. The great days of the industry, from which the lace trade also was to spring, belong to a later century.

Lee's village of Calverton was just one of a dozen that ringed the town.

Sherwood Forest still spread to the north and harboured stags to attract the sport-loving Stuarts. But even in the Robin Hood era it had never been an unbroken tract of greenwood. There were wide clearings and villages, some of whose parish churches are visible evidence of their antiquity – Strelley, with its fine fourteenth-century chancel; Gedling, with its needle-sharp spire built soon after 1300; and Calverton itself with Norman bits and pieces. There were the monasteries, too – not only Lenton on the town's doorstep and Newstead farther out, but Thurgarton, Beauvale and Felley, as well as the more distant houses of Rufford and Welbeck. What with the permitted felling of timber for this purpose and that, the charcoal-burning, and the enclosure of cleared land in 'assarts', the land north of Nottingham had long ceased to be a romantic outlaw country, though its villages were never as plentiful as those on the more open sides of the town – Bridgford and Edwalton, Wilford, Clifton and the rest.

Nottingham kept its ancient limits. But it would be wrong to picture a mysterious forest beyond the common fields. Many of today's outlying suburbs, such as Arnold, Basford and Bulwell, the last-mentioned already itself described as a 'township', were thriving little communities in their own right. The short walk to them was not through dense woodland but across the 'waste' of sandy moor. It was from such neighbourhoods, and from other more distant places, that people flocked in to the market every Saturday.

CHAPTER TEN

A Mayor and His Widow

So much for the scene. What of the characters who moved against this Tudor back-cloth? One family, that of Richard Mellers and his wife Agnes, has left a memorial more lasting than most of its contemporaries.

Richard Mellers was a bell-founder. The trade was long established in the town and was combined with the making of brass utensils. He had begun in a small way, if we can believe his tax assessment for 1472, when he was set down to pay $3\frac{3}{4}d$ compared with the $74s\ 7\frac{1}{2}d$ standing against the name of the plutocratic Thomas Thurland. But then Mellers was himself one of the Royal Commissioners appointed to make the assessments, for he was serving as a sheriff that year.

Since then, he had prospered. His bells chimed in half-a-dozen neighbouring counties. Some may still. There are certainly examples of his work preserved in honourable retirement, like the one that served St Giles's at West Bridgford until it was replaced in 1955.

There is no reason to suppose that he was anything but an honest, if keen and enterprising, business man. He may – probably inadvertently – have overcharged on some occasion, by supplying a bell of lighter weight than specified. There is no record of a dispute, though few people in those days hesitated to rush into court. But in April 1507 Mellers did apply for and obtain royal pardon for a technical offence against the Statute of Weights and Measures. As he died two months later, this looks more like a scruple of conscience than a fear of impending litigation. The most serious dispute he was ever involved in, so far as we can tell from

the Borough Records, was with another respected townsman
named John Wedirley, who had borrowed twenty shillings which
he would not repay. Mellers retorted by keeping some wine vats.
Hot words were exchanged. The then Mayor was brought in as
arbitrator. The two men were ordered to make friends and desist
from counter-accusations. If either broke the peace he was to pay
forty shillings to the fund for keeping the town bridges in repair.
There is no evidence that this penalty ever had to be exacted.
Mellers later bequeathed ten pounds to the bridge fund and his
widow left a legacy to Wedirley's son, so presumably the harmony
once restored continued.

As mayor in 1499, and again in the last year of his life, and as
a justice for many years before and between, Mellers was more
concerned with other men's disputes and misdemeanours than his
own. He was very likely on the Bench on 9 October 1497, when
the local vet, or 'horseleech', was summoned because in September he had thrown out 'a dead and putrid horse into the streets
of our said Lord the King at Nottingham aforesaid, to the
grievous nuisance of the lieges of our said Lord the King and
against his peace'. A few weeks later he may have been dealing
with complaints against a weaver, John Clitherow, 'a common
listener at the windows and houses of his neighbours to sow strife
and discord'. In August 1499, when Mellers must have been
already preening himself for his first mayoral election, there was
the graver case of Hugh Carrier, who combined the craft of glover
with the more profitable occupation of a fence, 'a common
receiver and harbourer of divers thieves with other folks' goods
unjustly taken by them'.

It was one thing to sit in judgement on such low-class neighbours,
but it could be embarrassing when personal friends were involved,
as in 1506 when the Prior of Lenton was sued for an unpaid wine-
bill. The Prior was clearly on the best of terms with the Mellers
family, and there must have been some relief on the Bench when
he produced the argument that, as an ecclesiastic, he was immune
from secular proceedings. The case was promptly adjourned so that
he could submit his charters as authority – and nothing more was
heard of the matter. Certainly the happy relations between monks

The Georgian town: part of Badder and Peat's map, 1744. Surviving landmarks are St Nicholas' Church (20), St Peter's (6), St Mary's (16) and Weekday Cross (14). The Castle lies just off the bottom left-hand corner. Back Side is now Parliament Street.

Jan Kib's East Prospect of Nottingham, 1707–8, showing the Duke's new castle, St Mary's Church and the

and Mellers were not impaired. When, in 1516, one of the sons, Thomas Mellers, was assaulted in the house of a fellow alderman, it is recorded that the other guests present were the Prior of Lenton and the Abbot of Dale, 'assembled in friendly manner and joyfully conversing and drinking wine'.

Local life was still dominated by a handful of families such as the Mellers, closely interwoven by marriage. They controlled the Merchant Guild, interpreting trade regulations and excluding outside competitors: they closed down the ironmongery business of Thomas Nix in 1578 because he had not served an apprenticeship in the town. The seven aldermen passed round the office of mayor and took care that, when death created a vacancy on the Bench, it was filled by some one suitable. With the help of the six lesser councillors, later increased to twelve, they directed the town's affairs with the legal guidance, where needed, of a recorder, who also sometimes represented the borough in Parliament, as Thomas Babington did in 1504. The full extent of their power may be gauged from the fact that, besides being *ex officio* magistrates, these seven were the obvious choices as tax-assessors and commissioners of array, deciding who should be called upon for military service. They controlled not only the town's common assets and revenues but also, especially after the Reformation, its charities. By that date, however, Mellers himself was dead.

The popular resentment against this self-perpetuating oligarchy did not weaken with the years. Towards the end of Elizabeth's reign there was a petition to the Privy Council. After leisurely investigation and consultation came a ruling from that body in 1606 (three years after the good Queen's own demise) that the burgesses should be given another twelve men to represent them. It made little difference. In essence Nottingham continued to be run for another two centuries and more, as it had been run a century earlier in Mellers' time, by a cosy group of prominent traders. Elsewhere in England it was much the same.

Mellers' humbler neighbours continued to make good use of the Mickletorn Jury, that treasured medieval survival which laid upon them the duty of 'presenting' abuses to be dealt with by their betters. It was still the best way of voicing complaints against those

same betters. Thus, in 1515, the Jury not only presented an outsider, Andrew Jackson of Newark, 'for selling of stinking salmon
in our market in Lent', but arraigned the Common Sergeant
'because that he looks not to the common muckhills and other
common lanes, according to his oath', adding, 'We often complain of his demeanour and hath no remedy.' They similarly
criticized 'the Pinder of the Woods and Corn Fields, that he takes
not heed of the cornfields, but suffers the beasts destroy the corn.'
Later, in 1577, the jurors managed to secure the expulsion of an
alderman from the Bench, for 'disporting himself with a naughty
quean'.

Despite the underlying tensions and occasional outbursts of this
social conflict, there is no reason to suppose that Mellers did not
thoroughly enjoy his term of office. It was something, in those
days, to be chief citizen even of a borough still comprising only
about three thousand inhabitants. He had his coat-of-arms, pun-
ning on his name, the three 'merles' or blackbirds that survive
perkily on the caps and blazers of the High School boys. As mayor
he walked the market on Saturdays, splendid in crimson gown,
attended by his clerk and servants, eyes and nose sharp to detect
abuses. If he went fishing, it was something of a public occasion,
with refreshment for his attendants and other expenses 'on the
town'. Not that Mellers had to worry about money. His family
were already provided for. Two sons were established in business
locally and his only daughter, Margery, was married to another
prosperous trader. A third son was at Oxford, taking Holy Orders.
Mellers was comfortable. Both he and subsequently his widow
had an abundant surplus to leave to charity.

Had he kept a diary of his mayoral year, it would have been
full of enjoyable occasions.

His election at Michaelmas was mainly a convivial formality.
It coincided with the Goose Fair, one of the biggest in the kingdom, attracting traders and buyers, quacks, crooks and enter-
tainers, from far and near. Its origins are lost, but it had been old
in Edward I's reign. In Mellers' time it lasted eight days. In my
own boyhood it still monopolized the centre of the city for three
days, paralysing the traffic and normal business but infecting the

community at large with a kind of hilarious St Vitus's Dance. It flourishes today as a mammoth fun-fair, but removed to the 'Forest' a mile away.

Mellers had no responsibility for the other great fair, held at Martinmas, a month later, in front of the priory gates at Lenton, but being on such friendly terms with the Prior he doubtless went out and shared in the junketings. Other Nottingham traders might resent the competition of the Lenton Fair, which interrupted their own business, but a bell-founder had nothing to fear from it. Indeed, Mellers would be more likely to win new orders from distant churches, especially when he had the Prior's goodwill to recommend him.

That was in November. Then came Christmas, always something of a gastronomic marathon among the Tudors. It is unlikely that the Mayor and his brethren denied themselves. The records show that they patronized the waits, and music would hardly be the sole ingredient in their celebrations.

Once Lent was over, the calendar filled with al fresco engagements. Easter Monday saw the Mayor leading his brightly robed procession on the annual pilgrimage to St Ann's Well just outside the town, an observance always followed by a good dinner at the public charge. Then came May Day, a more informal and popular festivity, but with the Mayor expected, no doubt, to show himself everywhere and beam benevolently. Even in London the milkmaids still garlanded their pails and danced in the streets, so it is easy to picture the ancient country customs being kept up in a much smaller town, where Sherwood Forest was close at hand for the traditional cutting of green branches and where the mummers announcing themselves as 'Robin Hood' and 'Maid Marian' would be accorded the special welcome reserved for local heroes. As the Tudor May Day corresponds to 12 May in our modern reckoning, there was a slightly better chance of warm weather for the proceedings.

Whitsun was the next event. In Mellers' time there would be the Catholic pageantry and the miracle plays, and on the Monday he would go on pilgrimage again with the aldermen and other dignitaries to make the town's Pentecostal offering at Southwell

Minster. As this was a journey of fifteen miles each way, no one would have expected them to make it without adequate refreshment.

The Midsummer Night Watch was another institution kept up until Charles I's time. The burgesses paraded at sunset and took an oath to see that the peace was preserved. Then, forming parties and wearing garlands, they spent the short summer night patrolling the streets, pausing at intervals to fortify themselves and to exchange amiable greetings with their female acquaintance looking down from upper windows.

And so the year rolled by, with lesser events to brighten the intervening weeks – saints' days and guild dinners and churchales, and, if all else failed, a turn-out of the trained bands, marching with pike and drum, always good for a laugh if we can accept the satirical picture given in *The Knight of the Burning Pestle*. The town may have been small in those days, but it can hardly have been sleepy.

Agnes Mellers is far better remembered than her husband. In her widowhood she founded the Nottingham High School, whose present buildings, with their Victorian façade, towered and flamboyantly battlemented, are a prominent feature on the northern skyline.

There are only tantalizingly vague references to local schools before this time, but there must have been some facilities: her own son Richard had gone on to the university at Oxford. Probably there was no establishment with any guarantee of continuity. So, as a rich widow with her children grown up and plentifully provided for, Dame Agnes resolved to fill the gap.

One problem had first to be overcome. The Statute of Mortmain prevented her establishing a corporate body, as she wished to do, and endowing it with property, unless she obtained a licence from the King. Luckily she had an influential contact, very close to the young Henry VIII. This was Thomas Lovell, who had been knighted by Henry VII after the Battle of East Stoke and had served as Constable of Nottingham Castle. He had held many other positions, including Chancellor of the Exchequer and

Speaker of the House of Commons, and in 1512 he was Treasurer of the Household. Thanks to his good offices the royal licence was made out at Westminster on 22 November of that year and the royal seal attached. It still exists, granting permission to 'our beloved Councillor, Thomas Lovell, Knight, Treasurer of our Household, and Agnes Mellers, Widow' to found a school, 'evermore to endure', for the 'education, teaching and instruction of boys in good manners and literature'. It is a beautifully illuminated document, with a stylized picture of Dame Agnes kneeling before the King, and the future school motto, *Lauda Finem*, 'Praise the End', which, as a boy enduring the longueurs of Speech Day, I used to think somewhat ambiguous.

The licence secured, Dame Agnes proved as businesslike as her late husband. She was prepared to endow the school herself but she meant to involve the whole town. A subscription list was opened. Long lost, the original document came to light not many years ago. It bears eighty-six names, an impressive roll-call of everybody who was anybody in Nottingham at that date, the gifts ranging from her own (five properties near St Peter's Church) and three acres of land from the serving Mayor, down to promises of fourpence a year each from Henry Hopkyn the tanner and several other townsmen of humble means.

Her arrangements for the governing of the school were equally consistent with her determination to make it a civic responsibility. She drew up ordinances for the school's conduct and appointed the Mayor, aldermen and Common Council to manage it. Only if they failed in their duties was control to pass to the Prior of Lenton and his successors. Dame Agnes knew human nature (she had had abundant opportunity) and she left nothing to chance. She gave most detailed instructions for the service that was to be held annually in St Mary's on her late husband's name-day, 16 June, the Feast of the Translation of St Richard, when Masses were to be said for his soul and in due time for her own. Twenty shillings would be distributed in appropriate proportions, starting with three shillings 'to the Vicar of the said Church personally being present from the beginning . . . to the ending thereof' and continuing with sixpence for the Mayor and fourpence apiece for the aldermen (always provided that they too stayed the course), twopence each to the Mayor's clerk and his two sergeants, and three shillings 'to the parish clerks for the great bells ringing eight peals after the customable length'. Four shillings were to be spent on bread, cheese and ale afterwards, an agreeable custom still kept up in the Lord Mayor's Parlour on Founder's Day, though now with rather more generous provision. 'If any be left,' continued Dame Agnes, forgetting nothing, 'I will shall be distributed to the poorest scholars of the said Free School to pray for our souls and all our friends.' There always is, and one can only hope that they do.

The school opened in February 1513, in the shadow of St Mary's, where it was to remain for the next three and a half centuries. That was the year of Flodden. As Lovell was back at the Castle, mobilizing troops, it is reasonable to suppose that he saw Dame Agnes and heard the latest news of the enterprise he had helped her to launch. In the spring of 1514 the good woman died, bequeathing further properties to the school. She was laid to rest beside her husband in St Mary's.

CHAPTER ELEVEN

The New Notables

WHEN Dame Agnes Mellers nominated the Prior of Lenton and his successors to take over her school if the Corporation ever failed in its duty, she could not have foreseen that within less than thirty years there would be no Prior and that the monastery would be a roofless ruin.

The storm was gathering in 1530, when the dying Wolsey paused overnight in Nottingham on his journey south to obey the King's summons. The next morning he could scarcely mount his mule, but he struggled on as far as Leicester, where he breathed his last in the Abbey. The whole monastic world in England was similarly tottering to its end. Soon Henry's conflict with the Church was fully under way. The smaller monasteries were dissolved in 1536. Rufford closed. Newstead purchased a brief respite for the sum of £233 6s 8d, which sounds less odd as 350 marks, the mark being two-thirds of a pound.

The turn of the bigger houses like Lenton came in 1538. Whereas most monasteries accepted their suppression quietly, the monks taking pensions or parish livings, Lenton displayed what would now be termed counter-revolutionary tendencies. The details are not known. One story says that the Prior, Nicholas Heath, together with eight monks and four local workmen, was convicted of treason at the Shire Hall, and that the Prior was hanged from his own gateway, while the others were hanged on Gallows Hill (where St Andrew's Church now stands), drawn, quartered and dragged on hurdles down the Mansfield Road. Dr Wood, in his scholarly *History of Nottinghamshire*, records only the execution of the Prior and one monk. Certain it is that the Priory came to a sudden and tragic end. The lead was stripped from the roof, carted to the Castle and then sent on to London. The buildings fell into decay and became a quarry for the neighbourhood, except for the church which served the parish of Lenton until Victorian times. Now, thanks to rebuilding, there is nothing left to see. Pevsner warns us that 'the so-called Priory Church in Gregory Street is a building of the 1880's'. The land was leased to Sir Michael Stanhope, one of the local landowning class coming more and more to the front in Tudor England. Newstead, similarly, was bought by Sir John Byron.

In the town itself the friaries went the same way. So did the chantries, the little chapels endowed for the saying of Masses, now pronounced superstitious. There was a chantry of this type attached to St Mary's: its endowment, along with others, was diverted to the maintenance of Trent Bridge. The chapel on that bridge was demolished, as were other Catholic monuments such as the Grey Friars' Cross.

Nottingham cannot be said to have shown much zeal in defence of the old religion, or, come to that, undue enthusiasm for the reforms. When Mary brought back the Catholic rites (she could not bring back Lenton Priory), the Rector of St Peter's, John Plough, was a staunch enough Protestant to seek safety in Switzerland. But he was exceptional. Neither clergy nor laity looked for trouble.

It was much the same with the Elizabethan Settlement. In August 1559 the royal commissioners arrived and took their seats in the chancel of St Mary's. All the clergy of the area were ordered to appear before them and take the Oath of Supremacy. Over forty did not appear, but nothing dramatic happened. During the next year or two the majority toed the line. Only a handful had finally to be evicted from their benefices. In this sphere, at least, Nottingham's tradition of protest was not followed with much vigour.

Back in 1523 a shoemaker had once interrupted a service in St Mary's, shouting 'malicious and contemptuous words against the Vicar', but he seems to have been impelled more by liquor than by doctrinal disagreement.

In July 1562 there was a great stir in the town. The Sheriff of Nottinghamshire let it be known that the Queen was coming on 3 September. Nottingham had not welcomed a sovereign since Henry VIII passed through in the summer of 1511. The Tudors were not great travellers and their famous 'progresses', though splendid enough, were mostly through the south-eastern quarter of their realm. The Castle, so much visited and improved by the last Plantagenets, had fallen into a sad decay.

Now it looked as though the great days were come again. It was to be no ordinary visit. Elizabeth had a special purpose: to meet Mary Queen of Scots, at that time of course still free and the ruler of her country. Their combined trains would amount to four thousand persons, rather more than the town's normal population. Elizabeth's favourite, Lord Robert Dudley, was in supreme charge of the arrangements. He warned the Sheriff, who passed on the information to the town authorities, that there would be a full programme of masques and entertainments and a tournament to which 'all lusty young knights' were invited. Had all this gone off as planned, the Nottingham visit might have become a legend to rival that of Kenilworth. But this early 'summit conference' was cancelled, and in all her long reign Gloriana never rode across Trent Bridge. There is a mistaken belief in some quarters that she once visited Sir Francis Willoughby at the old Wollaton Hall. This originates from a warning, conveyed to Willoughby in a letter from Sir Francis Knollys in July 1575 that 'Her Majesty is determined to tarry two days at your house, that is to say tomorrow night and Thursday all day. . . . You had need to consider how your provision of drink, etc., may hold out.' But on that day Elizabeth was in Warwickshire (it was the time of the Kenilworth visit) and without seven-leagued boots she could not have reached Nottinghamshire by 'tomorrow'. The mystery is solved by the recollection that the Willoughby family had another house, Middleton Hall in Warwickshire, from which they later took their title. The Knollys letter does not name the house.

The Willoughbys serve, however, to typify the stratum of country knights and squires who in Tudor times, along with the merchant oligarchy of the town, formed the upper class of

Nottingham and its neighbourhood. If royalty played no part in the local history of the period, the great nobles impinged upon it hardly any more. Nottingham was a place for the 'new' men, building fresh fortunes out of the ruins of medieval society. Between landed gentry and traders there was still no harsh division. They were friends and neighbours, for in that era of atrocious roads a man whose estate lay ten miles away would often find it worth while to maintain a town house as well.

Such were the Willoughbys, originally the Bugges of Willoughby, dividing their time between their estate on the border of Leicestershire and their town house, Bugge Hall, on High Pavement. In Edward III's reign they acquired, by marriage, their lands at Wollaton, much closer to Nottingham, but it was a long time before they moved there, and their earliest memorial in Wollaton Church is the brass commemorating Richard, who died in 1471. The most widely famous member of the family was Sir Hugh, who was frozen or starved to death with his ship's crew in 1554, seeking the North-east Passage to China between Russia and the Pole.

Sir Francis was an equally thrustful character, though in a less conventionally romantic way. Not for him the high seas: he sought his treasure no further than Wollaton itself, where the shallow pits and primitive mining-methods of the day produced 20,000 tons of coal a year, half the output of the shire. The local customer was always well served: the Nottingham householder, it was written in 1641, 'who at night when he goes to bed has not a handful of fuel, may the next morning in the shortest day of winter have coals brought to his door . . .' This facility won the town a bad reputation for smokiness, and an old rhyme ran:

> I cannot without lye and shame
> Comend the Town of Nottingham.
> The People and the Fewel stinke,
> The Place is sordid as a sinke.

But Sir Francis aimed at wider markets. He had schemes for sending his coal to London via Hull, and he tried out new pumping-equipment to increase output. Not content with coal

alone, he owned ironworks and experimented with glass-manu-
facture and the growing of woad for the dyers. He was perhaps
the first big Nottingham capitalist with thoroughly diversified
interests.

Like many a later tycoon, he was not so successful in the direction of his private life. He had twelve children, and when he had
disposed of his business worries he had still to cope with a complaining wife, a bevy of headstrong girls, and in due course their
husbands. A revealing glimpse of Elizabethan family life is provided by a letter Lady Willoughby sent him when he was away. She
warned him that their youngest daughter was set on marrying a
Cavendish of Hardwick; she was so brazen that she had her young
man continually in and out of the house, and would go off into the
forest with him for a whole day's walking. 'If you can come,'
urged Lady Willoughby, 'make an end of it, which being done on
the sudden you may save cost which otherwise she means to put
on you, for she talks of many new gowns which she intends to have
of rich stuff.'

There is a strangely modern ring about these informal goings-
on, yet it is clear that life with the Willoughbys had a stately and
authentically Elizabethan side. A family history was written in
1702 by Cassandra Willoughby, later Duchess of Chandos, in
which she quoted the rules Sir Francis laid down for his servants
at Wollaton in 1572. A large staff was maintained, headed by
Foxe, the usher, 'an officer of great trust and credit . . . above
either cook, butler, yeomen of the chambers, or porter'. Sir Francis seems to have kept open house, for Foxe was 'diligently to have
good regard of every person that comes into the hall, to the end
that if they be of the better sort, notice may be given to the master,
or some head officer that they may be entertained accordingly.
If of the meaner sort, to know the cause of their coming . . . to
the end that they may be answered of their business.' Yet Foxe,
though enjoined to send away any 'rascal or unseemly person',
was to ensure 'that no stranger be suffered to pass without offering
him to drink'. It is not surprising that household expenses
averaged the then astronomical sum of a thousand pounds a
month.

It is hard not to picture Foxe as a real-life Malvolio, if not in character at least in demeanour. When dinner was ready he had to head the procession of servers, attended by a torch-bearer and 'carrying a little fine rod in his hand'. As he went, he was to cry, 'Give way, my masters!' ('albeit no man be in the way') and, if the chatter grew too loud, to quell it with a decorous, 'Speak softly, my masters.' No guidance was given, however, on the subject of yellow stockings or cross-garters.

The spirit of that age survives nowhere more remarkably than in the flamboyant Wollaton Hall, the new home which Sir Francis commissioned in 1580 and which Pevsner has called 'the most important Elizabethan house in Notts and one of the most important in England'.

Today, it is very much part of the expanded city, close neighbour to the University and the cycle-works depicted in *Saturday Night and Sunday Morning*. A portion of its great walled park has been taken for housing, but the remainder, green and pleasant, complete with deer, lake and lime-tree avenue, has been preserved for public enjoyment. The Hall itself, fantastical with its spikes and pepper-pots, mullioned windows, balustrades and classical busts, now houses the city's Natural History Museum. But when it was built – its slender chimneys must have been topped off in the Armada year – this was essentially a country house, far out beyond Lenton, whose priory ruins supplemented the Ancaster stone fetched by packhorse in return for Wollaton coal. The house was eight years building. John Thorpe is often named as its designer, but it now seems that Robert Smythson was correctly described as its 'architector', doubtless with considerable interference from his idiosyncratic client. Italian craftsmen were employed, and there is a delightful (if perhaps far-fetched) suggestion that the stone rings carved near the base of the walls were unthinkingly included for the mooring of gondolas. In general there is less Italian influence traceable in the building than there is French, and what Pevsner describes as 'gaudy Netherlandish ornament'.

There was another interesting household at Newstead, where the Byrons had replaced the monks. The second Sir John, known as 'the Little Sir John with the Great Beard', was the illegitimate son of the original purchaser. He therefore had to succeed by deed of gift, and the Queen knighted him in 1579. He made Newstead famous for spectacular hospitality, keeping his own troop of players, who sometimes performed in the town. The Corporation often sponsored such visits from actors, sometimes setting up a stage in the Guildhall itself. The Chamberlain's accounts for 1573 record a visit by an Italian troop of *commedia dell' arte* players, who received five shillings 'for certain pastimes that they shewed before Master Mayor and his brethren'.

Other local families included the Cliftons at the village whose name they bore and which is now part of Nottingham: Sir Gervase died in the Armada year, 'an excellent person', wrote Thoroton, 'that he was generally styled "gentle Sir Gervase"'. Less gentle was Sir Charles Cavendish of Welbeck, who had a feud with another local family, the Stanhopes: riding one summer morning with two friends, he was assailed by John Stanhope galloping at the head of twenty followers, and a mêlée ensued in which two were killed. Pierreponts, Chaworths, Parkyns, and others made up the roll of country gentry whose lives were involved with the town in greater or lesser degree. Some had been honoured in the shire for centuries. Others had come from outside or had risen from obscurity.

One of the newcomers was William Holles, son of a self-made London merchant who had been Lord Mayor in 1540. From his father he inherited lands at Basford and other places in Nottinghamshire, at one of which (Haughton) he made his principal home and became a byword for goodness and generosity. For their town house in Nottingham the family bought Thurland Hall, a house destined to play an important part in local history during the next two reigns. Another county family, the Hutchinsons of Owthorpe, had a town house on High Pavement not far away. Their name, too, will recur frequently in the Stuart period.

CHAPTER TWELVE

The Road to Standard Hill

IF the Tudors had neglected Nottingham, James I made up for them, though he used the town chiefly as a stopping-place on his trips to hunt in Sherwood. The forest was shrinking. The oaks could still be reckoned in tens of thousands, but many were past their best and there was as yet none of the systematic replanting that some of the nobility were to practise a few generations later. Despite wholesale clearances, however, the greenwood still provided royal sport.

Mostly the King stayed at Newstead or Rufford, sleeping a night or two at Nottingham en route. The Castle was by this time quite unfit to receive him (he had already disposed of it to the Earl of Rutland) and he was always the guest of Sir John Holles at Thurland Hall. As this mansion boasted forty-seven rooms with fireplaces it could accommodate a party of considerable size.

Even a flying visit involved the town in formidable expense. The Council minutes for 10 July 1612 include the entry: 'Debating upon the necessary charge to be employed about His Majesty's entertainment, it is thought convenient that there should be £150 borrowed upon interest till the town shall be able to pay it.' Two councillors were sent to London to buy a suitable gift. They came back with three 'fair gilt bowls' and a bill for £61 6s 8d. The King's one-night visit cost the public funds another £54 11s 3d.

Subsequent visits were less expensive. There was no gift on the next visit in August 1614, and the other expenses were cut by half. On yet another occasion we hear of the King and his courtiers riding out to St Ann's Well, where they 'drank the wood ward and his barrels dry'. What the individual hosts spent on hospitality can be imagined, but their resources were deep and in the end they may have felt that they got value for money. Sir John Holles was eventually created Earl of Clare in 1624, having bought his way into the peerage with two further lump sums totalling £15,000. Sir William Cavendish became a viscount under James and Earl of Newcastle under Charles I, whom he later twice entertained most sumptuously at Welbeck, with banquets and elaborate masques written by Ben Jonson. In these same years several county families bought themselves high honours. The sons and grandsons of men who had been happy with knighthoods in Tudor times blossomed forth, Pierrepont as Earl of Kingston, Stanhope as Earl of Chesterfield, and Chaworth as a viscount. Sir John Byron achieved only a barony, and that not until 1643, but at least his honour was earned on the field of battle at Newbury. The Byrons (unlike some of the other families that outstripped them) were unswerving in their loyalty to the Royalist cause. No fewer than seven of them, it is said, fought at Edgehill.

How much did these brief royal visits mean to the town as a whole? A glimpse of pageantry, of cavaliers and their ladies, fine horses and self-important servants . . . snatches of muted music and illustrious laughter through the casements of that mansion standing on the little rise above the Market Place, where now the soberer activities of banking and chartered accountancy are carried on . . . a welcome break for apprentices and schoolboys . . . a moment of glory for the schoolmaster and other local notables given unwonted prominence. When Charles and Henrietta Maria spent five whole days at Thurland Hall in 1634, the task of welcoming them with a Latin oration was delegated to Samuel Lightfoot, usher, or assistant master of the Free School, who had to be provided with 'a suit, cloak, hat, stockings, garters, shoes, and all accoutrements', a further expense to the town of £8 6s od.

Expense, in fact, must have been the most lasting effect of the visits, and there may well have been curmudgeonly citizens who sighed for the days of cheeseparing Queen Bess who had never bestowed upon them the costly sunshine of her smile. For the 1634 visit the whole town was given what would now be termed a face-lift. The aldermen had to go round their respective wards and see that every house was repainted or freshly plastered by its owner, and the street cleared of obstructions. The chamberlains were made responsible for the condition of the paving, the wall dividing the Market Place, and the various crosses, this being at the town's charge. What with the hospitality involved, and the gift of plate expected by the King, the Council was compelled to take out a £200 mortgage on some of the public lands. A few years later, on the eve of the Civil War, Nottingham was in debt to the tune of £550, a desperate situation relieved by nearly all the councillors making individual contributions and by the fixing of a yearly payment by burgesses holding parts of the common fields.

The extra clean-up provoked by the royal visit can have done no harm. There was plenty to do, as is clear from the recurrent items in the town records. There were anti-social individuals who turned their pigs into St Mary's churchyard or let their children 'annoy the street with filth' or threw refuse into the open sewer in front of some one else's house. But the sheer frequency of these complaints by the Mickletorn Jury shows that there was a strong public feeling on such matters, and it was in these early Stuart years that the town appointed its first scavengers.

Even at this date the problem of overcrowding was recognized. In 1612, the year of the first royal visit, the Council passed regulations against the building of new cottages or the adaptation of barns without a licence equivalent to our own planning permission. At the same time the letting of accommodation to strangers was to be controlled, Jacobean Nottingham having a dislike of 'immigrants' even from a mere twenty miles away.

'Forasmuch', declared the Council,

> as it is found by daily experience that by the continual building and erecting of new cottages and poor habitations, and by the transferring of barns and such like buildings into cottages and habitations within this town, and also by the great confluence of many poor people from foreign parts ... to inhabit here, and likewise by the usual and frequent taking in of inmates into many poor habitations here, the poorer sort of people do much increase, to the great charge and burthen of all the inhabitants of the better sort within this said town; by occasion of which

inconveniences, many grievances and great burthens have arisen here, as well in time of visitations of pestilence as otherwise, in daily charges to support and maintain so great a number of poor and needy people ... to the great increase of idleness and to the committing of many misdemeanours. ...

And so on, and so forth. We can almost see the heavy-jowled sanguine aldermanic heads nodding in ponderous agreement or simply in drowsiness.

In short, what worried the 'better sort' was not so much hygiene or humanitarian concern as the threat of an unemployment problem, of personal infection, and (as has been noted elsewhere) of business competition from interlopers. In the context of the period, when a man looked for help to no one but God and his immediate neighbours, it would be unfair for us to sneer at this preoccupation with self-preservation.

The pestilence was an all too real danger. It came every few years. Isolation seemed the most promising safeguard. At Christmas in 1586, when there was an outbreak at Derby, the Council forbade Nottingham people to go there, and banned Derby people from entering Nottingham. In 1603 they similarly put Lenton Fair out of bounds. More than once in James I's reign the Free School was either closed or evacuated. 'It is agreed', declares a minute, 'that Master Braithwaite, the usher, shall teach at some place a mile or two of the town, if parents will board their children at such a place.' In 1606 arrangements were made for huts to be built in Gorsey Close (presumably near the modern Gorsey Road, on the Mapperley hillside) to provide for the isolation of sufferers. One of the regular aldermanic duties was to keep watch for suspected cases, and it was not unknown for tenpence to be given 'to a poor man that was suspected to have the plague, to avoid the town'.

Another aldermanic duty was 'to make search in his ward weekly or once in a fortnight at the least, to weed out idle persons'. Now that there were no monks and friars to dispense charity the burden fell on the town and its three parishes. In 1627 the Council took over one of the old religious foundations, St John's Hospital – its endowments had long ago been assigned to the maintenance of Trent Bridge – and set up a spinning-school for pauper children. This social experiment continued for a long time, the Council furnishing raw materials and a shilling a week per child for food, and at one time it was extended to include the adults. But so far as outsiders were concerned, whether their affliction was poverty or plague, the town preferred just to get rid of them if it could. In 1656, under the Commonwealth, one Leonard Wood was charged with 'skulking in our town of Nottingham' with his wife Ann. They confessed that 'their last abode and settlement was at Bridgford', the whole length of Trent Bridge away, so they were duly escorted thither and handed over to the Bridgford constable and overseers of the poor. Seventeenth-century England did not encourage the mobility of labour.

Such attitudes may seem harsh today, but again it must be urged that the town had to shoulder its own burdens. There were no grants and subsidies from Whitehall. The central government merely took, it did not give. Charles I's steadily mounting demands for money roused more and more resentment as the years passed. The Council 'willingly assented' to his forced loan in 1627, though many local people were shocked by the amount demanded and the absence of parliamentary authority. A succession of yearly levies for Ship Money (Nottingham's assessment being £200 per annum) did not amuse an inland town that was already deeply in debt through its lavish displays of loyalty to the Crown. In the circumstances perhaps the most remarkable thing is not that the burgesses were tight-fisted in their treatment of the unfortunate but that they ever gave a halfpenny they were not compelled to. Yet they did, even to the extent of paying student grants. In 1635, despite the crushing demand for Ship Money, a Council minute records the decision 'to give John Cooke, a scholar of Cambridge, and born in this town, 40s towards the taking of his degree'. It was not an isolated case.

So the mood became increasingly critical. The local gentry – some of them now the local nobility – were torn two ways. They enjoyed royal favours, but they paid through the nose for them. Forced loans, 'free' gifts, their individual assessments for Ship Money, an imposition which had been forbidden after the

Petition of Right a few years before. . . . So it went on. And whether they accepted titles or begged leave to decline, it could be expensive. Using the ancient device, Distraint of Knighthood, sensible enough in the Middle Ages but by then meaningless, Charles extracted nearly three thousand pounds from the gentlemen of Nottinghamshire alone.

When to these financial inflictions was added a dismayed disagreement with the way the country seemed to be going – first the unpopular policies of the Duke of Buckingham, then the King's disregard of Parliament and the suspected influence of his foreign and Catholic wife – the grumbles grew ever louder and loyalties were strained to breaking-point. The painful divisions within families at this time are often recalled by historians. There was such a division at Thurland Hall. The new Earl of Clare and his son John, who succeeded him in 1637, stood by the King, but the second son, the brilliant Denzil Holles, came out more and more openly as the opponent of the sovereign he had played with when Charles had been brought to Nottingham as a boy. It was Denzil who, in 1629, forced the Speaker to keep his seat and vowed that he should sit there till it pleased the House to rise. His erstwhile playmate clapped him into the Tower shortly afterwards and tried to repeat the operation in that dramatic scene in 1642, when Denzil was one of the 'Five Members'. The effect of these goings-on, both on the household at Thurland Hall and on the people of Nottingham, can be easily imagined.

As in other trading-towns Puritanism was now a growing force, though even in that age of religious fanaticism the inhabitants never seem to have been roused to excesses either way. There were the usual cases of non-attendance at church, then a legal offence. Lady Frances Pierrepont, described with the respectful restraint due to her status as 'of the age of 50 years at the least', was presented 'for not coming to her parish church for the space of 4 months at the least', but the charge was dropped, doubtless with general relief, when it was learnt that the lady was away. On another occasion information was laid against a couple in St James's Lane for having in their home an 'altar made with divers idolatrous pictures upon it' and another 'picture of a profane traitor that was in the Gunpowder Treason and, as they said, was canonised for a saint'. This was probably Father Henry Garnett, the Jesuit, whose father had been master of the Free School in Elizabethan times. Early Stuart Nottingham clearly had its Catholics and its Nonconformists, but they were discreet. When the *Mayflower* sailed she carried several Nottinghamshire people but none from the town itself.

Religious convictions were none the less deep and real, permeating men's political decisions in the critical years that loomed ahead. This is evident in every page of Lucy Hutchinson's *Memoirs* of her husband, and it is time now to look at the gallant Colonel's career.

John Hutchinson does not at all fit the old stereotyped conception of an earnest Roundhead. Even his appearance was all wrong: his widow recalls 'his hair of light brown, softer than the finest silk, and curling into loose great rings'. He was 'naturally cheerful', with 'eyes of a lively grey', and though she says that 'of country recreations he loved none but hawking' she must be thinking of blood sports, for he shared in many of the rural interests of his Cavalier neighbours. 'He took much pleasure in improvement of grounds, in planting groves, and walks, and fruit-trees, in opening springs and making fish-ponds', and he 'shot excellently in bows and guns, and much used them for his exercise'. He had the accomplishments of his class – dancing, fencing and music – and perhaps a more than average interest in 'paintings, graving, sculpture, and all liberal arts'. He must have had a lot in common with John Evelyn, and would have enjoyed a similarly quiet existence. Only the circumstances, and a streak in his nature that Evelyn lacked, made him a reluctant man of action.

The Hutchinsons were a respected and well-connected family with a country home at Owthorpe, about eight miles out, and the customary town house on High Pavement. John's mother had been a Byron of Newstead, who 'notwithstanding she had had her education at court, was delighted in her own country habitation, and managed all her family affairs better than any of the home-

spun housewives . . .'. She died when she was only twenty-six and
the boy was three. After some years Sir Thomas remarried,
choosing a bride from another of the leading local families,
Catharine Stanhope. She, says the Reverend Julius Hutchinson
who eventually published the *Memoirs* in 1806, 'lived to the age
of 102, and . . . dwelt in splendour at Nottingham', retaining her
faculties into the reign of Queen Anne. But during John Hutchinson's formative years his father was a widower, and the little boy
was at first brought up with his Byron cousins. In due time he and
his younger brother George were sent to the Free School, in which
their father took a great interest. They boarded with the master,
Robert Theobald, who, Mrs Hutchinson long afterwards recorded,
'was an excellent scholar' (he was the product of Westminster
and Trinity, Cambridge) 'but having no children, some wealth,
and a little living that kept his house, he first grew lazy, and after
left off his school'. Before Theobald resigned, however, to become
Rector of Colwick, the indignant father had removed his sons to
Lincoln. Here the master was 'such a supercilious pedant' that he
gave John 'a disgust of him, and he profited very little there'.
Happily Sir Thomas soon heard encouraging accounts of Thomas
Leake, the new young master appointed at Nottingham, and he
brought his boys back again. John found that 'the familiar kind-
ness of his master made him now begin to love that which the
other's austerity made him loathe; and in a year's time he advanced exceedingly in learning, and was sent to Cambridge'.

He would have been home from Peterhouse that August
in 1634 when Charles and Henrietta Maria paid their visit to
Thurland Hall. Sir Thomas had married again and settled in his
town house. When John finally came down from Cambridge, 'he
there enjoyed no great delight, another brood of children spring-
ing up in the house, and the servants endeavouring with tales and
flatteries to sow dissension on both sides'. He stayed some time at
home, amusing himself with such intellectual companionship as a
small town offered, friends such as young Doctor Huntingdon
Plumptre, 'a good scholar' with 'a great deal of wit, but withal a
professed atheist'. During the Civil War this Plumptre was to
become a thorn in Hutchinson's side, but he can scarcely have

been as black as Mrs Hutchinson painted him. Certainly he proved a generous master of the ancient family charity, rebuilding its ruinous Hospital in 1650 and increasing the cash allowances to the widowed inmates.

Hutchinson himself was serious, but broad-minded for that period, and certainly no fanatic in religion or politics. 'Having a great reverence for his father', and to avoid friction at home, he asked leave to go to London and enter Lincoln's Inn. The law did not hold his attention for long, but, being loth to return, he spent the summer at Richmond in a kind of guest-house where there were other young people. Here he fell in love with Lucy Apsley, whose father had been Lieutenant of the Tower in Ralegh's time. It is an idyllic episode as Lucy recalls it. If we allow for her partisanship, the pious phraseology natural in that century, and the special bias with which she speaks of the previous girls in his life, her *Memoirs of Colonel Hutchinson* (or 'Memories', as we should call them) can be enjoyed as one of the earliest truly personal books written by an Englishwoman. Her manuscript is displayed in the Castle Museum, the level lines of brown handwriting still beautifully legible.

In the autumn of 1641, when the Civil War lay less than twelve months ahead, the young couple moved down to Owthorpe. By then they had been married several years and had twin sons, but John had not settled on any career, assuming that as the eldest in the family he would be his father's heir. His younger brother, George, made them all welcome at Owthorpe. Sir Thomas was in London, serving in the Parliament which the King had been compelled to summon. He was a moderate, disapproving of the King's policies yet shuddering at the thought of rebellion. John, and his brother less markedly, had youth's dislike of compromise. Most of their relatives and neighbours were Royalists, but they had the inspiration of some notable exceptions such as Denzil Holles and their cousin, Henry Ireton of Attenborough, later to distinguish himself as a parliamentary general and to marry Cromwell's daughter. An analysis of political sympathies in town and county, that year, would have underlined the inadequacy of the old generalizations about 'Cavaliers' and 'Roundheads'. No class was solid for King or Parliament. Many individuals hesitated to declare themselves.

The spring of 1642, however, saw the issues slowly clarifying, and the committed parties jockeying for position. The King had left London, never (as it proved) to return except as a prisoner. He and his antagonistic Parliament were making contradictory appointments and pronouncements. If it came to a fight, each wished to control the militia and their munition-stores in the respective regions – these would be vital, since there was no regular army to win over, and the business would be settled by whatever forces could be improvised. The various lords lieutenant (who in Tudor times had taken over the military authority of the sheriffs) would be key figures in the situation, and both sides sought men they could rely on. In Nottinghamshire the office was held by Lord Newark, eldest son of the Earl of Kingston. As he was a known Royalist, Parliament replaced him with Denzil Holles' elder brother John, who had now succeeded their father as Earl of Clare and was thought to be of liberal views. But the Earl went off to join the King at York, and the people were left in some doubt as to whose orders they should take.

When Hutchinson rode into Nottingham, he found the town reflecting the same deep divisions as the rest of the kingdom. The Mayor, John James, was alone among the seven aldermen in resolutely supporting Parliament, though the rest of the Council gave him an over-all majority. Lucy Hutchinson describes him as 'a very honest, bold man' but adds, with her usual keen regard for class which nobody then would have called snobbery, that he 'had no more than a burgher's discretion; he was yet very well assisted by his wife, a woman of great zeal and courage, and with more understanding than women of her rank usually have'. The Mayor had to cope with a Town Clerk of opposite views: Robert Greaves decamped two years later to join the Royalist forces, and had to be dismissed from office, though he was reinstated in 1652. For the Deputy Recorder, Chadwick, Mrs Hutchinson reserves her most contemptuous comments, since he was to give her husband much trouble in the years that followed. He had 'purchased the honour of a barrister, though he had neither law nor learning,

but he had a voluble tongue, and was crafty; and it is almost
incredible that one of his mean education and poverty should
arrive to such things as he reached'. He 'kept up his credit with
the godly, cutting his hair, and taking up a form of godliness, the
better to deceive', but 'among other villainies which he secretly
practised, he was a libidinous goat, for which his wife, they say,
paid him with making him a cuckold; yet there were not two
persons to be found that pretended more sanctity than these two,
she having a tongue no less glavering and false than his'. Mrs
Hutchinson may not qualify as an impartial historian, but she can
be eminently readable. She certainly brings seventeenth-century
Nottingham before our eyes.

Late in July the King rode into the town with eight hundred
Cavaliers at his back. It was an embarrassing occasion for Alderman James. Twice he had ignored the royal command to present
himself in York, and he had failed to publish sundry proclamations with which he did not agree. Yet the moment for open
defiance had not come. Short of flight or a diplomatic sickness, he
had no choice but to offer the usual civic courtesies. Some thought
(and perhaps the Mayor himself shared their expectation) that
Charles in his characteristically high-handed manner would order
his arrest. But the King was possibly learning at last the futility of
such displays. With cold dignity he received the 'loyal' greetings
of the town, accepted the offered mace and handed it back. It was
noticed, however, that he did not hold out his hand for the Mayor
to kiss. The unctuous Chadwick, deputising for the Recorder –
that honorary office being held by the King's host, the Earl of
Clare – then stepped forward, knelt and presented the Prince of
Wales with a purse of fifty pounds in gold, a gift which the citizens
must have regretted deeply in the months that followed. The next
day, the King departed with his embryo army.

Matters were now coming to a head. In London Parliament had
just appointed the Earl of Essex as commander-in-chief, and both
Houses (or those members who had not departed elsewhere) had
sworn to live and die with him 'for the preservation of the true
religion, laws, liberties and peace of the kingdom'. A few weeks
before the King's visit to Nottingham, the Mayor and his sup-

porters had petitioned Parliament for the adequate protection of the town, and they had been given authority to enrol and train a local defence force. The royal visit coinciding, nothing much had yet been done.

Moderate men still hoped against hope. Hutchinson was one of a deputation who at this late hour followed the King back to York, petitioning him to return to Whitehall and meet his Parliament. At York Hutchinson met his Byron cousins, who 'were extremely troubled to see him there on that account'. Returning to Nottingham from this fruitless mission, he went to the Mayor's house to exchange the latest news. He found Mrs James in a flutter. Her husband was officially custodian of the munitions, principally gunpowder, belonging to the Nottinghamshire trained bands and stored (one might think somewhat imprudently) in the Guildhall. And now, explained Mrs James, Lord Newark had arrived with the High Sheriff, Sir John Digby, and a troop of Cavaliers, demanding the munitions in the King's name. The Mayor had protested. He was trying to delay them, while word was sent to his own supporters, but it was touch and go whether the neighbourhood could be roused in time.

Hutchinson hastened to the Guildhall. Sure enough, the Cavaliers were weighing and packing up the gunpowder. In respectful terms (if we may accept Lucy Hutchinson's verbatim dialogue as essentially if not literally accurate) he asked Lord Newark for his written authority. The Lord Lieutenant answered that he had one but he had left it behind. Hutchinson indicated that, while personally he accepted his lordship's word, 'the country' (Mrs Hutchinson's word when she meant 'county' or 'neighbourhood') 'would not be willing to part with their powder in so dangerous a time, without an absolute command'. There was indeed a crowd outside, growing every minute, determined to prevent the removal of the gunpowder and promising if necessary to 'go up and tumble my lord and the sheriff out of the windows'. Inside, the argument continued with superficial civility – these gentlemen had mixed socially all their lives – but with mounting emotion. At last the Cavaliers saw that, quite literally, they could not get away with it, and they departed empty-handed.

For Hutchinson and the Mayor it was a short-lived triumph. Within a week or two the Cavaliers were back in strength. Hutchinson heard the news at Owthorpe. He rode straight to Nottingham but was too late to do anything. The arsenal had been taken over. Individual townsmen were being stripped of their weapons to arm the King's followers. One man brandished an empty musket at Hutchinson, saying that 'he wished it loaded, and hoped the day would shortly come when all such roundheads would be fair marks for them'.

Charles had issued his fateful proclamation. All subjects who could bear arms 'northward of the Trent and twenty miles to the southward' were to assemble in Nottingham where he would set up his standard in ten days' time. Once more the strategic position of the town had earned it a vital role in an historic drama.

Hutchinson went on to his father's town house on High Pavement. It had been taken over as a billet for the Quartermaster-General. Hutchinson, though he had already been warned that he was on the Royalist black-list, showed remarkable courage – or obstinacy – in stopping to argue the point and actually persuaded Lord Lindsey, the general in question, to make do with one room. Hutchinson thereupon returned to Owthorpe and his wife, who was then expecting another child. A few days later the Cavaliers came searching for him and he had to escape into Leicestershire.

Meantime, on 19 August, the King reappeared in Nottingham. His two sons were with him, so that for the next few weeks three kings or future kings of England slept under the same roof at Thurland Hall, or Clare House as it was now sometimes termed from its owner's title. Rupert of the Rhine, and his brother Prince Maurice, were also in Nottingham to support their uncle.

The ceremony that opened the Civil War took place as scheduled three days later at six o'clock in the evening of Monday 22 August 1642. The standard was a silk pennon, emblazoned for the purpose by a local man. It was to be flown from a heavy flagstaff like a maypole, painted red. The chosen spot was a little mound just outside the walls of the derelict Castle, a spot known ever afterwards as Standard Hill and today covered by the General Hospital.

There was a certain element of anti-climax about the affair. The day had been wet and was still windy – the English August was August even in the most romantic eras – and it took twenty struggling men to hold up the too-massive flagpole. There were the requisite heralds, drummers and trumpeters, three troops of cavalry and a token army of some hundreds, local trained bands mustered by the High Sheriff of the county. The bad weather (if not political antagonism) had deterred any great assembly of townspeople. At the last moment, standing on the blustery hilltop, Charles called for a pen and began to rephrase his proclamation, so that the world should be in no doubt as to his motives in taking to arms. The herald found difficulty with the altered script and read hesitantly, much as the King might have done himself. But the proclamation *was* read, and the trumpets sounded bravely, and the plumed hats went up like a flock of birds.

It is said that soon afterwards the standard blew down in the gale. If so, the symbolism was most apt.

CHAPTER THIRTEEN

Colonel Hutchinson in Command

CHARLES stayed in Nottingham until 13 September. The response to his proclamation was disappointing. The first three weeks brought barely three hundred recruits. He accordingly set off for the West Midlands, where there was more enthusiasm for his cause.

That autumn most of the local people took up the threads of normal existence again and waited for news. It was assumed that the dispute would be settled elsewhere and soon, as it might well have been if the Battle of Edgehill had been a knock-out victory for either side or if the Cavaliers had pressed their subsequent advance on London. The year ended, however, with nothing decided. Clearly the contest was to involve more than two armies manœuvring against each other in the South: the North, too, was going to play a part (the Earl of Newcastle commanded powerful Royalist forces there) and if the North came into it so did the strategic crossings of the Trent. So, in December, the High Sheriff – that same Sir John Digby who had been so zealous in the matter of the gunpowder – occupied Newark with his tiny force of eighty local gentlemen and planned by a bold coup to seize Nottingham as well. Tiny indeed these numbers seem, at this stage of the war, but it must be remembered that the ordinary Englishman had had no military experience, whereas the gentry were at least good horsemen and trained in the use of arms, while not a few had seen active service as volunteers in foreign wars under generals such as Gustavus Adolphus. In the sort of hit-and-run operations which mainly characterized the Civil War in Nottinghamshire, a handful of dashing Cavaliers could dominate a whole region as effectively as any gang of Wild Western outlaws.

The townsmen of Nottingham did not mean to be so dominated. They were not enthusiastic supporters of the Parliament – Mrs Hutchinson admits that 'the town was generally more malignant than well affected' – but like many people in other localities, and with good reason,

> they cared not much to have cavalier soldiers quarter with them, and therefore agreed to defend themselves against any force which should come against them; and being called hastily together . . . about seven hundred listed themselves, and chose Mr George Hutchinson for their captain, who having lived among them, was very much loved and esteemed by them. The sheriff hearing this, came not to Nottingham. . . .

John Hutchinson was active in this hasty mobilization, having long ago returned home, and his wife cannot help explaining why his younger brother came to be preferred as leader. The arming of this force must have been a makeshift affair, for the King had taken away all the arms normally provided for the trained bands.

The vigilantes did not disband when the immediate emergency passed, for, 'having now taken up the sword', they 'saw it was not safe to lay it down again, and hold a naked throat to their enemy's whetted knives'. It was agreed to press on with the raising of proper regiments as required by Parliament. Sir Francis Thornhagh and his son made themselves responsible for the cavalry regiment. Francis Pierrepont, dissociating himself from his still uncommitted father, the Earl of Kingston, became colonel of the infantry regiment, which the Hutchinson brothers joined. John was commissioned lieutenant-colonel and soon found himself with a company of volunteers from the countryside. George became a major, with a ready-made company of the townsmen he had previously commanded. A young cousin named Poulton also served in the regiment. He was one of those who 'had seen some service abroad', but belonged to the minority of them who chose the parliamentary side. These commissions were issued by Lord Grey, commander-in-chief of the counties associated in the East Midland region. A large measure of local autonomy was unavoidable when the normally slow methods of communication were made even less reliable by the hazards of civil war.

For the same reason a local Defence Committee was set up in Nottingham, which virtually took over the functions of the (rather indignant) Town Council. The Hutchinson brothers were appointed to this committee. So naturally was the Mayor, that sound parliamentary supporter, and Ireton, who had come home for the time being to serve as major in the cavalry regiment. The actual defence measures undertaken included gates at Chapel Bar and Cow Lane Bar, a drawbridge over the Leen, and breastworks in front of the town. The Committee guaranteed the materials but the Council had to find the labour. They soon received orders to provide also a night guard of thirty townsmen. As events soon proved, the danger of surprise attack was genuine.

Nottingham was now an island in a hostile sea. Digby's Cavaliers held Newark and the whole countryside was dominated by the Royalist gentry. Mrs Hutchinson and the children were unsafe at Owthorpe. When Hutchinson decided they had better join him in the town he had to send a troop of horse to escort them, and then under cover of darkness, though the distance was only eight miles.

That May it looked as though the Earl of Newcastle might descend upon the district from the North. There was a hasty concentration of parliamentary troops in Nottingham, five or six thousand in all, including some 'rude troops out of Yorkshire' under a young officer named Hotham, a high-handed fellow keeping up his own private correspondence with the Royalists and later condemned as a traitor. Meanwhile, according to Mrs Hutchinson, the townspeople were

> more sadly distressed by their friends than by their enemies; for Hotham's . . . men not only lay upon free quarter, as all the rest did, but made such a havoc and plunder of friend and foe, that it was a sad thing for any one that had a generous heart to behold it. When the committee offered Hotham to assign him quarters for his men, because they were better acquainted with the country, he would tell them he was no stranger in any English ground. He had a great deal of wicked wit, and would make sport with the miseries of the poor

country; and, having treason in his heart, licensed his soldiers, which were the scum of mankind, to all the villanies in the country that might make their party odious.

When Hutchinson begged him to restrain his men from looting, Hotham merely replied that 'he fought for liberty, and expected it in all things'. Hutchinson found a more sympathetic listener in a certain Colonel Oliver Cromwell who had come in with the East Anglian contingent. They jointly despatched a confidential report to London, not merely complaining of Hotham but glancing at other weaknesses in the command. This unprofessional action produced from Parliament a surprisingly positive response: a new commander-in-chief, Sir John Meldrum, was sent down, and Hotham was placed under arrest in the Castle, whence he was sent off to London under escort, but managed to escape on the way.

The Earl of Newcastle's expected offensive never materialized, but there was some excitement when the Queen passed through the area, protected by five thousand of his men. Henrietta Maria had been in Holland, pawning the Crown Jewels. She landed in Yorkshire with the proceeds, partly in cash, partly in munitions, and was making for her husband's war-time capital at Oxford. She crossed the Trent at Newark, where for some reason she dallied two or three weeks. Perhaps Digby tried to persuade her to use her powerful escort against Nottingham. Mrs Hutchinson records a rather ineffectual demonstration, when

> the queen's forces came and faced the town; whereupon the cannon discharging upon them, the Duke of Vendome's son and some few others were slain. The parliament horse drew out of Nottingham to receive the queen's, but they came not on, after this execution of the cannon, for in the meantime the queen was passing by, and although the parliament horse pursued them, yet they would not engage, for it was not their business; so when they saw they had lost their design, the horse returned again to Nottingham, where the foot had stayed all the while they were out.

If Henrietta Maria had in fact resumed her march to Oxford, this Cavalier manœuvre can be explained as a covering action to anticipate any move against the convoy. But the two armies were so nearly matched in numbers that, as each had prior tasks assigned to it, neither was probably keen to risk a full-scale battle.

The major fighting of the Civil War was destined always to take place elsewhere. About this time, that hesitant Nottingham peer, the Earl of Kingston, had at last come out actively for the King and seized Gainsborough. He was captured and shot as a traitor – the elaborate civilities of 1642 were souring into brutal hatreds by 1643 – and the Roundheads who had captured him were in turn besieged in Gainsborough by the Cavaliers. Sir John Meldrum was ordered to relieve them, taking all the forces from Nottingham except a sufficient garrison to hold the Castle. Before going, he called a meeting of the Defence Committee to decide the awkward question of a commander for that garrison. It was awkward because Colonel Pierrepont had the senior claim to the honour – and Meldrum wondered if it was wise to entrust it to a man, however honourable, whose father had just been shot by a parliamentary general.

So it was unanimously resolved (Pierrepont concurring with as good a grace as he could manage) that Colonel John Hutchinson should take over, and on 29 June the appointment was made. For the rest of the Civil War the direction of Nottingham's affairs rested in the hands of the Colonel – hands that were, however, far from free.

It was an unenviable responsibility that Hutchinson took over. His military resources were slender for the position he was expected to defend against the forces that might easily come against it. His authority was ill-defined – the cavalry considered that they were not part of the garrison and their commander co-operated only when he thought fit. Hutchinson had wanted no more than the simple governorship of the Castle, but Parliament gave him also control of the town, which led to much ill-feeling. Perhaps his bitterest struggles were with his own committee.

Mrs Hutchinson has left a vivid description of the Castle as it was in 1643.

The castle was built upon a rock, and nature had made it capable of very strong fortification, but the buildings were very

Thomas Sandby's Nottingham

above: *Weekday Cross, 1741, with High Pavement winding away up to St Mary's, and on the right the Guildhall with jail beneath.*

below: *Chapel Bar, 1743. This old town gate was pulled down soon afterwards, and much regretted when Prince Charlie's wild Highlanders came as close as Derby in 1745.*

A WEST VIEW OF CHAPEL BAR

The Georgian houses at the top of Castle Gate are now preserved in a pedestrian precinct. On the right is Newdigate House, where Marshal Tallard, after his capture at Blenheim, beguiled his years of captivity with gardening.

The southern approach to Nottingham as Byron would have seen it, coming down from London in 1808. But the artist has badly exaggerated the west-to-east distance from the Castle to St Mary's.

The town the Luddites knew – a view from the north-eastern heights, published in Blackner's History of Nottingham, *1815.*

Nottingham in 1846, with one of the earliest trains chuffing past Castle Rock. A view across the Trent-side meadows. Haymakers, milkmaids and windmills were still there, but the factory-chimneys were appearing.

The Market Place, 1813, by Richard Bonington, drawing-master father of a more famous son. Left to right: Long Row, Smithy Row, the Exchange, the Poultry, Timber Hill and Beastmarket Hill, enclosing the space that was then the regular battlefield for troops, rioters and rival politicians.

ruinous and uninhabitable, neither affording room to lodge soldiers nor provisions. The castle stands at one end of the town, upon such an eminence as commands the chief streets....

After recalling the story of Mortimer's Hole, she goes on:

There is a little piece of the rock, on which a dove-cote had been built, but the governor took down the roof of it, and made it a platform for two or three pieces of ordnance, which commanded some streets and all the meadows better than the higher tower. Under that tower, which was the old castle [presumably the Norman keep], there was a larger castle, where there had been several towers and many noble rooms [the later, Plantagenet extensions] but the most of them were down; the yard of that was pretty large, and without the gate there was a very large yard that had been walled, but the walls were all down, only it was situated upon an ascent of the rock, and so stood a pretty height above the streets; and there were the ruins of an old pair of gates, with turrets on each side.

She recalls the Park 'had neither deer nor trees in it'. In the rock 'were many large caverns, where a great magazine and many hundred soldiers might have been disposed, if they had been cleansed and prepared for it; and they might have been kept secure from any danger of firing the magazines by any mortar-pieces shot against the castle'.

The Castle at least *could* be defended: the town could not. The Colonel began by making this unpopular but inevitable decision. He brought in the cannon from the outlying batteries where they might have fallen to the first Cavalier raiding-party, and had fresh gun-platforms prepared within the Castle precincts. The place had been, says Mrs Hutchinson, 'as ill provided as fortified, there being but ten barrels of powder, eleven hundred and fifty pounds of butter, and as much cheese, eleven quarters of bread corn, seven beeves, two hundred and fourteen flitches of bacon, five hundred and sixty fishes, and fifteen hogsheads of beer'. Though it was not easy to build up further stocks, when the surrounding country was so largely dominated by the enemy, he had to meet the complaints of the townspeople that he was leaving them at the mercy of the Cavaliers, so 'he made proclamation . . . that whatsoever honest persons desired to secure

themselves or their goods in the castle, should have reception
there, if they would repair their quarters; which divers well-
affected men accepting, it was presently made capable of receiving 400 men commodiously'.

Even so, the Colonel seems to have had considerable difficulty
in keeping his own garrison on the premises. His wife records that
he

> gave charge to all that belonged to the castle, being about three
> hundred men, that they should not upon any pretence whatever
> be out of their quarters; but they having, many of them, wives
> and better accommodations in the town, by stealth disobeyed
> his commands, and seldom left any more in the castle than
> what were upon the guard.

This was a highly dangerous situation. Nottingham was under
continuous threat, whether from the aggressive Cavalier forces at
Newark or from the main commanders, such as the Earl of
Newcastle or Prince Rupert, who would have been glad to control
this other passage over the Trent. The Earl tried to win over the
Colonel by bribery, offering ten thousand pounds in cash, a
peerage from the King, and a grant of the Castle itself in per-
petuity, with proportionate favours for George Hutchinson and
their cousin, Poulton. It was easy for a man of the Colonel's
principles to rebuff this approach, but an assault by Prince
Rupert's army would have been a different matter. Fortunately, if
we may accept Lucy Hutchinson's view of events, Providence
looked after the godly.

> The prince . . . was advanced within three miles of Notting-
> ham; when it pleased God to divert him from coming against
> the town by letters which were brought him from Oxford,
> which occasioned his hasty return into the south, without any
> attempt upon the place, which, by God's mercy, was thus
> delivered from this threatening danger.

The Cavalier raids from Newark were bad enough, especially
as there was plenty of Royalist sympathy – or at least anti-
parliamentary feeling – among the townspeople, who could be
relied upon by the enemy for passive if not active support. The
town had been divided from the start. Now the old criticisms of

the King were giving place to murmurs against the new order. How, men whispered, had these high-handed Parliament men improved matters? New financial burdens had been put upon the town. Defence works had been demanded – yet now only the Castle was to be defended. By the beginning of 1645 a kind of local conscription was coming into force, to man the night-watch. And every time some local personality suffered for his opposition to the new régime fuel was added to the burning indignation of those who liked and respected him. Men who had looked up to the executed Earl of Kingston, friends of the fugitive and dismissed Town Clerk, parishioners of Edmund Laycock, Vicar of St Mary's, who, with the Rector of West Bridgford, had been dispossessed and imprisoned early in the war – these, and countless other Nottingham people with individual causes for resentment, did not share Lucy Hutchinson's black-and-white picture of the conflict and were enough to make the town's loyalty to Parliament quite undependable.

It was an alderman, Francis Toplady, who was widely blamed for the Cavaliers' successful surprise of the town one September night in 1643. He was taking his turn to command the watch, and, whether through negligence or treachery, allowed the Cavaliers to pass the gates without firing a shot. The majority of the Castle garrison not on duty were, with their usual disregard of the Colonel's orders, sleeping at home. A large number of these were surprised in their beds and taken prisoner. It was all done so quietly that no alarm reached the Castle. Mrs Hutchinson says that her husband knew nothing of it until the next morning, when some of his men, coming off night-duty in the Castle, 'were going down into the town to refresh themselves' when they were driven back by the fire of Royalist muskets.

There were about six hundred Cavaliers, led by Sir Richard Byron, who then commanded at Newark. On the second day they were joined by four hundred from Ashby-de-la-Zouch, who withdrew again in pique when they found that they were too late for the plundering. Colonel Hutchinson found himself that first morning with only eighty men to defend the Castle ramparts, though the number gradually doubled as those who had escaped capture in the town managed to slip back to their posts by devious routes. The Colonel sent off urgent appeals to Derby and Leicester. It was lucky that the Cavaliers contented themselves with looting and keeping up a brisk musket-fire on the Castle, for if they had made a determined effort to storm it the depleted garrison could scarcely have kept them out.

To offset the Castle's dominating height, the Royalist musketeers climbed to the steeple of St Nicholas's, which 'so commanded the platform' that the Castle gunners 'could not play the ordnance without woolpacks before them' and 'the bullets played so thick into the outward castle-yard' that the defenders could not pass to and fro in safety until the Colonel had a trench dug during the night. One man bled to death because he could not be carried across this No-Man's-Land to Mrs Hutchinson, who was doing her best to treat the wounded as no surgeon was available. Afterwards, the Colonel insisted on the demolition of the church, which was not rebuilt for nearly forty years and never regained its spire. The present late-seventeenth-century church has, Pevsner remarks, 'much to remind one of New England', as does the warning boldly inscribed on the clock dial, 'It is time to seek the Lord.'

The Cavaliers held the town for five days. They offered to discuss terms. The Colonel defied them, running up a red flag (which then had no special political connotation) and discharging three cannon at the church steeple. It must have been a tiring week. The raiders 'durst not in all that time go to bed', asserts Mrs Hutchinson, adding with more first-hand authority that the defenders never slept at night and could only take snatches of rest in the day-time 'by the side of them that watched'.

At last, on the Saturday afternoon, the Colonel observed a long column moving out across the Leen Bridge, while simultaneously another body of troops was approaching from the other side of the town. Having satisfied himself that the latter were friendly (they were a relieving-force of four hundred men from Leicester and Derby), he 'sent out his brother, Major Hutchinson, with all the musketeers that could be spared, to help drive the enemy out of the town'. Instead of making sure of this, however, the musketeers, greedy of knowing what was become of their wives and houses, dropped so fast from behind him to make the inquiry, that they had left him at the head of only sixteen men, when Sir Richard Byron . . . followed by a whole troop of horse and a company of foot, came upon him. The major commanded his men to charge them, which they did, but shot over; yet falling in with them pell-mell, they had gotten Sir Richard Byron down, and they had his hat, but he escaped, though his horse was so wounded that it fell dead in the next street.

It is details such as Sir Richard's hat that make Lucy Hutchinson so splendid a witness on some matters, despite her bias in others.

This was not the only occasion when there was fierce street-fighting in Nottingham. On another, when the town lay under a thick cover of January snow, a force of a thousand Cavaliers advanced upon it. This time Hutchinson was forewarned. He sent down his infantry and cavalry to dispute the entrance to the town. But the horsemen, as usual, made their own estimate of the situation and retired to the Castle, where the infantry had to follow them when they realized they stood alone and would get no help from the townsmen either. The Cavaliers galloped in, occupied the houses facing the Castle, and opened fire. The Colonel thereupon treated his disobedient troopers to such a furious harangue that in shame 'they dismounted, and all took muskets to serve as foot' and helped the infantry to 'beat the cavaliers out of the nearest lanes and houses'.

This done, the Colonel got ready to launch a full-scale counter-attack. Meanwhile the Royalist commander, Sir Charles Lucas, was drafting terms of surrender: if Hutchinson would not immediately yield the fortress, at least he should send down the Mayor and aldermen, or otherwise the town would be sacked and burnt. Lucas could find no townsman willing to carry this letter, so the Mayor's wife was coerced into doing so. But, just as the frightened woman was starting out on her mission, there was an uproar in front of her and shouts that 'the Roundheads were sallying forth'. She sensibly dropped the letter and ran. It was no false alarm. The garrison was pouring down the narrow lanes from the Castle. The Cavaliers fled, though some made an effort to start fires by shooting pistols into the thatched roofs and setting matches to a hay barn. No great damage was done. Mrs Hutchinson claims that thirty or forty Cavaliers were killed in the streets and eighty taken prisoner, with a quantity of abandoned arms. Others were later found dead of wounds and exposure in the country outside. In this passage Mrs Hutchinson is both compassionate and generous to the enemy, acknowledging their initial gallantry at the capture of the town and their fortitude in 'such bitter weather', when, as they retreated, 'for two miles they left a great track of blood, which froze as it fell upon the snow'.

The irrepressible Cavaliers made another attempt on the town a month later. One Saturday morning a dozen of their soldiers appeared on Trent Bridge 'disguised like market men and women' but 'with pistols, long knives, hatchets, daggers, and great pieces of iron about them', and with more regularly armed comrades within call, once they had overcome the guards. Hutchinson had precise warning of this plan and was ready for it. The disguised Royalists were identified and seized. Ten others, who had advanced too closely on their heels, had to jump into the river. Five were drowned, four pulled out and made prisoner, and only their captain escaped by swimming to the Bridgford bank.

The parliamentary triumph at Naseby in 1645 did not at once relieve the pressure on Nottingham, for Newark became a rallying-point for the Royalists, stronger than ever, and the Colonel dared not relax his vigilance. But in 1646 the King surrendered to the Scots, who in due course handed him over to the Parliamentary Commissioners, and it was as their prisoner that Charles passed through Nottingham for the last time in February 1647 on the long sad journey that was to end on the Whitehall scaffold two years afterwards. Hutchinson was one of those who signed his death-warrant. He had been elected to Parliament to fill the vacancy left by his father's death some years before, and for a time he served on the council of state, but he more and more distrusted Cromwell's policies and he soon dropped out of public affairs. Poor health may have affected his decision, but the truth was that, even if the Colonel was not quite the saintly hero depicted by his wife, he was a man of integrity who did not enjoy party controversy and the moral compromises it demanded. He retired to Owthorpe and took up the life of a country squire.

Nottingham had been 'disgarrisoned' soon after the King's surrender. The town was not involved in the revival of hostilities known as the Second Civil War – its quiet was ruffled only by the passing of Cromwell's army on 3 August 1648, hastening northwards to defeat the Scots at Preston, and again in 1651, when on the ninth anniversary exactly of Charles I's standard-hoisting, Cromwell rode through the town to defeat his son at Worcester. The demolition of the Castle was ordered in that year. Cromwell is usually credited with the destruction of England's medieval fortresses, but in this instance it was Hutchinson who secured the order, fearing lest Cromwell might use such places to buttress a military dictatorship. The work was superintended by his cousin, now Major Poulton, and the proud (if decayed) Plantagenet stronghold, which had never fallen to military assault, went down before the demolition gangs. The stones disappeared in job lots for paving and domestic building.

The Commonwealth decade passed greyly without major incidents. Puritanism, of course, was rampant. The Sabbath was rigidly enforced. Those who loved sport and the famed strong ales of Nottingham had to take these and other pleasures more furtively. Christmas, football, church organs and stage plays were all abominable in the eyes of the extremists, and were alike made illegal. Some bans were harder to enforce than others, and doubtless the unregenerate members of the community kept some sparks of the old Merrie England aglow in Nottingham, if only behind closed doors, in back alleys, or in the pleasant fields and thickets round about. To take a hand at cards, for instance, was a safe enough way to defy the Puritans. An added relish came from giving the cards a political significance. Thus, the ace of diamonds stood for the High Court of Justice, more familiarly known as 'Oliver's Slaughterhouse'.

Church life was remoulded on Presbyterian lines. St Mary's was governed by eight elders, including Francis Pierrepont and other leading townsmen of similar persuasion. The pulpit, which had lacked a regular minister for two years, was shared by two ardent preachers brought in from Bedfordshire, the Reverend John Whitlock and his friend, the Reverend William Reynolds, now termed the Lecturer. It was some time before their appointment that George Fox paid an uninvited visit to the church. The Leicestershire weaver's son had recently started upon that career of itinerant preaching which led to the foundation of the Quakers. In 1649, he recalls in his *Journal*, 'I went to the Steeple House at Nottingham, during the time of divine worship, addressed the people, and was committed to prison.' This was the first of his many conflicts with the law, but he made good use of his time in custody to convert the Sheriff, John Reckless, to his views. Hutchinson too, Fox records, sent down soldiers from the Castle to disperse the mob demonstrating against him. Hutchinson agreed with Cromwell at least in a resistance to the Presbyterians' excessive claims to run the country. In Nottingham, however, they were in control. The minister at St Peter's, the Reverend John Barrett, worked closely with Whitlock and Reynolds, and the parishioners of the demolished St Nicholas's also sat under him. When a new master was appointed to the grammar school in 1657, the successful candidate was interrogated by five local ministers, and it was not long before he was acting as an elder at St Mary's – but this may indicate diplomacy rather than dogmatic conviction, for in later years he was ordained in the Church of England.

The town's secular affairs went on much as they had before the interruption of the war, except that the royal arms had to be taken off the mace. The fugitive Town Clerk was forgiven and restored to his office, and for a short time the experiment was made of employing a Town Treasurer at two pounds per year. The Council was chronically short of money. In 1650 it made the last of several attempts to find coal at the Coppice, part of the common lands, but in vain – if there was no gold in those Mapperley Hills, coal would have been the next best thing, the councillors doubtless reasoned, thinking of the Willoughby opulence at Wollaton. But the only revenue they could develop from the town lands was the annual rent they had begun to charge in 1640 for each allotment or 'burgess part' rented to individual citizens.

Cromwell's death raised hopes of a return to 'the good old days'. In some districts Cavaliers attempted unrealistic rebellions. Nottingham saw one of these fiascos. Lord Byron, who as Sir Richard had led the raid of 1643, mustered about a hundred followers in Sherwood Forest, six miles north of the town, but the demonstration ended in an ignominious gallop through the streets with the militia in fierce pursuit. It was an orderly restoration the people pined for, not a bloody counter-revolution.

In January 1660 General Monck passed through the town on his historic march from Scotland to London. More and more people agreed that the best course was to recall the Stuarts, but in a proper manner, through a new Parliament elected to replace the discredited 'Rump' surviving from 1640. By the spring, 'before the writs for the new elections came', says Lucy Hutchinson, 'the town of Nottingham began to grow mad, and to declare themselves so, in their desires of the king'. But the shadowy authority of the Commonwealth lingered a little longer, and two troops of Hacker's regiment, then quartered in the town, did their best to support it.

'The boys', she says, 'set on by their fathers and masters, got drums and colours, and marched up and down the town, and trained themselves in a military posture, and offered many affronts to the soldiers. . . .' Doubtless they taunted them with the news of how, elsewhere, their generals and comrades were changing sides. Perhaps they chanted the popular song of the hour:

> Ding a ding ding,
> I heard a bird sing,
> The Parliament soldiers
> Are gone to the King.

'One night', continues Mrs Hutchinson, 'there were about forty of the soldiers hurt and wounded with stones, upon the occasion of taking away the drums, when the youth were gathering together to make bonfires to burn the Rump, as was the

custom in those mad days.' The troops opened fire. Two respect-
able Presbyterians were accidentally killed, and a full-scale
conflict was averted only, she implies, by her 'chance coming into
the town' and timely intervention.

The Colonel was elected one of the town's two new M.P.s,
despite the rivalry of his old friend and enemy, Dr Plumptre. How
the new Parliament came to terms with Charles II, and brought
him back to England in triumph, is familiar national history. In
Nottingham, even before the official announcement, the exultant
Alderman Francis Toplady – he who had behaved so suspiciously
at the time of the surprise-attack in 1643 – lost no time in gathering the people and proclaiming the King with such a drumming
and shouting and discharge of guns 'as was to the wonderment
of all, and astonishment of those few Phanaticks in town'.

It seemed at first as though the Colonel would escape the
vengeance meted out to those still living who had put their names
to the late King's death-warrant. His moderate record, his dis-
sociation from Cromwell, and not least perhaps his cousinship
with the loyal Byrons, all worked in his favour. He was merely
disqualified from holding public office and retired quietly to
Nottinghamshire. In 1663, however, he was falsely accused of
conspiracy against the restored régime, and after nearly a year of
rigorous imprisonment, first in the Tower and then at Sandown
Castle in Kent, he died without ever being brought to trial. He
was just forty-eight. Almost at once Lucy sat down to write the
Memoirs she intended as his justification to posterity.

CHAPTER FOURTEEN

From Restoration to Revolution

IT was not the English way to embark upon orgies of wholesale revenge, and in Nottingham, as elsewhere, the general desire was to let bygones be bygones, whatever tragic memories and personal animosities lingered under the surface. Cavalier gentlemen came back to the estates they had not seen for years and rode up Low Pavement once more to reclaim their town houses – but not every ruined fortune could be restored as simply as a king and not every change wrought by the Commonwealth could be un-scrambled by Act of Parliament. At least, though, the constraints of everyday life could be relaxed. The sober-suited crowds were diversified with more and more bright colours and long curling wigs were eagerly donned by some who wanted to forget how recently they had gone with cropped round-heads. Fun and games were back in favour. Even church-going was livelier: St Mary's and St Peter's rang with music again after a decade of doleful unaccompanied psalms.

If there was anywhere a campaign of reprisals that really hurt, it was indeed led by the Church of England, though theology and politics were so intermingled in that age that it is hard to disentangle them. Not unreasonably, the Puritan ministers who had previously seized control of the town's parish-churches and put them under a Presbyterian system were now themselves ejected and replaced by orthodox Anglican clergy. It was a different matter, however, when the Corporation Act of 1661 required all mayors and councillors not only to swear their loyalty to the Crown but to accept Holy Communion according to the rites of the Church of England. We may judge how strong and sincere were the dissenting forces in Nottingham, for when the year's period of grace expired no fewer than six of the seven aldermen refused and were promptly removed from the Council. The seventh inevitably took over as mayor. His name, needless to say, was Francis Toplady.

There was some slight embarrassment over the mace, from which (it may be remembered) the royal arms had been removed. It had to be sold and a new one made. The two sheriffs had to manage without new maces until 1670, money being as always scarce. That problem was solved ingeniously without cost to the ratepayers: the first pair of sheriffs personally put down the money, and, on relinquishing office, received that sum (less ten shillings each) from their successors. This procedure was repeated annually until the total amount was wiped off.

The Church of England was not content, however, with the restoration of its own establishment and the control of local as well as national affairs. The dissenting preachers who still refused to conform were harried by the Five-Mile Act of 1665. Whitlock and Reynolds had at first been befriended by Sir John Musters who housed them rent-free at Colwick Hall, but this was far too close to St Mary's to be allowed under the new law, and they had to move to Mansfield, which, not being a corporate town, became a popular refuge for such ministers. John Barrett, who had officiated at St Peter's, went to Sandiacre, just outside the five-mile radius. They remained marked men until the Glorious Revolution. Whitlock and Reynolds were both put under preventive arrest at the time of Monmouth's rebellion in 1685.

Despite repression, Nottingham's tradition of Nonconformity had come to stay. In 1669 the Church itself estimated that the town had four or five hundred Presbyterians meeting in private houses for worship, as well as two hundred Congregationalists (the old Independents, whom both Cromwell and Hutchinson had favoured) and even a hundred of George Fox's converts, the Society of Friends. These last suffered more persecution than anyone, because their uncompromising views on everyday issues kept bringing them into conflict with the authorities.

Among the local magistrates most zealous in persecuting Quakers was a man remembered in other respects with the warmest gratitude: Robert Thoroton, the village doctor at Car Colston, whose interest in local history set him collecting records at a date when few people realized their possible importance. As a result of Thoroton's efforts, the county possesses a body of early material which is the envy of most other regions.

Thoroton's life was spent in and around the quiet village just off the Fosse Way, though it is believed that he may have been born in Nottingham (where his parents were married at St Mary's) and he must certainly have been a frequent visitor to the town, especially when the end of the Civil War restored its normal communications with the surrounding countryside. In 1646, when he was twenty-two, Thoroton took his Cambridge M.A. and was licensed as a physician, and within two or three years he had found a bride in Anne Boun, a lawyer's daughter, living on High Pavement at Bugge Hall, the erstwhile town house of the family which had long since changed its name to Willoughby. His father-in-law seems already to have toyed with the idea of a county history, but the incident which spurred the doctor to action was an encounter with Sir William Dugdale, whose famous *Antiquities of Warwickshire* had come out in 1655 and pointed the way down a whole new avenue of scholarly authorship. Dugdale and his host, the squire of Thrumpton, urged Thoroton to attempt something similar for his own shire.

To men of their class and century local history had a more limited meaning than it has to us today. It meant, primarily, the pedigrees of the old county families such as their own, and the sort of information preserved in legal documents. The 'Nobility and Gentry', to whom the work was eventually addressed, were not interested in the common man. The modern historian of the county, A. C. Wood, warns us not to look for the things which Thoroton would never have dreamed of including. At the same time, he pays tribute to the 'astonishingly competent and complete' work which this local physician did carry out in his spare time for more than ten years, inside the narrow limits he had marked out for himself. When the *Antiquities of Nottinghamshire* was published in 1677 – just in time, for he died a year later – it was a massive folio volume of more than five hundred pages, with specially drawn illustrations by Richard Hall, engraved by the veteran Czech émigré, Wenceslaus Hollar, and in every way a production worthy of its individual dedications to the Archbishop of Canterbury (Thoroton's one-time neighbour) and to Dugdale who had first inspired him.

Everyone who has tried to write about the past of Nottingham and Nottinghamshire owes a debt to Thoroton and also to the Thoroton Society, founded in 1897 to commemorate him and to carry on his work with similar zeal and fidelity but in the wider context of local historical studies as they are now understood. By searching out and preserving records of all kinds, and by making their discoveries available in annually published *Transactions*, its members provide the material without which the history of a locality cannot be written.

Happily the interest some men devote to history is matched by what others lavish on geography. In 1675, while Thoroton was completing his collection of old records, Nottingham was visited by the topographer, Thomas Baskerville. He was charmed with Nottingham, which seemed, 'as a man may say, Paradise restored'. Milton's poem, of rather similar title, had come out four years earlier. 'Here', continued Baskerville, 'you find large streets, fair built houses, fine women, and many coaches rattling about, and their shops full of all merchantable riches.'

Other travellers were to support this eulogy. The town was undergoing a conspicuous transformation. It had been only in 1615 (according to Deering) that the first brick building, the Green Dragon Inn, had appeared among the half-timbering of Long Row. Now there were brick houses everywhere, often with curved gables fronting the street, and tiled roofs were fast replacing thatch. The Pierreponts had built their Stoney Street mansion as early as 1650, but it was after the Restoration that things really began to move, Lord Mansfield leading the way with a house in Wheeler Gate. Almost nothing of what Baskerville saw now remains. Out at the suburb of Bulwell, then a separate 'township', there is Strelley House in Commercial Road, built in 1667 as a grammar school with curved and stepped Dutch gables, the whole design, according to Pevsner, 'very characteristic of Nottinghamshire brick building at the date'. But in Nottingham itself most of the fine town houses that survive were yet to come, such as Newdigate House in Castle Gate which, with its graceful proportions, elegant wrought iron, and interestingly varied window pediments is a poignant reminder of much other beauty that is now lost forever.

There was a special reason for this efflorescence: the fashion set by a remarkable octogenarian, the Duke of Newcastle, who had begun to rebuild the Castle as a residence. Nottingham had previously possessed its genteel society in miniature, headed by the Holles family at Thurland Hall, but there had never been a resident duke to set the tone. The Castle had been a fortress and a port of call for medieval kings, but never, like some castles, the permanent apex of the region's social pyramid. In 1675 it promised to become so.

The Duke was that same William Cavendish who, as Earl of Newcastle, had led the King's northern armies and advised Prince Rupert against fighting the Battle of Marston Moor. After that, in understandable pique, he had retired from the struggle and gone abroad. He was a man of almost incalculable riches. His second wife, who made an attempt at calculation, reckoned his losses in the Civil War at precisely £941,303, the translation of which into modern values would set any mind boggling. She described him as 'courtly, civil, easy and free', yet with 'something of grandeur, that causes an awful respect for him'. He would have taken a poor view of democracy and popular education, complaining even in those days that 'when most was unlettered, it was much a better world both for peace and war'. He had been Charles II's boyhood governor, and his old pupil made him a duke in 1665.

He was a versatile man. Besides playing patron to Jonson, Davenant and other authors, he collaborated with Dryden in translating Molière's *L'Étourdi* and wrote plays himself, as indeed his wife did. Pepys saw his comedy, *The Country Captain*, and commented in his diary: 'So silly a play as in all my life I never saw.' But then Pepys was not an infallible critic. A few months later he was decrying *Romeo and Juliet* as 'the worst that ever I heard'.

Newcastle was also absorbed in horsemanship. During his exile, when he was often at his wit's end for money, he ran a riding-school at Antwerp and wrote a manual on dressage. When he returned to Welbeck and began to set in order the estates which had been confiscated under the Protectorate, he laid out a race-course and held monthly meetings. The Nottingham races must have originated about this time, for they were well established by 1690, when the Corporation offered a piece of plate to be run for. The town course was originally four miles round, passing over the Forest waste or lings and touching the three parishes of Basford, Lenton and Radford. Doubtless the old Duke enjoyed the sport here as well as on his own estate. Clearly he had an interest in Nottingham, or he would not have embarked on his plan to erect a baroque mansion on the summit of the Castle Rock. He was then eighty-two and had just buried his beautiful, eccentric wife. Was it perhaps a diversion from his grief? They had doted upon each other, she as much as he.

The Castle site had never even belonged to the Cavendishes. It had passed from the Duke of Rutland, through his daughter, to the Duke of Buckingham, from whom Newcastle bought it. Of the fortress Hutchinson had defended little remained but cellars and dungeons, which he now converted to domestic purposes. The ducal ovens can still be seen in the basement of the museum.

On this foundation Newcastle raised the mansion which, in its general features, allowing for the fire of 1831, survives today. To quote once more from the indispensable Pevsner: 'a palace . . . which looks at first . . . as if it stood in North Italy or Prague. . . . Everything is done to increase life and movement in the way in which the Continental Baroque tried to do it everywhere. Yet the English accent can nowhere be mistaken.'

Newcastle had seen much of Europe even before his involuntary travels during the Commonwealth. As a young man, he had been abroad with that enthusiastic pioneer of the Grand Tour,

Sir Henry Wotton. By now, the old man must have known what he wanted. He did not, alas, live to see it. He died in 1676, leaving two thousand pounds earmarked for the completion of the work by his son Henry. The total cost was fourteen thousand.

About twenty years later that indefatigable sightseer, Celia Fiennes, who was usually more interested in a new house than an old one, recorded her impressions of the Castle, 'which is a fine thing, stands very high on a hill and when you come to the Castle you ascend 40 steps to the Court and Hall, the rooms are very lofty and large, 6 or 7 state rooms, and a long gallery hung with fine pictures of the family'. She noted that the wainscot was mostly of cedarwood and that some of the rooms were hung with good tapestry, especially the Chamber of State, where the three tapestries contained so much gold and silver that they were worth fifteen hundred pounds. Celia Fiennes missed nothing, from the damask bed and the floor inlaid with ciphers and coronets to the view from the leads, 'a very fine prospect of the whole town and river', with meadows, cornfields and stately homes, stretching for more than twenty miles.

By the date of her visit the Castle had yet another master. The second Duke had left only daughters. One of these married John Holles, fourth Earl of Clare, who in 1694 had been made Duke of Newcastle by a fresh creation. So, not unfittingly, the traditions of Thurland Hall were blended with those of the Castle, and two great local families, Holles and Cavendish, merged their honours. There seemed, however, to be some kind of ill-luck about the ducal title, for again the male line failed, and later yet again. The Duke who provoked all the trouble in 1831 was of the fourth creation.

By the time of Celia Fiennes' visit Nottingham had made great progress. It was, she declared, the neatest town she had seen. The houses were 'lofty and well built' and the long streets 'much like London'. She was impressed by the market place, 'out of which runs two very large streets much like Holborn but the buildings finer'. She noted the 'Pyaza' (Long Row) 'with stone pillars for walking', though she exaggerated the length, for it was never 'a mile long', whatever it may seem to the weary shopper.

Celia Fiennes was a grand-daughter of the Roundhead peer, Viscount Saye and Sele, and her own sympathies were frankly Whiggish and Nonconformist, which may have enhanced her favourable opinion of Nottingham. Her tireless peregrinations of England had begun as a young woman's visits to far-flung friends and relatives, but they evolved into sightseeing tours. Her journals were not printed until 1888, when there was an incomplete edition entitled *Through England on a Side Saddle in the time of William and Mary*, but it was left to a Cambridge scholar, Christopher Morris, to edit a definitive text in 1947. And very sprightly it is.

Celia was thirty-five when she approached the town via Newark, pausing to sample, as she entered the county, 'the strongest and best Nottingham ale that looked very pale but exceedingly clear'. For seven or eight miles she rode along the bank of the Trent, which she found 'very pleasant'. She passed 'several pretty houses by the river side', casting an approving eye at their 'good gardens'. Lord Kingston's house at Holme Pierrepont looked fine amid its woods.

Celia and her unspecified companions – sometimes she travelled alone except for servants – lodged at the principal inn, the Blackamoor's Head, where they were 'very well entertained and very reasonably'. Celia appears to have been a connoisseur of good ale and she knew that the town was famous for it. Insatiably curious, just as she had climbed to the roof of the Castle, she insisted on descending the sixty steps into the rock cellar of the Crown Inn and sampling the brew there.

She was a remarkable young woman for her time. She moved easily and confidently among aristocracy and bourgeoisie alike. She had no sentimental admiration for the past and her contempt for what were then ancient buildings equalled that of the most iconoclastic property-developer today. She preferred the new. She was interested in land drainage, mining, manufactures, and the marble-seated water-closets in royal palaces – an amenity which presumably even the Duke of Newcastle had not been able to command at the Castle, or she would surely have mentioned it.

At Nottingham she observed that 'the manufacture of the town mostly consists in weaving of stockings', a statement of some importance because it records the progress of the framework knitting industry which was to play such a conspicuous part in the town's subsequent history.

Lee's invention had gradually found its way back to the district where it had originated. In London the framework knitters had become a company in Cromwell's time and had then renewed their charter under Charles II. As the industry spread to the provinces (by 1660 there were a hundred frames working in Nottinghamshire) there was a growing resentment against the Londoners' efforts to maintain control of the trade. Just before Celia's arrival in Nottingham, the company had petitioned Parliament for help in enforcing its restrictions, and the Nottinghamshire framework knitters had sent up a counter-petition, complaining that the company was run by a clique in London who wasted its resources on city banquets, ornate Thames barges and other traditional trappings. From this date the Nottinghamshire industry expanded rapidly, with low production-costs based on its flouting of the apprenticeship system and the other by-laws which the company sought to impose.

Stockings were still made as Lee's prototype machine had made them a century before, and apart from minor improvements the method continued for another hundred years. The frame itself was a subtle and costly piece of apparatus and took several highly skilled men to produce it. There was a framesmith to make the steel parts, a sinkermaker to provide the thin plates of iron, and of course a needlemaker. Then a 'setter-up' was called in to assemble the whole machine, and the subsequent maintenance provided constant work for all these specialist tradesmen. Altogether there were more than two thousand parts.

It was a man's job, operating such a frame. Hands and feet were in constant and tiring movement – in the early days, indeed, most men needed a semi-skilled helper. Women and children could assist only with the lighter work, like the seaming of the flat stockings as they came off the frame and other tasks requiring hand stitching. It was a trade that could be carried on at home, and that was why it developed greatly in the villages outside the town, but a machine of such complexity was too expensive for a poor man to own. He therefore hired it from a master, and in the same way, instead of buying his own raw material, he fetched yarn from a hosier's warehouse and took it back as stockings, receiving the rate for the job. In due course middlemen appeared, saving him the long walks to and fro by delivering yarn and collecting the finished work from the cottages. Then these middlemen began to provide workshop space, and the trade was ready for the invention of power-driven machinery and a fully fledged capitalist system.

All this lay far ahead when Celia Fiennes explored the neat town and quaffed its famous ale. But the change had begun. When she died, at nearly eighty, there were twelve hundred frames owned by fifty master framework knitters, and hundreds more in the surrounding villages. As a consequence the tanneries and some of the other trades had declined.

Baskerville had observed the fine shops. There was money about. That was evident as more and more tall sash-windowed houses went up around St Mary's and in the streets running down from the Duke's gatehouse to the Market Place. There was money about, but until this period no bank to take care of it.

Thieves, footpads and highwaymen were a real menace. The southern approaches to the town were particularly troubled by the handsome young Edward Bracey, who seduced a farmer's daughter, Joan Phillips, and eloped with her, taking all the money and plate from the house. Joan herself had a fine figure and striking looks. She became his active accomplice, riding with him in men's clothes, with pistols in her holsters. After a series of successes, they held up some gentlemen in a coach on the Loughborough road and met with stiff resistance. Joan was captured, Bracey fled but was killed in an attempt to arrest him. Joan was tried at the Spring Assizes in 1685 and hanged at the end of Wilford Lane, near the scene of the hold-up. She was only twenty-nine. If these were the most romantic villains of the period, they were certainly not the only ones. Men with business in Nottingham must have dreaded a late homeward journey with large amounts of cash, and, highway hazards apart, the increase in sophisticated financial transactions, loans, mortgages, letters of credit and the like, made some sort of banking facilities essential.

On a corner of the old Market Place, facing the blank stare of the municipal lion on the Council House steps, stands Smith's Bank, now part of the National Westminster, but still remembered as a milestone in banking history. Near this spot Thomas Smith was conducting business in 1688, six years before the establishment of the Bank of England. It was not till 1750 that his example was followed in the provinces, with the foundation of the Bristol Old Bank.

Hitherto, a system of safe-deposits and credits had been developed by the goldsmiths. Smith, however, was a mercer. It was the deep rock-cellar under his original place of business that drew him, by degrees, into an enterprise more profitable than his drapery. In the troubled aftermath of the Civil War, when no one quite knew when the town might see looting and street-fighting again, he had more and more customers looking for a safe place for their valuables. There must have been many instances, too, when the confidential mediation of a man like Smith was invaluable – when, for example, a tenant wished to go on paying rent to his Cavalier landlord in exile, prudently foreseeing a day when that landlord would return.

Smith's sideline developed into his main business. He moved to the bank's present site at the south-east corner of the square, supplementing his bolts and bars with two fearsome-looking brass blunderbusses which have been preserved to this day. The drapery was discontinued about 1727.

The pioneer himself died in 1699, but he had founded a financial dynasty more durable than the Duke on Castle Rock. Soon the first Abel Smith was opening a branch in London. In 1960, Cecil Roberts records in *The Growing Boy*, seventeen of Thomas Smith's descendants 'held between them eighty-eight directorships in seventy-nine companies', while various members of the clan had married royalty, entered the House of Lords, and made their mark in the armed services.

They were prominent in the life of Nottingham for at least another century. One, Abel Smith, was a Whig Member of Parliament in 1779 and championed the framework knitters in their demands for legislation. After his early death his brother Robert won the seat. It was after one of his victories, at the 1790 election, that the infuriated Tories smashed the windows of the bank, along with those of the Exchange across the road.

A pleasant reminder of the family can be found on Angel Row at the far side of the Market Place. Bromley House was built for Sir George Smith in 1752, and remains, an unexpected gem of Georgian elegance, its unobtrusive and well-mannered doorway sandwiched between modern shopfronts. Walk in, and you have stepped back two centuries. The door is open during normal weekday hours, for the fine staircase mounts to the rooms occupied since 1820 by the Nottingham Subscription Library, itself something of an historical survival but more cheerful than the phrase suggests. Windows offer a glimpse of green garden. More stairs lead to the headquarters of the Thoroton Society. 'Very civilised', is Pevsner's judgment of the building, 'and not at all provincial, as indeed all these best Nottingham houses are.'

But it is time to step back yet another century, to the Nottingham of the first Mr Smith, before the Glorious Revolution.

Perhaps the greatest local excitement of those years was stirred up by the 'battle of the charters', as Duncan Gray termed it in his short history of the town's municipal evolution, *Nottingham through 500 Years*. He gave a full account of this affair drawing freely on the verbatim records of the Court of the King's Bench, under Lord Chief Justice Jeffreys of bloody memory, whose frequent and characteristically crude interventions did much to enliven a case which reads comically now but was no joke for those involved.

The story begins in June 1681 with a royal letter recommending the Corporation to elect a certain William Petty to the aldermanic vacancy caused by the death of Alderman John Parker senior.

If it seems surprising that Charles II, with his many other preoccupations, should interest himself, let alone interfere, in a municipal by-election, certain more general matters should be borne in mind. M.P.s at that period were elected by a mere handful of substantial citizens in each locality and the town councils virtually determined who should be sent up to Westminster. Charles desperately needed a Parliament more sympathetic to him. For three successive years, starting in 1679, the Commons had passed the Exclusion Bill, disqualifying the King's brother from succeeding to the throne (on the grounds of James's Roman Catholicism) and providing that the crown should pass to his Protestant daughter Mary or, failing her, the younger daughter, Anne. Charles could prevent this bill from becoming law by dissolving Parliament and calling another, but after three such attempts, with each fresh House of Commons as obstreperous as its predecessor, it was clear that something must be done to select a more pliable type of M.P. The new party names came in at this time. The Whigs, strong for parliamentary authority and the Protestant religion, promoted the Exclusion Bill, while the Tories, High Anglican or near Roman in sympathy, with all the old Cavalier instincts, backed the King in opposing it.

Nottingham's mayor, that summer, was Gervase Rippon, a Tory. He put the King's nomination to the meeting, but to his dismay the favoured William Petty received only a single humiliating vote from his fellow townsmen. John Sherwin topped the poll. William Toplady – another member of that family so active in the town's affairs – came second. Even the most loyal mayor could scarcely declare Petty elected. Rippon did the best he could. He got Sherwin disqualified on the grounds that he went to dissenters' prayer-meetings and was 'a very busy factious turbulent man' opposed to the interests of His Majesty. Toplady was duly made alderman.

At this rate, however, it was obviously going to take years to produce a subservient corporation. The Tories therefore worked out an ingenious procedure whereby it could be accomplished in

a single stage. Just as, in 1661, the various town councils had
been purged of all but Church of England communicants, now
they should be restricted to safe individuals actually nominated
by the King. But whereas the purge of 1661 had been put through
by the Cavaliers as an Act of Parliament, the Whig majority were
not going to vote for their own extinction. There was only one
way to do it: the towns must be induced, by hook or by crook, to
surrender their ancient charters and accept new ones from the
King, embodying the change.

In Nottingham the first step was to ensure that Mayor Rippon
should be succeeded in September by someone prepared to play
the King's game. The new Duke of Newcastle used his considerable influence. Gervas Wylde was duly elected mayor. The
Corporation plate still includes a silver-gilt loving-cup and two
silver tankards, the Latin inscriptions on which commemorate
His Grace's goodwill towards His Worship. Early in 1682
rumours began to spread through the town of what was being
planned. Three hundred burgesses signed a protest to the Mayor,
an impressive number from a population still under ten thousand,
most of whom had no civic rights anyhow. The Mayor ignored
the protest and continued his confidential discussions with the
Duke. The people made equally ineffectual representations to
the Lord Chancellor and the Attorney-General. Both the Town
Clerk and the Recorder were very properly alarmed by a proposal
to give away the town's ancient right of choosing its own officers
and councillors. So was the Rector of St Peter's. So were most of
the town's leading families and the gentry living round about.
Charles Hutchinson of Owthorpe (half-brother of the Colonel),
Sir Thomas Parkyns of Bunny, Henry Plumptre, George Gregory
and many other respected local names occur prominently in the
story. And Alderman William Greaves, the Whig choice for the
next mayor, naturally rallied his fellow councillors.

Gervas Wylde went boldly ahead with his scheme. The Duke
supplied him secretly with a draft instrument of surrender, which
he produced without previous notice at a Council meeting on 25
July. There was an angry debate. The question was put. There
was a tie, fourteen to fourteen. The Mayor gave his casting vote

in favour. The town seal was taken out of its box with due solemnity – it was wisely kept locked, with three different locks and keys held by separate persons, and was never to be taken out except in Council. The fatal document was sealed. Later there was an anti-climax to this scene, for the instrument was found to contain legal flaws and a revised document had to be drawn up. The Mayor thought fit not to trouble his brethren with this tiresome detail, so he broke into the box, used the seal privately, and despatched the amended instrument to London.

Two months passed. Everything had been carefully timed. The mayor-making was always on 29 September. Left to themselves, the councillors would choose Greaves, not the comparatively junior alderman, William Toplady. Toplady, however, would be named by the King in the new charter, which would be dated 28 September but would arrive in Nottingham with remarkable promptitude on the following morning, just before the election took place. The charter would similarly name all the men approved as councillors, and it would be made clear to the Town Clerk and the Recorder that in future they would hold office only while their conduct satisfied the King. In case of trouble, Charles instructed the Duke (who was conveniently Lord-Lieutenant of the county) to be in residence in the Castle with suitable forces at his disposal.

That Michaelmas morning must have been about as lively as any in the robust history of the town.

The formal election of the Mayor was preceded always by a service at St Mary's and it was there that the Council's own nominee and his supporters were mustered. At eleven o'clock, however, the retiring Mayor lingered at his own house like some reluctant bride, for the licence, in the shape of the new charter, had not arrived. His own faction were there in strength, but soon they were joined by uninvited Whigs, clamouring to get on with the programme.

'We do expect a charter,' protested one of the Tory aldermen, 'and if we should go on to the choosing of a Mayor we should be all in confusion'.

Soon after that the Sergeant-at-Mace arrived with the vital

document. The Tories sent word to the Town Clerk, who was at
the church with the Whigs, to come down and read it. He refused.
The Tories then moved to the Council Chamber, in the Town
Hall, and another summons was sent to the Town Clerk. He
still refused, saying that 'he knew there was an old charter, and
what he was by that charter' but 'he did not know of any new
one'. The Tories accordingly proceeded on their own account, so
that Wylde could be formally sworn in for the closing minutes of
his year (resworn, that is, under the new charter) and then conduct
the election of Toplady as his successor.

Before these ceremonies were completed the Whigs burst into
the Council Chamber and there was considerable disorder, with
'shoving and crowding' and a struggle to seize the mace. 'I have
been a member of the Corporation and have been present at these
elections for eighteen years,' protested one Tory, 'and I never
saw such a thing as this. I could almost cry to see these dissensions
made among us.'

The Tories, being thrown out of the Town Hall, returned to
the Mayor's house, where they duly 'elected' Toplady and the
other approved candidates for sheriff, coroner and chamberlain.
These were being proclaimed at Weekday Cross, according to
custom, when they came into conflict again with the Whigs,
prominent among them that same Sherwin who had been barred
from office the previous year. He was leading the cry of 'No new
charter! It is not worth a groat!' A free fight ensued. The
Sheriffs' Sergeant received 'a full swop over the face' and the
Tory ex-mayor Rippon had a waistcoat ruined in his struggle to
protect the charter. 'At last we got away through them,' he told
the King's Bench later, 'but if I touched ground, I wish I might
never see my wife again.' Judge Jeffreys could not help inter-
jecting, 'Now whether that be a curse thou layest upon thyself
or no, I can't tell.'

Order was restored only by the appearance of the Duke and his
men from the Castle. Twenty-three Whigs were prosecuted and
all but one found guilty of riot, fined heavily and bound over for
a year.

So, for a few years, the civic freedom of the town was extinguished. When James II succeeded his brother, the royal control became more complete. A Privy Council order of 13 January 1688 removed the Mayor, one of the sheriffs, two aldermen and eleven councillors. Within two months all the rest had been dismissed and the Corporation entirely reconstituted. On 1 September the King signed another new charter, more repressive than his brother's.

But it was 1688 now, and that autumn brought William of Orange and the Glorious Revolution.

If the second Duke of Newcastle was the mainstay of the local Tories, his kinsman William Cavendish, Earl (and soon to be Duke) of Devonshire, was equally strong for the Whigs. He was, indeed, one of the seven notables who that summer despatched the historic invitation to the Prince of Orange. Forty-eight, tall and handsome, a fine classical scholar whose love of dead languages was surpassed only by his taste for live women, he was, in Lord Orford's words, 'a patriot among the men, a Corydon among the ladies'. Out of favour at James's court, he had withdrawn to the country and had just embarked upon the building of Chatsworth, a superb architectural enterprise from which his attention was temporarily diverted by the crisis in national politics.

William, as we now know, landed in Devon on 5 November. At the time, however, he had been expected to cross the North Sea and come ashore on the north-east coast, in which case Nottingham would have once more assumed its traditional strategic role. It had therefore been agreed that the Earl of Danby should seize York while the Earl of Devonshire made sure of Nottingham. When they heard that the Prince was in the West Country, they judged it best to carry out their own part of the programme, and on 22 November they occupied their objectives without any trouble.

The Duke of Newcastle was at his country home at Welbeck, and powerless to prevent the seizure of Nottingham and his own castle by the Whigs, who set up their headquarters however at the Feathers Inn in Wheeler Gate. In vain the Duke ordered the county militia to mobilize at Southwell. They ignored him, and a timely raid by the Earl of Danby's son robbed him even of arms and horses for his own retainers. Meanwhile, the jubilant Whigs in Nottingham were joined by Lord Delamere, who had ridden in from Cheshire with several hundred mounted men, occupying Manchester on the way. Another regiment of horse had been recruited locally by Sir Scrope Howe of Langar, a comparative newcomer to the shire whose family was, however, to become prominent in its annals. Twelve years later, William III created him Viscount Howe.

At the Saturday market, two days after the occupation of the town, Devonshire appeared at the Malt Cross, supported by Delamere and Howe, and explained to the assembled populace what was (or was supposed to be) happening. After the events of the past few years, during which a predominantly Whiggish town had had a kind of Tory dictatorship imposed upon it by an unpopular monarch, the enthusiasm was wild and to a great extent genuine.

It was stirred to fresh fervour a week later, on 2 December, by the arrival of the twenty-three-year-old Princess Anne, in flight from her father's capital. The events of the past few weeks must have been inexpressibly painful to her, with her loyalties divided between the King and her sister's husband. When her own husband, that Danish nonentity Prince George, followed Churchill's example by deserting to the Orange banner, she judged it time to go. Slipping out of her apartments in Whitehall like an eloping girl, she stepped into a hackney coach which the Bishop of London had ready for her. Not for nothing had the Bishop been a dashing cornet of dragoons in his youth. Next day he rode north beside her coach with sword and pistols ready for action. 'I have been forced to lay aside the Bible at present,' he told the welcoming assembly at Leicester, 'but I hope very suddenly to take it in my hands again.' Hundreds of armed riders joined them as they travelled. It was a little army that rode into Nottingham to fraternize with the Earl of Devonshire's men. The bells pealed in welcome.

The future Queen Anne was driven to the Castle, where only

the owner was lacking to do the honours. Celia Fiennes was shown, a few years later, the bedroom that had been occupied by the illustrious fugitive. Devonshire played host. He borrowed some of the Corporation's pewter plates and dishes for her entertainment. They vanished, as things are apt to do in revolutions, though the Mayor did his best to recover them. But there were a great many strangers in the town just then, perhaps a thousand armed men, a dozen of them peers of the realm, and everybody was rather excited.

A local tradition maintains that a nearby public house, the Royal Children, is so called because the Princess's children played with the landlord's family. Unfortunately, there is no record of an inn with this name until 1799, and the Princess in 1688 had no living offspring. Nor is she known to have revisited Nottingham. Except for the poor young Duke of Gloucester (1689-1700) none of her subsequent children survived to an age when they could play with anyone.

Her sojourn at the Castle in 1688 lasted just a week. Then came news that the Prince of Orange was advancing on London and meeting no resistance. Her husband, the dull Prince George, was not so dull as to be absent from William's side. If Anne set out at once, she could join them at Oxford. She drove forth across Trent Bridge, Devonshire and his fellow Whigs escorting her in triumphal procession. The Glorious Revolution was over, bar the shouting, but there was a good deal of that.

CHAPTER FIFTEEN

Georgian Grace

'I MIGHT enter into a long description of all the modern buildings erected lately in Nottingham,' wrote Defoe with manifest approval in 1726. His words, if not his approval, could be echoed by any visitor today.

The steady transformation of the town had already been commented upon by Thoroton. It had continued and showed no signs of slackening under the Georges. The first part of the eighteenth century saw the reconstruction of the old half-timbered Guildhall and substantial extensions to the Free School, the provision of an entirely new town hall (the Exchange) fronting the Market Place, and the erection of the beautiful but now vanished Collin's Almshouses in Friar Lane.

This charity was established under the will of Abel Collin, an unmarried mercer who died in 1705. His father was Laurence Collin, master gunner to Colonel Hutchinson, who settled in Nottingham after the Civil War and tried to operate as a woolcomber, but was debarred at first on the grounds that he was not a freeman of the town. A direct appeal to the Lord Protector removed this disability, and Laurence Collin prospered, building himself a fine house at 39 Castle Gate, and marrying his daughter (prophetically baptized Fortune) to the widowed Thomas Smith, the pioneer banker. In such circumstances the bachelor son could well afford to bequeath his own wealth to the endowment of almshouses.

Much as these new public buildings adorned the town, the most notable development was in private housing. More and more gentlemen's town houses went up along the Pavements.

Willoughby House, with its Ionic columns, dates from 1738, just after Defoe's visit. Castle Gate was equally fashionable, and the smart congregation earned St Nicholas's the nickname of 'the drawing-room church'. The full flowering of Georgian elegance coincided with the publication of Dr Charles Deering's *Nottinghamia Vetus et Nova* in 1751.

Deering brought a foreigner's objectivity, not to say a German's thoroughness, to the study of his adopted town. Born in Dresden, educated in Hamburg, Leyden and Amsterdam, he had studied medicine in Paris and spent two years in London as secretary to Peter the Great's ambassador. When he was about forty, a childless widower, he came to Nottingham and established himself in a house opposite St Peter's churchyard.

Surprisingly, he seems to have fallen in love with the town. Surprisingly, not because the place was not lovable – it goes to one's heart to think what Nottingham must have looked like in those days – but because Deering's own circumstances might excusably have soured his judgment. He was sophisticated yet unsuccessful, poor and an outsider. His views on the treatment of smallpox did not recommend him to his professional rivals. He suffered from gout and asthma, for which the hilly streets and the mists coming up from the rivers cannot have provided the kindest environment. But fortunately he had a passion for botany, and in the fields and woods that still lapped closely round the little town he was able to indulge that passion and assuage his loneliness.

'Were a naturalist in quest of an exquisite spot to build a town or city upon,' he asked 'could he meet with one that would better answer his wishes?'

Within three years he had prepared a catalogue of the local flora that for the first time put the subject on a scientific basis. It was published by a friendly printer, George Ayscough, whose father had established in 1710 the town's first press and its first newspaper, the *Weekly Courant*, one of the earliest in England, from which the present *Nottingham Guardian Journal* can claim unbroken descent.

Deering had another sympathetic friend: the John Plumptre of his generation. The Plumptres lived in one of the grand new houses built on the site of their previous home beside St Mary's Church. In Italy it would surely have qualified as a *palazzo* with its coat-of-arms and impressive façade, topped by an ornate balustrade, but it was not out of place in the Nottingham of those days. The nearby Pierrepont mansion, if we can trust another contemporary drawing, had formal gardens worthy of a miniature Versailles.

The Plumptres, however, were interested in more than material show. They carried on the intellectual tradition of the witty and contentious Huntingdon Plumptre two generations before, and they started young, as is indicated by a formidable tablet in St Mary's:

> Here lyes interr'd HENRY eldest son of John Plumptre Esq. Born 22 July 1708 deceased Janry 3, 1718/9. In these few and tender Years he had to a great Degree made himself Master of the Jewish Roman and English History, the Heathen Mythology and the French Tongue, and was not inconsiderably advanced in the Latin.

Another Henry Plumptre was President of the Royal College of Physicians in Deering's time, but it was John who befriended the lonely German doctor, just as he befriended two local boys whose artistic talent he noticed, Thomas and Paul Sandby, then living close by in Stoney Street. It was his recommendation that helped to launch them into the wider world.

John Plumptre was interested in the history of the town and he infected Deering with his enthusiasm. The German took over his friend's materials and obtained permission to inspect the Corporation records. The same systematic attention he had previously given to the hedgerow flowers was now turned to the streets he traversed every day. The resulting book, *Nottinghamia Vetus et Nova*, was well titled, for it included the new as well as the old. Deering is an invaluable witness, because he brought the fresh vision of a stranger and the standards of a travelled man.

He did not live to see the publication of his book, which might have won him esteem in a community that had never appreciated him. He died in 1749, owing money to Ayscough and his other

Fun and games

Rowlandson's robust portrayal of a street-scene outside the Swann Inn in 1807.

Decorous play-time for the sons of mid-Victorian gentlemen: Chestnut House Academy at the northern suburb of Arnold in the eighteen sixties.

The golden age of the lace trade. The magnificent warehouse of Thomas Adams, the devout Evangelical who provided a chapel for the moral fortification of his pretty work-girls.

Sailing-barges still plied on the River Leen as late as 1885. High Pavement Chapel rises between the Castle and the town's mother-church — in some respects more dominant than either.

friends. The printer took over the manuscript, Plumptre checked it, and it appeared as a quarto volume with suitable illustrations. Thanks to these, and to the increasing flow of other drawings and maps from this date onwards, it is easy to visualize the eighteenth-century town.

The elder Sandby was twenty when he left Nottingham, so he had more time to depict the local scene than his better-known brother, four years his junior. About 1741, the year of their departure, Thomas did a drawing of the medieval west gate at Chapel Bar, a shocking bottle-neck even for the traffic of those days. It was understandably pulled down by the far-sighted Corporation – and almost immediately regretted because they had not been far-sighted enough to foresee the 1745 rising and the advance of Bonnie Prince Charlie's wild Highlanders to within a day's march of the town.

Sandby shows a lone horseman in tricorn hat galloping towards the pointed archway, and through the narrow opening is glimpsed the Market Place, which is displayed panoramically in its full Georgian glory in another drawing, attributed to him, in the British Museum. Here stretches the entire colonnaded length of Long Row, then mainly inns and taverns, the Talbot, the May-pole, the Black Boy and more than a dozen others. To the right, facing them, is the noble row of elms screening Timber Row (now South Parade) and reminding us that, for all the spate of building, this Nottingham was still a green town, and even the customers of Smith's Bank or the Flying Horse approached their business beneath a vaulting of foliage. In the centre is the Exchange, built as a town hall in the seventeen twenties and replaced by the present Council House two hundred years later. Even in Sandby's time people could not quite decide which building to treat as the centre of local government, and in 1744 the Corporation rebuilt the Guildhall for its everyday business, reserving the Exchange for activities involving the public at large. The equivalent modern buildings have kept this division of functions.

Early in William and Mary's reign the Corporation recovered the rights lost under James II, and though they remained a closed (if not always cosy) little circle elected by a minority of the inhabitants, they were at least elected by somebody and not nominated by the King. They had not a modern council's vast powers to shape the life of the community, but within the limitations of their period they did not do badly for this town.

They repaved the Market Place and removed the dividing wall which had so long obstructed it. They widened a few streets, not before time: today's drivers are at least spared the problem of backing a hay-waggon confronted by a coach-and-four, and the pedestrian, though risking death in other ways, is not frequently squashed slowly and painfully between wheel and wall. Another form of obstruction had been the tradesman's sign standing on a post in front of his premises. The Corporation banned this and ordered signs to be hung from wall-brackets. They also introduced house-numbers. Street-lighting came in by very slow degrees – first, a light outside the home of the serving mayor, then lamps in front of the Exchange and at the Hen Cross, but no general scheme until 1762, when a private Act of Parliament was promoted to get it. The streets were patrolled at night by blue-coated watchmen carrying bells. Since there were a hundred and thirty-two inns and alehouses serving a total population of about ten thousand it was probably not easy for every citizen to find his own way quietly home. Another form of disturbance was reported in the *Tatler* in 1710:

> Whereas by letters from Nottingham we have advice that the young ladies of that place complained for want of sleep by reason of certain riotous lovers who, for this last summer, have very much infested the streets of that eminent city with violins and bass viols between the hours of twelve and four in the morning. . . .

The fires of love, however, rated low among the Corporation's responsibilities. Other kinds of conflagration were a different matter. In Queen Anne's reign every parish was called upon to acquire a fire-engine, that newfangled apparatus which had been introduced from Holland, like so many other ideas about this time, in 1676. The engine was housed in St Mary's Church and supplemented by a dozen leather buckets hung in the Guildhall down the street. Later, each of the seven wards had its own smaller appliance in the charge of its alderman, and in 1764 the town was presented with an additional small engine by the Sun Fire Office, which had an understandable interest in the problem.

Water was obviously essential, to refill the buckets and to pump through the leather hoses. As early as 1696 there was the modest beginning of a piped supply. A private company was formed and the Corporation bought six of its thirty-two shares. The water was pumped up from the Leen to a cistern near Standard Hill, whence it ran down through pipes to the premises of subscribers. These were relatively few. The wells and pumps, and the door-to-door service of the water-carrier, continued for some generations to supply the average resident.

It was indeed a green town. Part of what is now Lower Parliament Street, then Coalpit Lane, had cherry orchards to right and left. Upper Parliament Street, then known more tersely as Back Side, was lined with poplars, and in Stoney Street the grammar-school boys loitered in the shade of elms. Willows were planted along the banks of the Leen, where the ground had been levelled and laid out with a bowling-green, paths and arbours for the recreation of the people: Deering even refers to this area rather grandly as a 'spaw'. From there the meadows stretched away to the main river, renowned for the wild crocuses that carpeted them each spring. Well might Robert Sanders write in *The Complete English Traveller* in 1772: 'Many gentlemen of great fortune reside here, which is not to be wondered at as the prospects from the streets, over the fields, and the windings of the Trent are so delightful that it even exceeds imagination.' The reverse view, from the far side of Trent Bridge, was equally pleasing. The 'south prospect of Nottingham', with strollers, anglers and cows in the foreground, was a favourite subject with artists. In those happy days there was no reason to assume that a town made a blot on the landscape.

Defoe noted how the Duke of Newcastle had 'laid out a plan of the finest gardens that are to be seen in all that part of

England', designed to cover sixty acres adjoining the Castle. This Duke was the great Whig, Thomas Pelham, who eventually became Prime Minister: the dukedom had again been extinguished when John Holles had fallen from his horse while stag-hunting in Sherwood Forest in 1711, but it was revived a few years later for Pelham, who was his nephew and part-heir to his estates. He has been described as 'a peculiarly muddle-headed man, and unhappy if he had not more to do than he could possibly manage'. As he is said to have managed both Houses of Parliament with some success, it is not surprising that his grandiose gardening-scheme, described by Defoe as 'not yet finish'd' and requiring 'an immense sum to go on with it', never seems to have been fully executed.

At the other end of the scale Defoe admired the garden at Newdigate House, where the captive Marshal Tallard had 'amused himself with making a small but beautiful parterre, after the French fashion'. But Tallard had returned to France in 1712, after adorning the polite society of Nottingham for the best part of eight years, and Defoe noted that the garden did not 'gain by English keeping'.

The names on old street-maps help to conjure up a picture of the sylvan town. Walnut Tree Lane and Rosemary Lane survive within a short step of the Marshal's wrought-iron gate, but the delightful Gillyflower Hill has become 'Castle Hill'. These old maps show, too, with their neat little rows of toy-like trees, what a patchwork of orchards and paddocks, as well as private gardens, still found space within the ancient boundaries. There was even a diversity of little burial grounds, for Quakers and others excluded from the churchyards, which made further oases of quiet amid the street-cries, the clop of hoofs and the rumble of wheels. Or they should have done. For it is typical of public indifference to children's needs in those days that in all this garden city there was no provision for play, and the graveyards, being open, offered the handiest open spaces. A Grand Jury in 1755 recorded its desire 'that some active, nimble constables be sent to the church-yards every Sabbath day to prevent boys playing; complaints being made that the constables sent have been inactive and the boys run away from them, which makes greater disturbances than if none was there'.

For the adults, on the other hand, there was amusement for every taste, a rich menu of the rural and the urban, the cultivated and the crude.

London was brought nearer by improved stage-coaches and more gradually improving roads. In 1760 'the flying machines with steel springs' (as an advertisement in the *Nottingham Courant* described them) used to leave the Swan with Two Necks in London each Monday and Thursday at five o'clock in the morning, and after an overnight halt at the Angel, Northampton, drive through the yard gates of the Blackamoor's Head the following evening – 'IF GOD PERMIT', added the proprietors with a humility that some modern timetable-compilers would do well to copy.

As communications improved, provincial towns began to lose some of their old insularity. There was a developing interest in what was being said – and worn – in the capital. In Nottingham the gentry crowded the Assembly Rooms in Low Pavement for cards, music and dancing, producing their own microcosm of London and Bath society. The bourgeoisie set up a rendezvous of their own in Thurland Hall, now no longer a nobleman's private residence, and on special occasions enlisted the catering expertise of Mr Simpson, landlord of the Blackamoor's Head across the street, who put on a menu of nearly forty different dishes for their banquet celebrating the hundredth anniversary of the Glorious Revolution. Even the Castle might become the scene of public revelry, as on 14 June 1776, when a ball was held there in honour of the newly formed Nottinghamshire Regiment, the 42nd Foot, which had just completed its first month's training on a parade-ground north of the town. The military were no strangers to Nottingham throughout this period, and with good reason, as will appear. Barrack Lane, on the edge of the Park, commemorates their quarters.

In 1760 an elegant-looking theatre was built in St Mary's Gate. Burnt out in a 1941 air raid, it was later demolished. As in more recent times, the strong Puritan and utilitarian traditions of the

Georgian town made any theatrical venture an excuse for violent controversy. Just after Christmas 1763 the proprietor abolished admission charges for six days, whether for publicity reasons or from pure generosity, but this action only inflamed the opposition. Their leader, an alderman and *ex officio* magistrate, issued a warrant for the arrest of an actor named Wheeler, who was playing the lead in Addison's famous play, *Cato*, which had been politically topical fifty years earlier but was now itself presumably harmless enough. Wheeler was seized, interrogated for three hours in the magistrate's house, and then marched off by seven constables to the lock-up which occupied the ground-floor of the Guildhall. On the way, however, an enthusiastic theatregoer, Mr Whiteley, led a successful rescue bid – successful, at least, in so far as the unfortunate Wheeler got free, although Mr Whiteley was seized and thrown into a cell by way of substitute. There he relieved his feelings in verse, which he began:

> Dear Town of Commerce, once the Muse's seat,
> Where Players tasted happiness complete
> Till Dark Stupidity usurped the throne. . . .

Despite the occasional *contretempts* of this kind, and the ups and downs familiar in the annals of most theatres, this early playhouse must have contributed much to the urbanity of the Georgian town. Sometimes it was used for music, and in 1772 a week-long festival was directed there by the organist from St Mary's, *Messiah* and two other Handel oratorios being performed.

Nottingham had its miniature Vauxhall and Ranelagh in such outlying resorts as the Lenton Coffee House, where a Mr George Wombwell opened his pleasure gardens each summer, and Radford Grove, later known as Radford Folly, which a Mr Elliott laid out in 1780 with an ornamental lake, classical temples and shrubberies, 'a little paradise' in which, no doubt, innocence was sometimes lost. Before these places became fashionable there was always St Ann's Well, that time-honoured objective for a short excursion, where the inn provided music and there was dancing in the open air. For quieter amusement one could drive out to play bowls on the famous green at Holme Pierrepont, where the company was considered more exclusive than at the Bowling-green Inn at Basford. Clifton and Wilford were then peaceful riverside villages. Wilford was a favourite retreat of the youthful poet, Henry Kirke White, whose promise had been recognized by Southey before he burned himself out with overwork, dying in 1806 at twenty-two.

Two packs of hounds were kennelled in the town itself, and the still bloodier blood sports had their keen followers. The White Lion on Long Row owed much of its fashionable repute to its cock-pit: one match arranged by London and Nottingham gentry in 1761 was abandoned when it was discovered that the London birds had been given sedatives. Bull-baiting was a regular spectacle for many years, but was discontinued in Nottingham long before its abolition by law in 1835.

The local love of cricket developed early. There was a match between Nottingham and Sheffield in 1771, sixteen years before the foundation of the M.C.C., when curved bats were only just going out and the middle stump had not been introduced. In 1791 a match against a neighbouring county attracted ten thousand spectators, equal to almost half the town's population at the time. This game was played in the upper meadow. The associations of Trent Bridge were still with swimming. Even ladies could indulge in river bathing, and a stretch of water near the bridge was screened off for their use. Men and boys were less organized, and scandalized the godly by plunging into the water on the Sabbath, though Corporation officers patrolled the banks to prevent them. Two other and most innocent English pastimes had many devotees – gardening and the country walk. The Ancient Society of Flowerists was formed in 1761 and held a yearly show. The footpaths encircling the town afforded a ten-mile walk by river-bank, hill and coppice.

These were the regular recreations, and many of them could be enjoyed by the working man, even after the ten-hour day then considered reasonable. When the Industrial Revolution arrived a generation or two later, and the framework knitters found themselves working sixteen and even eighteen hours, it was a different story.

High days and holidays were dotted through the calendar. The King's Birthday was usually celebrated with fireworks and bonfires at the Corporation's expense – and sometimes at additional expense to others, as in 1780, when some Guards officers clashed with the crowd and were chased back to the Blackamoor's Head, one hundred and sixty-eight sash-windows being broken. Victories over the French were similarly commemorated, with ox-roastings, illuminations and music, though on these occasions a red coat more likely earned a free drink than a brickbat. At Christmas time it was customary for employers and traders to entertain the work people in the alehouses, and parliamentary elections, though a rather special type of public entertainment which must be dealt with separately, bore a strong superficial resemblance to the other junketings.

Goose Fair, curiously enough, was not then the annual carnival of pleasure it afterwards became. It was still the great trading-occasion it had been since the early Middle Ages, and as late as 1813 the authorities were excluding 'those disgraceful and dangerous machines called merry-go-rounds', which were also stigmatized as 'instruments of folly, immodesty and danger'. Though the name 'Goose Fair' dates from at least Henry VIII's reign, geese were not always the main commodity. The Fair was especially noted for the immense cheeses brought in by the farmers, and the year 1766 went down in local history as the year of the cheese riot. That autumn the farmers were asking twenty-eight and even thirty shillings a hundredweight, and trouble flared up, as it was always apt to do in Nottingham Market Place on the slightest provocation. Some of the big round cheeses were sent rolling down Wheeler Gate and one of them bowled over the Mayor himself. The Dragoons were summoned and opened fire. Many people were wounded and one man killed, an innocent one as so often on these occasions, who was only trying to protect the cheeses.

It was not the Fair but the Races on the Forest that provided the great event of the year. ''Tis a most glorious show they have here,' said Defoe, 'such an assembly of gentlemen of quality, that not Bansted Down, or New Market Heath, produces better company, better horses, or shows the horse and master's skill better.' After comparisons with the Olympic Games and the chariot-races of Rome, he went on:

> But the illustrious company at the Nottingham races was, in my opinion, the glory of the day; for there we saw, besides eleven or twelve noblemen, an infinite throng of gentlemen from all the countries round, nay, even out of Scotland itself. . . . Nor is the appearance of the ladies to be omitted, as fine and without comparison more bright and gay, tho' they might a little fall short in number of the many thousands of nobility and gentry of the other sex; in short, the train of coaches filled with the beauties of the north was not to be described; except we were to speak of the garden of the Tulleries at Paris, or the Prado at Mexico. . . .

In Nottingham, as everywhere else, Georgian elegance existed side by side with extremes of coarseness and crudity.

It was all very fine for the gentry to sow their wild oats, and indeed lesser folk might do so, provided they paid for their amusement. But woe betide the girl who produced an illegitimate baby chargeable to the parish. She was whipped at the House of Correction, then paraded via Stoney Street, High Pavement, Bridlesmith Gate and the Malt Cross, and finally bound to the ducking-stool. It was not so much the immorality that upset the citizens as the consequent expense to the ratepayer.

Property, not virtue, was sacred. It was not only unmarried mothers who were flogged and paraded. A girl of nineteen, who had obtained goods under false pretences, was taken to the Market Place on market day, stripped to the waist and thrashed. An old man of eighty, who had stolen some hay, was whipped from Weekday Cross to the Malt Cross. Perhaps they were lucky to get off so lightly, for innumerable offences carried the death penalty. A lofty gallows was a permanent landmark on the crest of the Mansfield road, near the present St Andrew's Church. Prisoners were made to listen to a 'Condemned Sermon' at St Mary's, before being taken to try their ready-dug graves for size. Then, sometimes already swathed in their shrouds, they were taken up the long hill in the execution cart, pausing for the traditional last drink on the way. Among the many who suffered the ordeal of this public spectacle was a fifteen-year-old maid-servant, Elizabeth Morton, who seems to have been impelled by delusions into strangling her employer's child. Thousands watched her own last struggles. William Horne was a rare case in that he was a gentleman of means who none the less suffered the extreme penalty. As a concession to his status, he was allowed to be driven to the gallows by his own coachmen. His neighbours and tenants turned out in force to pay their respects.

Clearly not all crime sprang from poverty, but much of it did. Defoe had noted that by now 'the chief manufacture carried on here is frame-work knitting for stockings, the same as at Leicester', and some of the other trades had declined, while an attempt to establish cotton-spinning was never a success, the local spinners being unable to equal the yarn spun at Tewkesbury and in India. The frame-knitters themselves suffered from trade slumps, notably during the American War of Independence. In such times, if a man was determined to remain 'poor but honest', he was apt to end in the workhouse which each parish was com-pelled to maintain. It was not much use his leaving Nottingham to seek work elsewhere which did not exist. He could see for himself how many impoverished strangers drifted into his own town on the same hopeless quest. All lodging-house keepers were bound to report such arrivals within twenty-four hours to the churchwardens and overseers of the poor. It was the old fear of outsiders' becoming chargeable on the rates. Insularity was so extreme that the three town parishes could not be induced to combine their efforts. A community which believed fervently in the deterrent principle had little desire to improve the relief given to the down-and-out. In 1795 St Mary's workhouse was 'dark, verminous, ill-ventilated', and appallingly overcrowded. Its hundred and sixty-eight inmates included seventy-seven boys and girls under twenty years of age.

Well-to-do folk might complain of the improvidence of the poor, but it was an unfair generalization. In that same year the town had over fifty friendly societies in which the workers, when they had work, could save their pennies in mutual protection against misfortunes to come. But in such an uneven society, with some enjoying vast and virtually untaxed incomes, while others reared families on less than seven shillings a week, no working class could ever insure itself unaided against mass unemployment.

John Wesley paid generous tribute to the workers of Nottingham – generous because at first both he and his brother were met with insults and violence when they tried to preach in the Market Place and it was twenty years before the first Methodist tabernacle, the Octagon, was established. He wrote in his *Journal* in 1777:

> There is something in the people of this town which I cannot but approve of; although most of our Society are of the lower class, chiefly employed in the stocking manufacture, yet there is generally an uncommon gentleness and sweetness in their temper, and something of elegance in their behaviour, which when added to solid vital religion make them an ornament to their profession.

A few years later he came to open a second chapel.

The Church of England tended here, as elsewhere, to doze through the eighteenth century – though even the Vicar of St Mary's was stirred to indignation when the Archbishop of York, having confirmed a number of candidates, retired to the vestry demanding a flagon of ale and a pipe of tobacco. One lasting achievement stands to the Church's credit, the opening of a charity school in 1707, which came to be known (and still is) as the Bluecoat School after the boys and girls changed their original grey uniforms in George I's reign. But largely it was the chapels that ran the town, in particular the Congregationalists of Castle Gate and the Presbyterians of High Pavement, who went solidly Unitarian during the first half of the century.

High Pavement Chapel was the focus of Nottingham's intellectual life, especially after the appointment of the Reverend George Walker as assistant minister in 1774. Walker was a mathematician of repute, a Fellow of the Royal Society, a man who knew Priestley and Adam Smith and could talk brilliantly on many subjects, notably the need for parliamentary reform. For twenty-five happy years he was the natural leader of the local intelligentsia, but he did not lack worthy companions. One was Gilbert Wakefield, whose father had been Rector of St Nicholas's and who had himself held a Cambridge fellowship. A fine classical scholar, Wakefield quitted the Church (which in those days meant quitting his fellowship), and returned to his native town as a Unitarian. He and Walker ran a discussion-group which met in various houses.

High Pavement School started in 1788 as 'a charity school for the children of poor persons belonging to this Society', the Unitarian congregation that is to say, who felt that the Bluecoat School was too exclusively a Church of England foundation. The educational programme was much the same – the three Rs plus needlework for the girls. The latter wore brown ribbons in their bonnets, but the boys had not even that much uniform. Funds were low, provided in large measure by an annual collection following a celebrity sermon. One January Sunday in 1796 this was preached by Coleridge in a blue coat and white waistcoat – the twenty-three-year-old poet was then stumping the country on a fund-raising venture of his own. The first three headmasters were on a part-time basis, one being a tailor and another a clock-maker. It was not until 1805 that a proper schoolroom was built behind the chapel, on the edge of the old sandstone cliff that had attracted the Saxon settlers long ago, and the first whole-time master was appointed in 1816.

Meanwhile, in Stoney Street close by, the ancient grammar school had fallen into decline as so many similar foundations did during this period, and many of the well-to-do families began to send their sons, as well as their daughters, to the numerous little private academies that were set up. The grammar-school masters were nearly always Cambridge men and not without scholarship, but they were often in conflict with their governors, the Corpora-tion, and their efforts seem not to have produced any memorable successes.

Paradoxically, it was perhaps the best scholar among them, Richard Johnson, who did the place most harm. Johnson was an outstanding Latinist with a caustic wit such as Housman possessed in a later era. A fearless controversialist, he took on the great Bentley himself. As a result, he neglected the school, which dwindled to five boys. The Corporation dismissed him. To facilitate the process of getting rid of him, they imprudently gave him a warm testimonial, which he then produced in court against them to prove that he was being unjustly removed. Johnson won that round, but the end of the story is sad.

'They write from Nottingham', reported a London newspaper in November 1721, 'that some days since, the Rev Mr Richard Johnson, lately Master of the Free School there, being a little Melancholly, took a walk into the Meadows, and drowned himself in a Pit near the Old Trent.'

Such were the lights and shadows of the Georgian town. Not all who beheld 'the south prospect of Nottingham' saw the same view as Dr Deering.

CHAPTER SIXTEEN

'That Political Pandemonium'

LATE in the summer of 1798 the new Lord Byron arrived in Nottingham, a ten-year-old grammar-school boy with a strong Aberdonian accent, a conspicuous limp and an embarrassing mother. To her intense disappointment, Mrs Byron had found Newstead Abbey unfit to live in. The Wicked Lord, her son's eccentric great-uncle and immediate predecessor, had allowed both house and estate to go to ruin. So, for the next year or two, while she dashed to and fro between London and Newstead, striving to achieve some kind of order and solvency, the boy stayed mostly in Nottingham. Sometimes he was with his relatives, the Parkyns, a well-known local family with their country house at Bunny, and at other times, left to the casual care of the maid who had come down with them from Aberdeen, he lodged with a Mr Gill at 76 St James's Street. It was while he was there that his deformed foot was subjected to agonizing and ineffectual treatment by a self-styled surgeon, a Mr Lavender, who was in fact trussmaker to the General Hospital which had been established near by about seventeen years before. The boy's interrupted education was taken over by a tutor, an American Loyalist named Dummer Rogers, who lived near Hen Cross on a British government pension.

In Byron's later years, after Harrow and Cambridge, by which time Newstead Abbey was habitable (though by no means in the good state visitors see it in today), the poet was frequently in Nottingham. When Hobhouse stayed with him in 1808 the young men attended balls and masquerades in the town, for instance the Infirmary Ball in October of that year. On another occasion

Byron employed a Nottingham tailor to make up, from a London pattern, an elaborate Turkish fancy-dress with turban at a total cost of £11 9s 6d. When he staged his wild parties, passing round the monk's skull converted into a loving-cup, the company wore habits obtained from a masquerade warehouse, doubtless a local establishment.

There is something symbolic about that 'Infirmary Ball'. A change was creeping over Nottingham society. The quality were forsaking their elegant town houses, now that the improved turnpikes put London itself within easy reach of their country estates. The Duke no longer came to the Castle. By 1795 he had removed his pictures and most of his furniture, leaving little but some threadbare tapestries. Parts of the mansion were let to private tenants. For a time one portion became a boarding-school. There were thus no special ducal entertainments to provide the highlights of the social season. Instead there was the far-from-exclusive Infirmary Ball.

Money there was in plenty. The bankers, tradesmen and manufacturers grew ever wealthier. There was no income tax until 1799, and even then it was regarded as a temporary war-time measure, abolished (men confidently thought for ever) after Napoleon's defeat. While landed nobility like the Byrons struggled against bankruptcy, a brass merchant on Long Row like Humphrey Hollins was so rich that, it was said, he could have paved the Market Place with his gold.

The Nottingham Byron knew at the turn of the century was already deeply advanced into the Industrial Revolution. To the casual eye it looked much the same as before. The wild crocuses still carpeted the meadows and along the northern ridge thirteen windmills spread their sails like one of Nelson's fleets arrayed for action. A man could still follow the footpaths Deering had loved, for the town's commons remained inviolate, a green belt slowly turning into a strangler's cord.

In the half-century since Deering the population had multiplied: from 10,000 in 1750 to 25,000 in 1793. Yet it was practically impossibly to extend the ancient limits. In the 1787 election a candidate had proposed enclosing some of the town fields for building, but the crowd had burned his effigy in derision and paraded his few supporters through the streets in muck-carts. Where the town was not bordered by its own common lands expansion was barred by the Castle Park and Lord Middleton's deer-park at Wollaton. Only on the east side, looking towards the old village of Sneinton, was there a stretch of ground on which, swampy and undesirable though it was, the builders were thankful to lay hands. Here, from 1803, New Sneinton was rapidly developed. Otherwise, apart from a thin ribbon of houses allowed to creep out along the Derby and Mansfield roads, there was only one way to accommodate the swarming inhabitants, and that was by the 'in-filling', with cramped and insanitary courts of working-class hovels, of those gardens and orchards that had made Nottingham the green place beloved by earlier visitors.

Textiles were the basis of the town's development. There had been a time when Nottingham had looked like becoming a great cotton centre. James Hargreaves had arrived from Lancashire with his spinning-jenny in 1768, closely followed by Richard Arkwright. The latter, in partnership with Samuel Need, had established the world's first spinning-mill at Hockley, near the site of the modern Central Market, using horses to turn the wheel, but he very soon removed to Cromford in Derbyshire. Hargreaves set up a small mill in what is now Wollaton Street, and there were half-a-dozen such establishments at the end of the century. For varied reasons, however – geographical, climatic and others – Nottinghamshire was not fated to rival the Lancashire cotton industry.

One factor that hampered the development of big mills and power-driven factories of the new pattern was the sheer difficulty of finding space for them. Just as, for generations, much of the frame-knitting had been done in surrounding villages, so the new enterprises were driven to Lenton, Basford and places much farther afield. The early history of the Hollins company is significant. It began in 1784 as a partnership between Henry Hollins, of the Long Row brass business, his brother-in-law Thomas Oldknow, a draper on Beastmarket Hill opposite, and three other men. But the mill they set up was at Pleasley, across the Derbyshire boundary, and though the company sold its products in Nottingham it did not manufacture there until the second half of the nineteenth century when the expansion of the town began in earnest. Today Viyella House stands on Castle Boulevard, obliterating the spot where once the barges loaded at the Duke's Wharfs.

Problems of space might prevent industrial Nottingham spreading to the extent of a Manchester or a Birmingham, but even Lee's ancient stocking-frame, clacking away with its 'shee-shee – chockerty-chock' in small workshops and cottages, gave direct or indirect employment to thousands. In times of bad trade, notably during the American War of Independence, ingenious workmen had thought of ways to adapt it to other purposes such as the making of simple lace nets. In 1808 John Heathcoat patented a bobbin-net machine, following it with an improved model a year later, and this laid the foundation of the industry for which Nottingham became famous. Examples of these early machines and the lace they produced can be seen in the city's new Industrial Museum, in the courtyard buildings at Wollaton Park.

Apart from hosiery and lace manufacture, the town possessed foundries, glassworks, brickyards, and a tannery. From the near-by Wollaton colliery, and from the other mines of Nottingham-shire and Derbyshire, coal was shipped down the Trent to Hull and Gainsborough, as much as a million and a half tons during 1816. Lace and hosiery were exported to the Continent by the same waterway. The Duke's Wharfs (where the Grey Friars had built their smaller wharf on the Leen many centuries earlier) lay along the Nottingham Canal made in 1796 to link the Cromford Canal with the Trent and its associated waterways; and those wharfs were heaped high not only with coal but with timber, corn, building-materials, and other bulky commodities. Notting-ham was a thriving inland port, well placed to take full advantage of the boom in canal-building which preceded the railways. Regular boats left twice a week for Liverpool and Manchester via the Grand Trunk, and every evening at nine o'clock a 'fly boat' set out for London by way of the Grand Junction and the

Grand Union. It is not always realized how much these waterways were used for passenger traffic so long as a horse-drawn coach was the fastest alternative. In 1797 one could voyage smoothly to Cromford, amid the foothills of the Peak, for five shillings in the best cabin or three-and-sixpence second class. There were four boats a week to Leicester with similar fares. Twenty years later there was the Nottingham Steam Packet sailing down-river to Gainsborough twice a week.

The very excellence of these waterways, and the strength of the canal-owning interests, caused Nottingham to lag behind when the railway era began. Some say that economic and geographical factors foredoomed the town never to enjoy that prominence in the railway network its importance seems to demand. However that may be, the canal-proprietors *did* fight bitterly to obstruct their rivals, and there was a strong public conviction (which lingers) that an opportunity had been thrown away. A speaker at a Council meeting in 1836 declared:

> Nottingham from its geographical position might and ought to have been made a point through which the direct line of railway from south to north should pass. That benefit has been lost to the town in consequence of the neglect and indifference with which the subject has been treated. The neighbouring town of Derby has completely outstripped us in the race for railway advantages.

Travellers still echo his sentiments as they 'change at Derby' and travel like suburban commuters the last few miles to one of the largest cities in England.

Public indignation did not always stop short at councillors' protests. Until well into the nineteenth century the townsmen were always ripe for violence. In the year of Byron's arrival a gentleman complained that 'he had lived seventeen years in the town of Nottingham, and during that time there had been seventeen riots', and Byron himself wrote in 1806 of 'that *political Pandemonium*, Nottingham'. Any excuse turned the Market Place into a battle-ground: the high price of cheese (or meat, or bread), low wages, unemployment, or the French

Revolution. The magistrates answered by enrolling hundreds of special constables and calling out yeomanry, dragoons, or hussars, as available. The Barracks stood handy on the edge of the Park.

Whatever the pretext, these regular explosions were caused by the conditions under which many people lived and the frustration of a political system which denied them any say in local or national affairs.

The town's government continued, as in medieval times, to be run by a small group of intermarried families, now with the additional bond of the same Unitarian chapel on High Pavement. In 1833 out of forty-two councillors and Corporation officials no fewer than eleven were drawn from two families. At that time the rates brought in £6000 and another £7000 came from rents, tolls and such-like, yet more than a third of this total went in 'management expenses'. Corporation business was largely transacted at lively evening parties, and besides enjoying this regular hospitality at the public charge the members were able to share out among themselves the contracts for supplying the workhouse and prison along with similar perquisites. As Stanley Pigott says, in *Hollins: a Study of Industry 1784–1949*, this clique 'anticipated the methods of Tammany Hall' and circumvented the dangers of popular election 'either by holding no elections at all, or by distributing appointments in such a way that any election result was ineffective'.

When it came to parliamentary elections the prospects for democracy seemed brighter. Those qualified to vote, all burgesses and possessors of a forty-shilling freehold, totalled about three thousand, a considerable number for those days, but the procedure still left scope for unlimited corruption.

The town was a two-member constituency. The election was held at the Exchange, where the returning-officer accepted nominations and announced if a poll were necessary. A wooden booth was then set up in the Market Place outside and voting began, continuing for several days (once, it is said, for ten) unless one side, possibly encouraged by threats of violence, conceded victory. There was no secret ballot before 1871. Officers recorded each man's name, address, occupation, qualification to vote, and the way he voted. These facts were later published in a poll-book, an invaluable record for future historians but an embarrassing one for the citizen at the time. The Whig and Tory organizations set up their headquarters in rival inns. As the polling slowly proceeded from day to day, enterprising electors often chalked up on the shutters the price at which their votes were for sale. Those without strong personal preferences held back in the early stages, studying the market trend like stock-exchange speculators, and entering the booth at the moment they judged most profitable.

It would be a mistake to suppose, however, that party feeling did not run high. Many electors, whatever their motives, were enthusiastically committed from the start. There were extraordinary scenes in May 1803 following the previous year's election which had been so blatantly corrupt (even the returning-officer behaving improperly) that it was annulled so far as one seat was concerned, though oddly enough the other result was allowed to stand. When the contest was refought, the Tory candidate, a Derbyshire barrister named Coke, arrived in Nottingham attended by sixteen hundred horsemen riding six abreast and an uncounted horde of foot-followers, all decked with blue ribbons, carrying fifty-two flags and heartened by the music of a band packed into a carriage lined with blue silk and drawn by four horses. It was a parade that would have overshadowed Charles I's arrival in 1642, but it was matched by the show put on by Mr Birch's Whig supporters the next day. It was, of course, a by-election. Both multitudes must have been swollen by partisans from outside the constituency, for they far exceeded the number on the electoral roll. Mr Coke got in by 1359 votes to 1164.

Politics were not all bribes, beer and bludgeons. There were thoughtful people in all classes, fighting the usual uphill battle against reaction and ignorance. The Corporation itself, spurred on by the feelings of the whole town, had presented an address to George III indicating its opposition to the use of force against the American colonists. As early as 1780 the Duke of Portland chaired a meeting in support of Parliamentary Reform, including universal suffrage, the secret ballot and all the other points that the Chartists were still urging sixty years later. The prime mover of that Nottingham meeting was Major John Cartwright, who has been called 'the Father of Reform', and was no less an innovator than his brother, the Reverend Edmund Cartwright, whose invention of the power-loom was inspired by a visit to Arkwright's cotton-mill.

The working class had its own leaders, by far the most remarkable being Gravener Henson, of whom it was said that he was connected with every trade combination in the region between 1808 and 1840, during much of which period (it should be remembered) trade unions were illegal and alternately repressed or connived at according to circumstances. Henson had been an apprentice stocking-maker, then a maker of point net, employing eleven skilled hands, and, when that trade diminished, a bobbin-net maker. Clearly he was adaptable. He was also articulate, a forceful but reasonable negotiator, and well versed in industrial law, a man who knew what it was to run a business himself. In due course he came to give all his time to the interests of the workmen, making frequent visits to London and receiving a weekly allowance to live on. Very likely he was the first full-time paid organizer in trade-union history. Needless to say, his name was anathema in reactionary circles. They swore that he was behind the Luddite troubles, even that he was the mysterious 'King Ludd' himself, but no charge was ever pinned on him. Henson seems rather to have been an intelligent, responsible man, often privately dismayed by the blindness of his own followers, and would have made a valuable, if not always a comfortable, member of a modern Labour government or the T.U.C.

Conditions were bad enough. In 1819 the frameworkers worked sixteen to eighteen hours a day for earnings of four to seven shillings a week. There was frequent unemployment. Thousands of men and women trudged through the streets with banners inscribed 'Pity Our Children' and 'We Ask for Bread'. The charitable responded by raising a relief fund of ten thousand pounds and helping three hundred destitute families to emigrate to South Africa. The Government characteristically sent Nottingham several cartloads of ammunition and six companies of infantry to back up the garrison. Three members of the frameworkers' committee went to prison for conspiracy.

Gravener Henson used to make his headquarters at the Sir Isaac Newton. The more radically minded foregathered at the Rancliffe Arms, kept by a self-educated frameworker, John Blackner. He wrote for the *Nottingham Review* and probably edited it when its founder, Charles Sutton, a Methodist printer, was jailed for twelve months in 1816 after publishing a letter offensive to the Home Secretary. It was Blackner too who, in this atmosphere of political bitterness, yet found heart to compile his *History of Nottingham*.

Other public houses served as places where workmen could meet freely, exchange ideas and read the newspapers, which the tax made prohibitive to buy at sevenpence a copy. Several of these establishments served as the first lending libraries, housing collections of books built up by the regulars and lent out on Wednesdays and Sundays. Later, this function was taken over by the Artisans' Library system. There was another library in the Mechanics' Institution, founded in 1837 as part of a general movement which in a few years had spread as far as Sydney and Melbourne. The gentry had their own Nottingham Subscription Library, founded in 1816 and still flourishing on the elegant first floor of Bromley House.

Some workers who could save a little were already forming building societies. Space being almost unobtainable in the old town, their cottages began to spring up in outlying suburbs like Carrington and Hyson Green.

Everyone has heard of the Luddites, but most people are hazy about the motives of the machine-breakers whose violent and mysterious activities disturbed Nottinghamshire and neighbouring counties at frequent intervals from 1811 to 1817.

The name 'Luddites' is often invoked in modern denunciations of trade-union prejudice against new methods, and it is mistakenly assumed that they were ignorantly opposing the new power-driven machinery. But as Professor Chambers has shown in *Nottinghamshire in the Eighteenth Century*, Luddism 'had no connection with the introduction of steam power' and he regrets that Ernst Toller's famous play, *The Machine Wreckers*, 'revived this delusion'. The movement took its name, almost irrelevantly, from Ned Ludlam, a Leicester apprentice, who smashed his stocking-frame in a fit of temper. Really it was 'a matter of bare cupboards and empty bellies'. England suffered four bad harvests in succession, so that wheat stood at famine prices. Simultaneously the export trade was slashed by Napoleon's ban on British goods entering Europe and by a dispute with the United States which soon developed into war. Unemployment among the stockingers rose to twenty per cent and the earnings of the rest were cut. The men who banded thmselves together to attack mills at night and destroy the stocking-frames and lace machines were not, in the main, besotted fanatics blindly smashing the means of their own livelihood, but a disciplined secret organization, concentrating on hosiers who paid below the agreed rates. Often they gave their opponents a fair warning to mend their ways. Their letters and proclamations were signed 'Ned Ludd' or 'King Ludd'. The identity of this shadowy leader has never been established.

Sneinton, Arnold and Bulwell saw many of these midnight attacks. The Luddites used to meet in Sherwood Forest and proceed in orderly bands to their objectives. Like all guerrillas they relied on the sympathy of the population. Rewards of fifty guineas offered to informers, together with free pardons for offenders willing to betray their comrades, seem to have had little effect. A bill was brought in to impose the death-penalty instead of transportation. It evoked Byron's famous opposition speech in the House of Lords, when he spoke vehemently of 'these men, as I have seen them – meagre with famine, sullen with despair, careless of a life which your Lordships are perhaps about to value at something less than the price of a stocking-frame'. He had just returned from Turkey, he said, where he had never 'beheld such squalid wretchedness' as he found in 'the heart of a Christian country'. Even if the bill were passed, they would still need to find 'twelve butchers for a jury, and a Jeffreys for a judge!'

The young poet could not sway the peers. The bill became law. But the hare had to be caught before he could be hanged, and at this the authorities were singularly inept. They drafted thousands of troops into Nottinghamshire. A camp was set up in the Forest and redcoats were quartered in every village inn, while in Nottingham itself a curfew was proclaimed and soldiers marched even to church parade at St Mary's with their bayonets fixed. Six Luddites were hanged in 1817, but it was rather the pendulum-swing of economic conditions that caused the campaign of sabotage to die away.

Never did the pendulum swing more violently than in the brief lace-boom that started in 1823, with the lapse of Heathcoat's patent. Now any skilled mechanic could copy his machine, and there were plenty of speculators eager to pay him five pounds a week, even ten pounds, to do so. Country squires, parsons, bankers, lawyers, doctors and shopkeepers scurried to put up capital as if it were some sort of a gold-rush, and the resemblance was heightened by the workmen flocking from Birmingham, Sheffield and Manchester to earn unheard-of wages as twist hands. A contemporary ballad ran:

> With rum and gin and brandy-o, we made the people stare,
> And horse and gig so handy-o to take the morning air,
> And then with single-breasted coats and spanking new top-
> boots,
> And pockets lined with five-pound notes, we were the merry
> shoots.

> The bobbin and the carriage-hands they scarcely would look
> down,
> Or bend their portly bodies for to pick up half a crown,
> And if it had but lasted long I think they wouldn't stoop
> To poor beefsteaks and onions but they'd dine on turtle soup.

> The cobbler left his soles and heels and wouldn't be so mean
> As to stick to wax and 'taching ends but bought a twist
> machine.
> The tailor left his board and goose, the miller left his grist.
> Tag, rag and bobtail all got loose to get into the twist.

And servants left their mop and broom and wouldn't go to
  place,
But set their dainty hands to work to purl and mend the lace.
But to tell the long and short of it and so to end my song –
Among so many twisters, sir, they've twisted it too strong.

One wonders what Byron, with his blend of aristocratic prejudice and radical sentiment, would have made of this sudden
reversal in the fortunes of the famished workers. He never saw
this altered Nottingham with its lace-workers riding to their
factories on horseback and tossing off a pint of champagne at the
end of their shift. Byron was dying in Greece at this time. It was
on 15 July 1824, at the height of the boom, that his body lay in state
at the Blackamoor's Head in Pelham Street, having been refused
burial in Westminster Abbey, and on the following day that it was
taken the last few miles to the family vault in Hucknall church,
near Newstead, escorted by a vast concourse of mourners such as
only a Winston Churchill would draw together in our own day.

The lace boom lasted until the end of 1825. Then it burst like
the South Sea Bubble. There was a run on the local banks, of
which the town had four, each issuing its own paper money as
was the custom then. But the businessmen got together sensibly,
formed a committee under the Mayor, and restored confidence.
No bank failed.

The golden age was over. The dizzy workers returned to cruel
realities. A few, however, had made good use of their brief
opportunity. Such was Richard Birkin, later a name to conjure
with in the lace trade. Birkin was a Derbyshire youth who came
to Basford the year before Heathcoat's patent expired. He learned
to work a bobbin-net machine and, having intelligence and
character, spent his evenings reading, drawing and experimenting
with technical improvements. The high wages of the boom period
allowed him to save a little capital and in 1825 his employer
offered him a partnership. He went on to build up the company
that still bears his name, and to found one of those industrial
dynasties so typical of Victorian England. He himself was four
times Mayor of Nottingham, and his son Thomas went on to
become High Sheriff and a baronet.

It was to be expected that the independent-minded citizens of Nottingham would share fully in the agitation for Parliamentary Reform which gripped England in the early months of 1831. The new Prime Minister, Lord Grey, was pledged to introduce the bill, and in March a mass meeting in the Exchange supported it. At the election in May the Reform candidates were both elected, and when rival petitions were circulated there were twelve thousand signatures demanding the change and only four hundred against.

The man who presented the anti-Reform petition to the House of Lords (and the supreme antagonist of Reform throughout the controversy) was the Duke of Newcastle, who now became a sort of absentee bogeyman to the town over which his derelict Castle still lowered. Its last tenant had moved out a year or two before and its park had been let for grazing to the local butchers.

Henry Pelham Fiennes Pelham Clinton, fourth Duke of the latest creation, was in his middle forties. He had strong ideas on what it meant to be a duke, and, having inherited when he was ten, little notion of what it meant to be anything else. He was cold and pompous even to his own family. Wellington, not himself exactly progressive, declared that 'there never was such a fool'. He had once persuaded himself, and tried to persuade the Home Secretary, that the Luddite troubles were caused by Napoleonic agents. He was a big man with a loud thick voice and passionate gesticulations. At Newark he had evicted a number of his tenants for voting against his own nominee. His thunderous answer to criticism was the rhetorical question, 'May I not do what I like with mine own?' He admitted complacently, 'I have only to show my face to cause a riot.'

He had no need to show his face in Nottingham. It sufficed that he was the leading opponent of the Reform Bill in the House of Lords, which threw out the measure in the early morning of Saturday 8 October. At Nottingham, crowded for Goose Fair, the stunning news reached only a handful of people that night, but next morning, when the mail coach clattered in from London, the whole town knew that the Lords had defeated the Prime

Minister and defied the nation's wishes. And every one knew whom to blame.

There were rumours of disorder in Derby. A detachment of the Hussars stationed in the Park rode off to deal with it. The rest were called out in Nottingham by evening, after the wilder elements had begun to attack the premises of known anti-Reformers and the Mayor had been compelled to read the Riot Act. On Monday twenty thousand people thronged the Market Place and voted a loyal address to the new king, William IV, praying him to support his government in the cause of Reform. The meeting passed off without any trouble, but soon afterwards a party assailed one of the windmills on the Forest, the property of an opponent, and there was a good deal more window-smashing elsewhere. The affair only began to grow serious as the autumn twilight came down.

The burning of the Castle seems to have been planned: some of the other incidents were either spontaneous acts of the mob or cunning feints to draw away the military. Usually, in those days, Nottingham's protests were cut short by the sabre, and historians have devoted considerable discussion to the puzzling questions presented by the affair. Why was it all so easy? Could not the Castle really have been saved?

The rioters began the evening by marching on Colwick Hall, home of John Musters, a well-known opponent of Reform. They broke up iron railings for weapons as they rampaged through Sneinton. Musters was away, but his unfortunate wife (Byron's boyhood love, Mary Chaworth) cowered in the shrubbery while they tried inefficiently to burn down the house. Her death soon afterwards was attributed to this experience. Turning back into Nottingham, one party attacked the House of Correction, which was strongly defended by Hussars and several hundred special constables. The rest of the rioters, estimated at six hundred, made straight for the Castle, turning out the street-lamps as they went.

Almost incredibly, the Duke's mansion was entirely undefended. In no time the lodge-gates were broken down and the attackers swarmed up the steep slope to the great baroque mass looming square against the night sky. They smashed in doors and

windows and ranged through the desolate apartments. The
incendiarism was thoughtfully organized. Some men hacked holes
in the floors, poked in broken banisters, and set them on fire.
Others descended to the basement kitchens, heaped up piles of
furniture, and set them ablaze. There was little to loot, even if
that had been the motive. Some of the marauders did make off
with the old tapestries, and these were later sold to souvenir-
hunters in squares for three shillings a yard. But essentially the
destruction of the Castle was a political act, a planned reprisal
against a reactionary duke.

Soon the air was sadly fragrant with the burning of that cedarwood wainscotting which Celia Fiennes had admired so long ago,
and the lead roof, from which she had surveyed the 'fine prospect
of the whole town and river', was pouring down as bright molten
metal. Heavy rain was falling. A contemporary painting shows
people watching the conflagration from the meadows below, the
firelight unromantically gleaming on the tops of their wet um-
brellas. But no rain could quench such a blaze, and by morning
only the blackened walls stood up against the sky.

There was an ironical sequel. The infuriated Duke begged the
Government to make him chairman of the commission set up to
punish the miscreants, but they wisely refused him even a seat on
it. When, as in this case, it was impossible to exact compensation
from the people who had actually done the damage, the law
held the ratepayers as a whole responsible for their failure to keep
order in their area. By an odd quirk of history the residents of
Nottingham were held innocent, for, ever since Henry VI's
charter, the Castle had been expressly excluded from the town's
boundaries. The Duke's compensation was therefore extracted
from the 'Hundred of Broxtowe'. Bulwell, Basford and Arnold
had to contribute large sums, but at least they may have contributed a few of the untraced culprits. It was distinctly hard,
however, on the worthy people of Mansfield, miles away but part
of the Broxtowe Hundred. They had to pay £2,903, more than
the other three places put together.

The Reform Bill went through in 1832. Grey asked the King
to create, if necessary, enough new peers to push it through the

Lords, and William IV, for all his nickname 'Silly Billy', was not so foolish as to refuse. Events in Nottingham and Bristol had shown that there was a real chance of revolution. The mere threat of new peers brought the Upper House to its senses, and Wellington persuaded the Lords to pass the bill.

In Nottingham the news was signalized by the hoisting of a flag over the Exchange and the repeated discharge of two cannon in the Market Place. Processions formed, bands played, bonfires blazed far into the night, and fireworks exploded in all directions. When the town's two M.P.s returned from London they were welcomed with another monster procession in which fifteen or twenty thousand people paraded. And, so that the children should remember the day as long as they lived, they were given not only a bun apiece but a mug of ale.

In point of fact, the first Reform Act still left two men out of three without votes, since they lacked the property qualification, and Nottingham now threw itself wholeheartedly into the Chartist campaign for universal male suffrage.

This and the other Chartist demands (except for the one requiring a General Election every year) have long been part of the system we live under, and might seem incontrovertible by any reasonable person, but at the time they were regarded with the horror that Communism inspired a century later. In this connection it is fair to remember that the Chartist movement had a powerful wing that was understandly pessimistic about the effect of mere propaganda and petitions, and talked in violent revolutionary terms.

There were plenty of these advocates of physical force in Nottingham, and in the crucial summer of 1839, when a 'Sacred Month' or general strike was threatened, the town was packed with troops. Fortunately they were under General Sir Charles Napier (the same whose statue adorns Trafalgar Square), an extraordinarily humane and level-headed soldier, who was deeply sympathetic to the ideas of the Chartists. From his headquarters in Wheeler Gate he commanded the whole of the North.

'I like Nottingham,' he wrote. 'The poor people are good and

were they fairly treated they would be perfectly quiet. . . . The
people should have universal suffrage – it is their right.'

He had, however, to do his duty. 'If the mob break the peace,
I will break their heads. We will have no burnings, no disgraceful
proceedings which the honest part of the Chartists deprecate.'

The Chartists held a mass parade on the Forest. Napier
favoured such safety-valves, but he had to be tactful in his deal-
ings with the local authorities. 'The magistrates here want to act
rightly,' he noted, 'but have been bullied by the county magistrates into a proclamation against meetings. . . . This is unwise.'
He knew that some of the Chartist pickets were carrying pistols,
but held his hand. 'Seizing these men could do no good. It would
not stop Chartism if they were all hanged. Chartism cannot be
stopped. God forbid that it should. What we want is to stop the
letting loose a large body of armed cut-throats upon the public.'
Even when a trigger-happy idealist shot at a dragoon, fortunately
missing, the General restrained his men from reprisals. 'Let us
shut our mouths,' he ordered, 'and the thing will be unnoticed.'
Later he was able to write: 'Thank God we have had no row and
not a drop of blood spilled.' Characteristically he gave the main
credit to 'the good heart and good sense of [William] Roworth
the Mayor', who had certainly co-operated admirably during
the months of tension. He spoke warmly, too, of the local bankers,
the Wrights, 'one family here that would save a city from God's
wrath'.

The tension continued into 1840. November 1839 saw the
Newport Rising, when the Monmouthshire Chartists were shot
down and their leaders transported for life to Australia. Nottingham remained calm, though Napier's troops stood to at nightfall
and his dragoons patrolled the town until daybreak.

There was real trouble in the summer of 1842, by which time
Napier was unfortunately far away in India. As a prelude, there
was a by-election in July, when a Quaker, Joseph Sturge, backed
by the Chartists, opposed a Tory democrat, John Walter, editor
of *The Times*. Feeling was feverish. Sturge had the embarrassing
support of Feargus O'Connor, a wild Irish barrister fresh from
a term in prison for sedition. Walter was aided by a renegade

Chartist, the Reverend J. R. Stephens, and it was the clash of these lieutenants that produced the strongest drama. They held simultaneous meetings in the Market Place, thronged with sixteen thousand people. While the Quaker and his quieter supporters watched from the windows of Bromley House, the waggon from which O'Connor was ranting in his stentorian voice was pushed to within fifteen yards of Stephens, who looked down from his own with folded arms and a disdainful expression. Finally O'Connor leapt to the ground, like some Homeric hero quitting his chariot, and battled his way with flailing fists towards his erstwhile ally. Stephens, at the last moment, prudently dived into the headquarters of his own candidate, the adjacent Bell. The sequel was that Walter won narrowly by 1885 votes to 1801, Sturge having refused to give any bribes whereas the *Times* editor had given them so generously that he was in due course unseated. As Asa Briggs blandly observes in *Victorian Cities*: 'Nottingham had an extremely interesting electoral history, not least on account of the tradition of corruption which existed there.' The ebullient O'Connor himself won one of the Nottingham seats in 1847, was declared insane in 1852, died in 1855, and was honoured in 1859 by the statue in the Arboretum.

The narrow Chartist defeat in the 1842 election was followed a few weeks later by disorders culminating in 'the Battle of Mapperley Hills'. The trouble started with a strike meeting at five o'clock one morning. It was broken up, resumed and broken up again, whereupon hundreds of men marched round the factories calling the workers to come out. The Riot Act was ripped from the magistrate's hands, and the police charged, arresting a number of men. For several days there were marches and riotous assemblies at Radford, Basford, Bulwell, Arnold and elsewhere. The climax was the massing of thousands on Mapperley Hills. Some were doubtless trying, as Professor Chambers says, to produce a general strike 'until the document known as the People's Charter became the law of the land', while others were merely demanding, as Roy Church says, 'a fair day's wages for a fair day's work'. The authorities did not stop to discuss their views. Police and dragoons charged. After a brief scuffle the strikers ran. Four hundred were rounded up, handcuffed, and marched off to the House of Correction. The people in the streets stoned their captors. The dragoons had to gallop to and fro with brandished sabres. Napier might have handled things differently.

Despite all these agitations Nottingham was able, the next year, to offer a loyal welcome to the young Queen Victoria, who seems to have been the first reigning sovereign to visit the town since William III was banqueted by a grateful Corporation in 1695. Victoria arrived at the recently built railway station, her 'luxuriant fair hair simply braided' under a 'bonnet of white straw trimmed with blue ribbons and a white feather'. She was greeted with triumphal arches, military bands and gun-salutes from the Castle Rock, and accompanied by Prince Albert, whose 'distinguished looks', Anne Gilbert recalled more than half-a-century later, 'were enhanced to my girlish eyes by the moustache he wore, a labial ornament I had never seen except in the presence of Signor Assolari, our French and Italian master'.

Five years later in 1848, 'the year of revolutions', Nottingham shared the tension preceding the fiasco of the great Chartist parade in London. Local sympathizers planned mass meetings. The authorities prepared for the worst. Sixteen hundred special constables were enrolled, troops prepared to defend the jail, shop-windows round the Market Place were boarded up, detachments of Yeomanry moved to key points at Trent Bridge, Wollaton and elsewhere. It was specially feared that the gasworks would be an objective, so the premises were barricaded, loopholed and provisioned for a siege, boiling tar being made ready to discourage attackers in the best medieval tradition. But in Nottingham, as elsewhere in England, the day passed uneventfully, giving scant comfort to Marx and Engels, who had just written their *Communist Manifesto*.

Trade was improving. Discontent died down. When it boiled up again it found more orderly expression in the formation of trade unions, co-operative societies and finally the Labour Party. The Hussars and Dragoons were not needed again in the streets of Nottingham.

The Market Place as D. H. Lawrence depicted it in his early novels. Twice a week it became a sea of canvas awnings, the greatest open market in the country.

The horse-and-cart parade in 1911. On Long Row, behind, a single taxi appears as an omen of the transport revolution.

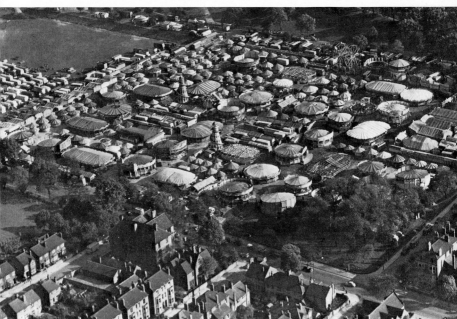

Goose Fair – then and now

above: *In 1926 the ancient Fair still crammed the Market Place, but its days there were numbered. The Exchange had been demolished and the Council House was soon to rise in the gap seen here above the tops of the merry-go-rounds.*

below: *Since 1928 the Fair has been held in a corner of 'the Forest', which, despite the name, is only a mile from the old site in the heart of the city.*

CHAPTER SEVENTEEN

Progress and Philanthropy

FOR a special reason that will appear, the middle of the nineteenth century happens to form a conspicuous watershed in Nottingham's history. The town was one thing in the eighteen forties and quite another in the eighteen sixties. Yet it would be foolish to exaggerate the change (great though it was) and to suggest that there was nothing but riots before 1850, nothing but committees and commissions thereafter.

With so much happening in the last chapter it was hard to do justice to the action and the actors without neglecting the background against which they ranted and postured. It is time to pause and see how the town itself had changed as it moved into the early Victorian era.

Its population was still increasing, 53,091 in 1841, multiplied five times in less than a century, twenty times since the Middle Ages, yet without any addition to its area. As a result, Nottingham was about the unhealthiest and most overcrowded town in England, with an especially appalling death-rate for children in the poorer quarters. In the spring of 1832 a cholera epidemic began, which reached its climax in the September, when 137 people died. There were nearly a thousand cases that summer, one-third of them fatal. An emergency Board of Health was formed. Led by the Unitarian Thomas Wakefield, its members, including William Enfield the Town Clerk, a Quaker grocer named Samuel Fox, and a Roman Catholic priest, worked devotedly and fearlessly in the most noisome alleys of the town, but official inertia returned as soon as the danger passed.

In the following year a count revealed 4283 persons living in

883 houses within an area of less than nine acres, a density of almost a hundred houses and five hundred persons to the acre. Twelve years later, in 1845, a commission reported: 'It is common to find 15 to 20 children in a low garret, 12 feet square, working for 15 hours a day.' The commissioners, who were studying all the large towns, declared: 'Nowhere else shall we find so large a mass of inhabitants crowded into courts, alleys and lanes as in Nottingham. And those too of the worst description . . . clustered yard within yard and lane within lane.' This was what had happened to the gardens, paddocks and orchards of the once green town. There were thousands of back-to-back houses. Two hundred cellar dwellings had been gouged out of the sandstone below them. Up to a dozen human beings slept in these holes measuring about twelve feet square, with the roof of rock barely clearing a tall man's head.

Sanitation, as now understood, scarcely existed. Twenty or thirty people shared one privy, usually sited so that it was in itself one of the worst hazards to health. The Mickletorn Jury, which had been so watchful for nuisances in days gone by, survived into late Victorian times, but it was a sentimental anachronism, either impotent or indifferent in the face of the massive problems created by industrialism. It would assemble on a fixed date to beat the bounds and march off singing a song written for it by a local poet. The chorus in 1850 ran:

> Shoulder your spades and march away,
> The sun shines bright, 'tis a glorious day!
> Our Foreman's the King, whom we all obey,
>   When we serve on the Mickletorn Jury.

Refreshments were provided at frequent stops along the route, which did not pass through the most unsavoury of the slums, and a few days later the jurors were further rewarded for their efforts with a public dinner at the Maypole Inn, by which time it would have seemed ungracious to trouble the Council with complaints.

There were, however, men who had grasped the importance of plumbing. Thomas Hawksley, who has been described as 'the greatest of water engineers for all time', was born at Arnold in

1807 and went to the old grammar school in Stoney Street. He was good at mathematics and developed a private interest in geology and chemistry, outside the classroom. He was articled to a local architect who undertook engineering work, and it was in this field that he found his true bent. At twenty-three he became engineer to the new Trent Bridge Water Works Company.

Many households still depended on water-carriers charging a farthing a bucket. Hawksley provided a piped supply for a penny a week, and with a staff of one man and a boy maintained that supply to eight thousand dwellings and innumerable business premises. 'He was the first', claimed a B.B.C. broadcast in 1927, 'to provide a constant supply of water by mains always under pressure, and Nottingham was the first place in the world to be so blessed.' He dealt also with gas-mains and sewers, and given the chance would have installed central drains throughout the slums at a cost of six shillings per house.

The town was lucky to keep him for twenty-two years, but even when he moved to London in 1852 he remained its water engineer, serving altogether half-a-century in that capacity. He became President of the Institute of Civil Engineers, and the *Encyclopaedia Britannica* credits him with the provision of one hundred and fifty water-works, including those of Liverpool, Sheffield, Stockholm and Bridgetown in the West Indies. It can hardly be a coincidence that, when cholera reappeared in 1849, Nottingham suffered nothing like the terrible mortality of 1832.

This, then, was the murky background (and contributory cause) of the violent events enacted in the period of Luddite, Reform and Chartist agitations, and Hawksley must stand as just one, if perhaps the most remarkable, of the individuals working in other ways to improve the lot of the community. Hawksley knew well enough that there were some things no engineer could accomplish until political action had cleared the way but he was aware of the obstacles to that action. 'The working classes', he observed bitterly, 'invariably vote contrary to their own interests.'

Working-conditions matched housing-conditions in horror. A cynic might have argued that housing was almost irrelevant since in many cases factory hours were so long that 'home' could be little more than a hole to creep into for exhausted sleep. The factory, however, was not the typical work-place in Nottingham until after 1850, though it was becoming commoner in the surrounding villages. Steam-power was introduced for bobbin net within a year of Waterloo. By the time of the Reform Riots there were twenty-two factories and a total of a thousand power-driven machines, but of the four major establishments only one was truly in the town, in Canal Street. It was the employers' determination to get every penny of profit out of these expensive steam-engines that condemned the people to such inhuman hours. The engines ran continuously from four o'clock in the morning until midnight, sometimes even all round the clock. Children were kept on hand, not ceaselessly employed but ready as required, from four or five in the morning until ten or eleven at night. There was a variety of jobs, 'suited' (at least in the opinion of the management) to every age. The boys, from five years upwards, could wind the thread on to the bobbins. The girls could start seaming when they were seven or eight, and thereafter go on to become menders, embroiderers, bleachers, dyers and dressers. Many of these processes were carried out away from the factories, in small workshops or at home, just as much of the original production was still centred in long-windowed attics filled with hand-operated machines. Conditions in such places were often worse than those in the factories.

It would be untrue to say that this state of affairs caused no concern to the middle class, but their indignation was aroused mainly by the danger to the workers' morals. Their protests have a strangely modern ring. 'In many instances,' complained Mr Barnett, the workhouse overseer, in 1843, 'a portion of the earnings allowed to young persons affords the means of indulging irregular desires.' Overcrowded homes were frowned upon mainly because they drove the young persons out onto the streets. Juvenile prostitution was rife, the illegitimate birth-rate twice that of Birmingham. There was a sad lack of parental control. Young working-class mothers knew nothing about bringing up children. A third of these people, estimated Archdeacon Wilkins, had no moral or religious feelings whatever. 'They go to no place of worship. They are kept in restraint only by the strong arm of the law, and live without God in the world.'

William Booth, who was born at Sneinton in 1829, recalled in after-life 'the degradation and helpless misery of the poor stockingers, wandering gaunt and hunger-stricken through the streets', and declared that his boyhood impressions had 'had a powerful influence on my whole life'. He early became a street-corner evangelist for the Wesleyans, and in a sense the Salvation Army was founded, in his heart at least, before he departed for London in 1849.

It was in 1846, ironically enough, in these same factories, that the supreme symbol of Victorian propriety – the Nottingham lace curtain – first came into production.

There was obviously a brighter side.

The Market Place was now lined with shops. John Townsend had come down from London in 1804 and set up on Long Row as a haberdasher and milliner, his business being taken over in 1866 by Zebedee Jessop. Nottingham's other old-established store, Griffin and Spalding's, began in 1846. There must have been a numerous top-hat and parasol society. The first afternoon of Goose Fair was called the 'gig fair' because it was patronized by the better sort. In 1826 nearly a hundred ladies and gentlemen were ready to pay half-a-guinea apiece for the thrill of a balloon ascent from the Market Place. By 1845 there were railway excursions as far afield as Calais and Boulogne, leaving at crack of dawn on Monday and returning on Thursday.

There were still crocuses in the meadows and horse-races on the Forest. At the very end of the century Anne Gilbert (who as a child had watched the Castle burning) could remember the Leen as a country river: 'In my dreams I find myself and my companions wandering by its streamlets, watching the fish in the clear waters and the dragonflies skimming along the surface, or gathering flowers that grew along the banks.' And a grammar-school boy of that period recalled how holiday afternoons used to be spent in the Castle Park, 'then a fine, open, breezy place, where cows grazed and bluebells grew'.

But the old fashionable quarter was becoming less and less suitable for a gentleman to live in, still less raise a family. Riots and cholera were always possible. Smoke, stench and noise were certain, as workshops and slums crept closer to Castle Gate and High Pavement. One by one the fine mansions near St Mary's were deserted, their spacious gardens built on, themselves finally demolished. Plumptre House came tumbling down in 1853 and Birkin's lace warehouse rose in its place. The whole area, the original Saxon town, began to turn into 'the Lace Market', and is still known by that name.

The well-to-do moved further out. In the eighteen twenties the Duke had begun to grant a few ninety-nine-year leases for suitably genteel houses to be built along the Derby Road fringe of his domain: the stuccoed villas we see now began to creep along the Ropewalk and Park Terrace soon after this date. But mostly the thriving business-class had to seek fresh air and space beyond the green belt of town lands.

Amid all the money-making there were many of these homes in which intellectual and aesthetic interests were pursued. The Lowe family, for instance, lived at Highfield House, now the residence of the Vice-Chancellor, and the contemporary *Hand-book to Nottingham* notes that 'the lake and park' (now the university campus) 'together form a very pleasing "coup d'œil" '. The walls of the mansion were hung with hundreds of pictures, including the work of Rembrandt, Rubens, Murillo, Velasquez, Claude, Watteau, Poussin, Gainsborough, Morland, and Bonington, the brilliant but short-lived Arnold boy, whose family had left Nottingham for France about 1817. One Lowe, at least, foreshadowed the scientific associations of Highfields. Born there in 1825, Edward J. Lowe became a Fellow of the Royal Society. Botany was only one of his diverse studies. He had a famous collection of ferns with three hundred named varieties.

At Basford there were the Baileys. Thomas, the father, was a wine merchant and a town councillor with progressive views. Local history was his hobby and in 1853, not long before his death, he published his useful but not wholly reliable *Annals of Nottinghamshire*. Many years earlier he had moved out to

Basford Manor House, which Pevsner judges 'a rare and good example' of the 1700 period, though today it is divided into flats and business premises. In this handsome seven-bayed brick manor, with its fine panelling, Thomas Bailey played the local squire, interested himself in good causes and compiled his four volumes of county annals, while his son, Philip James, whose bust adorns the colonnade at the Castle along with those of contemporary minor writers such as Kirke White and the Nature-loving William and Mary Howitt, interminably revised and expanded his philosophic epic, *Festus*, an ambitious treatment of the Faust theme designed to improve on Goethe.

The younger Bailey had been born in the old town in 1816. He entered Glasgow University and was later called to the bar, but never practised. From the age of twenty he was obsessed by his poem. Its first (1839) edition was praised by Tennyson and had a large sale both in Britain and in America. Later, Watts-Dunton granted it 'lovely oases of poetry' amid 'wide tracts of ratiocinative writing', and in our own century Louis Cazamian has remarked on the 'dreadful monotony' of its blank verse. However, Bailey retains a somewhat dusty little niche in literary history, where he is often labelled 'the father of the Spasmodic School'. He was certainly dedicated to his Muse. For fifty years he tinkered with his poem, doubling its length to 40,000 lines. In 1856, the year of his father's death, he was awarded a Civil List pension of a hundred pounds a year (poets of almost any quality were more highly regarded in those days) and continued to draw it until his death in 1902.

There were no pensions for the lace hands. Before the young poet was astir in his father's pleasant garden at Basford, the five-year-olds had toddled through the factory-gates at 5 a.m. Not that every poor man's son faced that destiny. In the most crowded slums two out of three babies were sure of dying before their fourth birthday.

The mid-century watershed in Nottingham's history was the 1845 Enclosure Act, secured after a long struggle.

Other places had long ago carried out their enclosures: Wilford in 1766, and then, with a rush in the seventeen nineties, Sneinton, Basford, Hyson Green and Carrington. In this last village six acres were awarded to the banker, Robert Smith, then M.P. for Nottingham and the close friend and financial adviser of Pitt, who made him Lord Carrington in 1796. The six acres, which lay in the angle of the Mansfield and Hucknall roads, Smith sold to his fellow banker, Ichabod Wright, who built on it and laid out the little triangular market-place, still to be seen there as a curious reminder of the days when lonely country stretched between it and the town market a mile and a half away.

For long after that, Nottingham, or rather its ruling group, resisted every proposal to enclose its own common lands. The Corporation controlled well over a thousand acres. On the Sand Field and the Clay Field, where crops were grown, plots were assigned to burgesses by seniority in return for a small ground-rent. Similar burgess parts were provided by the Hunger Hill Gardens. Here a lucky holder could usually sub-let his garden for about ten pounds a year, since there were more burgesses than burgess parts available. Any burgess, however, had the ancient commoner's right to pasture animals. The Waste, that is, the Forest and Mapperley Common, was open to him all the year round. After Lammas (the old Harvest Festival on 1 August) beasts could be turned on to the stubble of the cultivated fields, the Lammas Lands. He could use the Meadows similarly after haymaking at a charge of three shillings for a horse and half-a-crown for a cow. The Corporation also owned the Coppice, but this was let as a farm.

It is understandable that enclosure was resisted by various people for various reasons. Apart from the lucky minority who were allotted burgess parts, and the relatively few who actually exercised their grazing-rights, there were the property-owners who feared a drop in their site-values or house-rents if a vast new area became free for building development. Lastly, there were the disinterested amenity-lovers who saw the beauty of the threatened scene but not the misery of the overcrowded courts and alleys.

The balance was tipped by the Municipal Corporations Act of

1835. Swift on the heels of Parliamentary Reform, this Act ended the domination of the closed corporations. All ratepayers were given a vote in the town's affairs. Now things began to move. The new Council was induced to promote private bills at Westminster to allow the enclosure first, in 1839, of a mere fifty-two acres, and in 1845 of their remaining lands.

Some of the 'vested interests' had also been legitimate interests. The tangle of individual rights was too complex to unravel here. Four hundred claimants demanded an allotment of the area to be enclosed, and it took three well-meaning commissioners until 1865 to stake out the claims. Those awarded plots were allowed to build on them very much as they pleased, subject to certain rules about the width of streets and alleys, the provision of yards or gardens, and the location of privies, but these rules were often ignored by speculative builders, especially in the Meadows, where some appalling new slums were quickly created and the danger of floods was not sufficiently considered. The commissioners kept the old pattern of the field-paths, which became the main streets. Otherwise, it was a typically Victorian 'free-for-all'. A fine opportunity for town-planning, on lines that could have been studied at Bath or Cheltenham, was sadly thrown away. The town did, however, reserve a proportion of open space that is still envied by other cities.

Land had been taken for the General Cemetery in the eighteen thirties, for the needs of the dead were more clamant than those of the living. Across the lane that became Waverley Street the twelve-acre Arboretum was laid out by Samuel Curtis, from London, in 1852. He provided curved walks, shrubberies, flower-beds, and refreshment-rooms inspired by the Crystal Palace that had set England gaping a year before. Military bands played there, there were quadrilles and fireworks sparkling and hissing through the dusk, but soon came complaints, not unknown today, that the place was 'merely a huge playground for young boys and girls'. As a boy myself I used to look from its heights over the tree-tops and the hidden street to the cemetery rising opposite, its tombstones masked by its own exuberant foliage. Was it so fanciful to think of it as a lonely wooded valley? Though the

Market Place lay within a ten-minute stroll, in historical terms I was gazing, had I but known it then, from the head of Wrendale into Larkdale.

Beyond the northward ridge the Forest's seventy-seven acres, already long dedicated to horse-racing, were formally reserved for other public recreations approved by the Victorians. There, on a legendary if not indisputably historical day in 1865, a number of gentlemen gathered for their customary game of 'shinney', a painfully expressive synonym for hockey. Someone experimentally tossed a larger ball among them. They dropped their sticks and began to kick it about. For the next year or two they alternated shinney with the ancient but as yet uncodified game of football. Then shinney was abandoned and they became known as the 'Nottingham Forest Football Club'. They are the third oldest League club, but Notts. County, the 'Magpies', founded in 1862 are the oldest of all.

Thin ribbons of open space preserved some of the footpaths that had once encircled the town. Sadly urbanized though they now are, and in some parts depressingly shabby, these tree-lined walks – Robin Hood's Chase, Corporation Oaks, Elm Avenue and Waterloo Promenade – can still be combined with the Forest and Arboretum to make, with several street-crossings and one rather longer transition, an otherwise continuous mile-and-a-half pedestrian-route through nineteenth-century Nottingham. It would scarcely stir Deering's botanical enthusiasm, but it was an imaginative effort in the eighteen fifties.

The commissioners also spared the steeply terraced gardens on the Hunger Hills, from which the stockingers and other part-time gardeners used to despatch vast quantities of roses to the markets of Liverpool and Manchester. It is claimed that they held England's first rose show in a nearby public-house in 1860. It was honoured by no less a personage than Dean Hole, who was so impressed that he went off to see the gardens for himself. Later, that doyen of rose-growers described 'these tiny allotments on sunny slopes just out of the town, separated by hedges and boards, in size about three to the rod, such an extent as a country squire in Lilliput might . . . devote to horticulture'. Six foot three himself, the Dean must have looked well cast for Gulliver, his shovel hat, long-skirted coat and gaiters adding the right suggestion of the eighteenth century as he picked his way along the hillside paths.

The Coppice became in 1859 a mental hospital. The rest of the old town lands was submerged by the tide of bricks and mortar which washed over them as fast as the new site-owners could get the word to go ahead. The pleasant vicinity of the Arboretum became a specially coveted residential area. It is said that one house in Addison Street was fully decorated and ready for occupation six weeks after the first brick was laid. Along with this hectic housing-development went an equivalent industrial expansion. Between 1851 and 1858 Nottingham acquired 128 new factories and 67 new warehouses. The tide of building soon washed up to the edges of the former perimeter-villages, which had already trebled their own populations in the preceding twenty years. Now they were true suburbs, and their status was formally recognized when the town boundaries were extended to include them in 1877. This sent the town's population figures leaping to 186,575 in 1881. By 1897, when Nottingham was raised to the dignity of 'city and county' during the Diamond Jubilee celebrations, the population was nearing a quarter of a million.

This local building-boom in the eighteen fifties, combined with the national trade-improvement, contributed to the fading away of the Chartist agitation. Militancy was diverted into more profitable channels. The *Nottingham Review* wrote of the building-workers in 1853: 'Strikes are frequently threatened but are generally prevented by employers conceding what is asked.'

The old Duke of Newcastle, who had provoked so much trouble, died in January 1851. The local architect, T. C. Hine, who had set his hallmark on many other parts of the town, had just been commissioned to prepare a scheme for a superior housing-estate to be laid out in the Castle Park, and the work now went rapidly ahead. Crescents and drives and circuses were planned with a symmetry impressive on paper but obscured in reality by the ups and downs of the terrain. Professor Chambers writes feelingly of the 'complexity of the road plan which seems expressly designed to prevent the visitor from reaching his destination until he is quite sure that his journey is really necessary'. Nor was the symmetry of the roads (all fittingly known by the innumerable family surnames or possessions of the Newcastles) matched by any congruence of architectural style. The new residents were quite free to express their own highly eclectic tastes and to blazon the size of their bank balances. The result, as Professor Wood neatly expressed it, represents the 'transition from disciplined Georgian to variegated villadom'.

The fire-blistered Castle, still roofless, looked down on all this. The Park, primly defended by gates and lodges, barred to outside traffic and screened from all disturbingly vulgar intrusion, was the symbol of the new order, a precinct of privilege. It was 'the thing' to live in the Park. Here gradually congregated the best people, the 'warm men' of industry, above all the lace kings. For this was pre-eminently the age of Nottingham lace.

The town had no age-old reputation for hand-made lace. Its industry developed from the adaptation of the stocking-frame by men like Heathcoat, John Leavers and Hooton Deverill, but it did not copy the organization of the hosiery trade. The latter was relatively conservative, slow to accept steam power and other technical change, inclined to carry on the 'outwork' system and a rigid class barrier between framework knitter and master hosier. The lace trade, by contrast, was a new forward-looking industry, uncluttered by traditional practices, owing its very existence to the inventive talents and enterprise of individual workmen, who, like Birkin, found no difficulty in crossing the dividing-line and becoming employers. Power-driven machines were welcome from the start, and by 1850 the factory system was general.

If the lace trade was born of the mechanical ingenuity of the Midland workman, its development into a world export business owed much to the German Jews who emigrated to Nottingham in this period. In particular, there was Lewis Heymann, the pioneer of the lace curtain, who came over from Mecklenburg-Schwerin in 1834 and went into partnership with Alexander from Ham-

burg. From Hamburg also came Jacob Weinberg in 1849.
Warburg, Jacoby, Stiebel and Goldschmidt were other names
that soon became potent not only in the business life of Nottingham but also in the fields of charity, culture and local affairs.
Their contribution should be remembered whenever the general
question of foreign immigration is discussed. As Roy Church
records, 'having quit the great commercial centres of Europe to
which Nottingham merchants regularly shipped lace and hosiery',
they 'brought . . . zeal and vision, capital and a willingness to
risk it, world-wide connections and commercial judgement, without which, it has been claimed, a great deal of Nottingham lace
would never have been called into existence'.

These Jews integrated closely with the townspeople. Many
joined in worship with the Unitarians at High Pavement. Heymann, who became Mayor in 1857, seems to have been a well-
loved figure. He could be seen every morning, walking across the
old Trent Bridge from Bridgford Hall, where he lived from about
1840, to his business in Stoney Street, where he stayed until
half-past six in the evening. When he was Mayor, he invited all
the senior students from the School of Art to his reception. Such
men as Heyman did much to temper the inbred philistinism of
the natives, but their devotion to culture and education (with its
consequent cost to the ratepayers) was not universally admired.
Witness the following Valentine publicly addressed to the Chairman of the Finance Committee in 1881:

> Now, Goldschmidt, since you have an Alderman been,
> You are the most extravagant we ever have seen;
> We wish you had remained in your own Fatherland,
> Ere you had steered us to an Educational Strand.

Nothing could have more distinctly underlined the town's need
for better schooling.

The Victorians had an inexhaustible passion for lace. Most of
the Queen's dresses were trimmed with it, and although hers came
from Honiton she undoubtedly stimulated a mass-demand which
only Nottingham could satisfy. Veils, caps, collars, frills, ruffles,
were all in fashion. A typical afternoon dress of 1884 had flounces
of black lace, a cascade of lace over the bustle, and a long *jabot*

of the same material down the bodice. One skirt might use eighty
yards of trimming. And even when the mistress of the house was
one vast froth of lace there remained the tall windows to curtain
and a host of other household uses.

Orders for Nottingham lace streamed in from Berlin and
Buenos Aires, Sydney and San Francisco, and the industry
flourished until the First World War. Its prosperity was expressed
in the portentous warehouses of the Lace Market which replaced
the elegant town houses of the Plumptres and other families. The
new buildings were themselves almost like mansions. A magnificent flight of steps usually led up to the front door and the
partners' offices, while the myriad lace girls (who became
legendary for their fresh beauty) streamed in and out through the
equivalent of the servants' entrance. The warehouses Hine built
for Birkin and Thomas Adams survive as memorials to the boom-
ing eighteen fifties.

Hours, wages and working-conditions, however they might
appal people today, showed a distinct improvement on those of a
few years earlier. Many of the employers were benevolent auto-
crats, deeply sincere within the limitations of their Victorian
philosophy. Adams, a devout Evangelical, provided his warehouse
with a chapel as well as a workers' dining-room, a separate tea-
room for the men, and washing facilities. Morning prayers were
held every day at eight, in the firm's time, and Adams always left
his house on Derby Road (where the name of Adams Hill commemorates him) early enough to be there himself. Outside his
own business he was an active but modest philanthropist, often
giving a small subscription in his own name to hide a much
larger anonymous one. He was particularly concerned with the
churches needed for the newly created parishes of the expanding
town, and helped to build six of them. When he died in 1873,
ten thousand people went to his funeral. With all due allowance
for the Victorians' love of such occasions, that must have meant
something.

Adams, who in any case had eight partners to win over, was
not unique. The firm of Copestake, Moore and Crampton also
began the day in their own works chapel. Lending libraries,

religious in flavour, were as common as canteens and wash-places. There were works outings, brass bands and benefit clubs. Where employers chiefly disagreed was on the need for legislation. Adams wanted hours fixed by law: he himself operated a nine-hour day. Heymann, his equal in philanthropy, voiced a view more typical of his age: 'All legislation with regard to the employment of labour is, I think, objectionable.'

Towards the end of the century other industries began to loom larger in the picture, fortunately for the town, since they were later able to offset the decline in lace. Bicycle-making was an obvious opportunity for the individual mechanic with ambition, the type of man whose father or grandfather would have struck out for himself in the early lace industry. By 1868 a blacksmith moulder named William Humber was building bicycles in Nottingham. Though he moved and set up elsewhere, he was not the only one: three other local mechanics took a small workroom in Raleigh Street, and by 1887 were employing a dozen men, with a modest total output of three machines a week. At this point chance took a hand. Frank Bowden was forced by ill-health to come home from Hong Kong. One specialist gave him three months to live, another told him to take up bicycling, the fashionable panacea of the moment. The first specialist was certainly wrong. On the assumption that the second had been right, a grateful and rejuvenated Bowden sought out the makers of his miraculous machine. He saw the shed in Raleigh Street and saw what could be done with adequate capital. So the great Raleigh cycle undertaking was born. Within a few years it was employing nearly a thousand hands in what was then the largest cycle-factory in the world, and indeed still is. There were, at the end of the century, another sixty-seven small-scale bicycle-makers in the town, but today Raleigh Industries alone remain. Even Humber's company, which he had moved to Coventry, is now merged in the group centred in the city where he began, and where now about eighty-five per cent of British pedal cycles are made.

John Player, a solicitor's son from Saffron Walden, was another newcomer to Nottingham who brought a wider vision to a small existing business. In 1823 William Wright had started a factory to produce shag and twist. Those were the days before packaged goods and brand names: the tobacconist, like the grocer, weighed and wrapped his customer's requirements. The idea of pre-packing was still in its infancy when Player bought the factory in 1877. He not only developed it but immediately registered his first trade-mark, a drawing of the Castle, so that his products should be instantly recognized on every counter. The bearded sailor and the lifebuoy came a few years later. It was typical of Player's confidence and foresight that he then planned a large new factory at Radford, far in excess of immediate needs, letting out two of its three blocks to lace manufacturers until his own business had expanded enough to use them. When he died, his two sons carried on. By 1898 they were employing over a thousand workers and had taken over the other blocks.

Pre-packing was also (along with cut prices) the foundation of Jesse Boot's early success in pharmacy. Born in 1850, the son of a Nottingham herbalist, he lost his father when he was ten and at thirteen had to leave the grammar school to help his mother run their small herbalist's shop round the corner in Goose Gate. At twenty-seven he had taken control and moved to a bigger shop in the same street. His window proclaimed his policy in big letters: 'Drugs and Proprietary Articles at Reduced Prices'. He used that window for single, eye-catching displays. Once, having bought up a quantity of sponges, he sent off two hundred sixpenny telegrams to potential customers, 'Visit our special display of sponges', and cleared his stock. One of his earliest gambles was to buy a whole ton of Epsom salts and sell it at a penny a pound, the price his rivals were charging for an ounce. From Boot's one could buy a neat one-pound packet of soft soap for twopence three farthings, while elsewhere it was usually fourpence, ladled messily out of a barrel and wrapped in newspaper. Needless to say, he met with every sort of opposition in the trade from slanderous whispers to legal action.

In 1885 his health broke down. He put up his business for sale and went to the Channel Islands for a holiday. There he met Florence Rowe and married her less than a year later. In the meantime, his health and zest restored, he went back to Notting-

ham and cancelled the offer of his business. Within three years he
had started the Boots Pure Drug Company to supply his growing
number of branches. His wife persuaded him to add scent, cos-
metics and other goods, and it was she who brought back from
America the idea of including a library.

From about 1900 Boot was progressively paralysed by rheuma-
toid arthritis. In *The Growing Boy* Cecil Roberts describes the
millionaire in his mansion in the Park, able only 'to insert a
twisted finger in a small loop in the lapel of his coat, by which
he summoned his secretary'. The business went on growing. Boot
lived on until 1931, becoming Lord Trent in 1929, soon after
George V's opening of the new university college buildings. His
disability prevented him from being present at the ceremony
which his tireless interest, and not just his money, had largely
made possible. D. H. Lawrence sneered at the occasion in what
his own biographer, Harry T. Moore, admits to be 'a mean little
poem'.

Though Boot and his wife were outstanding among the numerous
benefactors of what became a fully fledged university in 1948,
the dream dated right back to the eighteen seventies, a period of
various cultural projects in the city.

The Corporation had obtained a five-hundred-year lease of the
roofless Castle and was engaged in repairing it. In 1878 it was
opened by the Prince of Wales, later Edward VII, as the first
municipal art gallery and museum in the provinces. His markedly
unintellectual Royal Highness then made a plausible display of
pleasure that Nottingham should have 'taken the lead in carrying
out one of the principal objects entertained by the Prince Consort,
my lamented father, when he established the National Art
Museum at South Kensington. . . .' Today, to quote a recent
Times article, its 'splendid suite of galleries . . . contains a
fascinating miscellany' not only of pictures – Boningtons, Mor-
lands, Sandbys and the earliest known Charles Le Brun – but of
other exhibits. These range from the Bronze Age canoes and
medieval alabasters to a collection of old English silver, begun by
a local jeweller, Frederick Gibbs, in the eighteen sixties and

presented to the city by his two young great-granddaughters in 1968, a superb gesture since it was by then valued at a quarter of a million.

Simultaneously there were discussions proceeding about a Natural History Museum, a proper public library to replace the rooms of the old Artisans' Library in Thurland Street, taken over by the town in 1867, and some kind of building to serve as a centre for adult education, a need which was becoming obvious since the support given in Nottingham to the 'extension lectures' provided by Cambridge.

One autumn Sunday in 1874 a local solicitor, Richard Enfield, was walking with one of the visiting lecturers, and, pointing to an empty factory, suggested that it might make such a centre. The don, aware of the other schemes afoot, thought that it would be better if the Corporation could be brought in and persuaded to provide one big new building, combining museum, library and lecture-rooms. Out of that conversation the whole grand project was born.

In one respect it was revolutionary. The earlier redbrick universities had been endowed by rich individuals and voluntary public subscriptions. Nottingham Corporation had to be talked into assuming responsibility for something which *The Times* prophesied would eventually develop into a University of Nottingham.

The acrimonious Council debates may be imagined. The scales were tipped by an anonymous offer, probably from Louis Heymann's son, William, though the secret has been well kept, to give ten thousand pounds if the Corporation would pay the rest. The original estimate was for thirty-seven thousand, but in the end, as always happens, the Corporation had to find sixty-one. Some suggested that the buildings should be put up in the Castle grounds, but a site was chosen bordering Shakespeare Street and South Sherwood Street. The foundation stone was laid in 1877, Gladstone speaking lengthily at the ceremony and again at the luncheon which followed, and the building was opened four years later, in a midsummer drizzle, by Victoria's youngest son, the Duke of Albany. D. H. Lawrence, who became a student there in 1906, depicts in *The Rainbow* 'the big college built of stone, standing in the quiet street, with a rim of grass and limetrees all so peaceful' and comments that its imitation-Gothic architecture, though 'foolish', was at least 'different' and recalled 'the wondrous cloistral origin of education'.

Impressive the building might be, but in its first years it was run on a shoe-string. One reads with sympathy of Professor Blake who occupied the Chair of Natural Sciences, surely a swivel chair, since he was expected to teach geology, biology, physiology, botany and geography. Even so, he was asked to resign during an economy drive in 1887.

Of students at least there was no lack, hundreds from the start, many in the day-time (thanks to the admission of women) and still more at the evening classes. The original association with the Cambridge extension lectures diminished as these students found that they could study for London matriculation and even a London external degree. Three years after Prince Leopold's opening speech, the first B.A. was won, and three years later a woman graduated B.Sc. This relationship with London University was the basis of the College until its own charter enabled it to confer Nottingham degrees.

Meanwhile the town's schools were expanding. The Bluecoat School exchanged its picturesque but cramped building at Weekday Cross for a mock-Elizabethan one, designed by the indefatigable T. C. Hine and erected in 1853 a little way up the Mansfield Road, where the school remained until moving out to its present Aspley site in 1967. The grammar school, which had had rather more downs than ups in the preceding decades, escaped in 1868 from the overshadowing warehouses of the Lace Market to the airy ridge beyond the Arboretum, where it still stands. Simultaneously it changed its name to the Nottingham High School. High Pavement School remained in its original place until 1895, when it too moved north, beyond the Forest, moving again sixty years later to the Bestwood Estate on the city's expanding northern boundary.

All these three old foundations were fortunate in their headmasters. To the High School in 1885 came Dr James Gow, an outstanding classical scholar but also an administrator and a man of character, who inspired in many of his pupils (though not noticeably in D. H. Lawrence) the mingled awe and affection with which Arnold was remembered at Rugby. Even Lawrence, according to F. R. Leavis, 'had a better education, one better calculated to develop his genius for its most fruitful use, than any other he could have got.'

High Pavement had its William Hugh, who came in 1861 as a certificated teacher of twenty-six and stayed till he was seventy, doggedly raising the status of his school by uncompromising standards. He was an old-style dominie, a massive fifteen-stone figure in frock coat and white choker, a martinet with the then fashionable admiration for Germany, which he visited every year. No one dared to knock at his study-door before eleven in the morning. He was reading the *Daily Telegraph*, secure in the knowledge that in his school nothing would dare to go wrong. Headmasters were headmasters in those days. Yet the terrifying giant could unbend and become the life and soul of the juniors' Christmas party, when the small boys arrived in cabs, fidgety in their stiff collars, white bow ties and white cotton gloves, and were taught to partner the girls whose hair they had pulled the day before and would pull again next term.

In the same year that Hugh took over High Pavement, John Williamson Curtin became head of the Bluecoat School, and outdid even Hugh in length of service, staying until his death in 1908 at the age of seventy-five. Under him, as indeed in most Victorian schools, morals and manners were given unremitting attention, but he must have been equally effective in knocking knowledge into the heads of his pupils. One of the 1889 vintage later recalled: 'As an indication of the zeal shown in Geography, I remember naming some thirty tributaries of the Amazon on one occasion.'

These were the great pioneering days of girls' education. Thanks to the enthusiasm of the then Vicar of St Mary's and other leading townspeople, Nottingham Girls' High School was founded in 1875, sixth of the thirty-eight schools started by the Girls' Public Day School Company (now Trust) in the space of only twenty years. Soon outgrowing its first home, near the present Playhouse, the school moved to a house in Arboretum Street originally built for a lace manufacturer, whose business interests are still reflected in the pattern of the front railings. The boys' High School was already established at the far end of the same street, a juxtaposition which has sometimes confused more than the postmen. In that golden dawn of feminine emancipation the zealots were determined that their girls should be denied no opportunity open to their brothers. On Mondays, Tuesdays and Thursdays the high-school girls hitched up their ample skirts and played football instead of tennis.

There were, of course, many other schools in the town. There were genteel private establishments like the Standard Hill Academy, which flourished especially during those periods when the grammar school was in decline. And, before the setting up of the Board schools under the 1870 Act, soon followed by compulsory attendance, roughly half of the working-class children were getting the rudiments of an education in fifty-eight schools run by the Church of England, the Nonconformist chapels or the Roman Catholics. Then, and thereafter, Nottingham followed the same course of development as the rest of England.

One of the architects of that development was a hosiery manufacturer, who, unlike the other local philanthropists, sought wider scope by entering national politics. Anthony John Mundella was the son of an Italian exile who had married a Leicester girl. Mundella himself came to Nottingham as a young man and was soon director of the Nottingham Manufacturing Company. He was a popular and progressive employer and got on well with the trade unions. He was specially interested in education, and, having studied the German and Swiss systems, championed the idea of compulsory school-attendance, which, as a Liberal M.P. and a member of Gladstone's government, he helped to put on the statute book. In 1899, two years after his death, his name was appropriately commemorated by the opening of Mundella School, which one of is earliest pupils, Cecil Roberts, remembers as 'bright and airy, terracotta in hue, set in the centre of playing fields bordered by the River Trent'.

Early in 1883 J. M. Barrie arrived in Nottingham to work as a
young leader-writer on the *Journal* as a plaque on its old offices
in Pelham Street commemorates. The town then had two morning
papers, now amalgamated, the *Journal's* Conservative rival being
the *Guardian*, originally a weekly started in 1846 by a group of
county gentlemen with a clergyman as editor. Barrie stayed
nearly two years, and used his experiences in an early novel,
When A Man's Single, but he gave his story a different setting
and has really left nothing of special local interest. 'Nottingham',
wrote his biographer, J. A. Hammerton, 'was never to be more
to him than a stage on the road south.'

It was different with D. H. Lawrence, Cecil Roberts and Dame
Laura Knight, all born in the district about that period. Their
novels and autobiographies are rich in verbal vignettes of Nottingham at the close of the century. 'The town itself would have
been fine to paint,' recalls Laura Knight. 'The market, the
Saturday crowds. . . .' But a certain shyness deterred her from
taking her sketch-book into a place where she was known.
Lawrence, in *The White Peacock*, makes us smell that market,
'the mingled scent of fruit, oranges, and small apricots, and pears
piled in their vividly-coloured sections on the stalls'. Roberts
evokes the 'earthy tang' of the vegetables and the 'leathery
odours' of the shoes. His 'first contact with anything Italian' was
his purchase of halfpenny ice-cream cornets from the generous
Mrs Capocci with her dark skin, glittering earrings and multi-
coloured shawl.

Elsewhere these writers offer glimpses of the Goose Fair, which
first stirred Laura Knight's life-long interest in painting acrobats
and other show people; the race-meetings still held on the Forest;
the banjo-noisy steamers puffing down the Trent to the Colwick
pleasure-gardens and the Hyson Green steam tram 'with a long
black funnel belching black smoke'; Vesta Tilley at the Empire
music-hall and the Carl Rosa in *Carmen* at the Theatre Royal
next door, the dress-circle patrons 'like giddy dukes' in their
evening formality. And there are quieter scenes. In *Sons and
Lovers* Paul and his mother pause in Carrington Street 'to hang
over the parapet and look at the barges on the canal below. "It's

just like Venice," he said, seeing the sunshine on the water that lay between high factory walls.' Leaning on another parapet, at the Castle, he tells Clara Dawes: 'The town's all right, it's only temporary. This is the crude, clumsy makeshift we've practised on, till we find out what the idea is. The town will come all right.' They have walked up from the surgical factory in Castle Gate (where Lawrence himself worked for a time) up the 'gloomy and old-fashioned' street with its 'low dark shops and dark green house-doors with brass knockers, and yellow-ochred doorsteps projecting on to the pavement'. On another occasion they walk along 'the elm-tree colonnade' of Clifton Grove, beloved by generations of Nottingham people for picnics and courtship. They look down on 'the full, soft-sliding Trent' and the 'water-meadows dotted with small cattle', and Paul remarks: 'It has scarcely altered since little Kirke White used to come.'

Other things were altering fast, but it would be unreasonable to seek a chronicle of municipal progress in the pages of these highly subjective writers.

While the town had been spreading outwards there had been a vast amount of demolition and reconstruction in the centre. For centuries the Market Place had been approached by the narrow lanes that had served in Robin Hood's time. In 1865 Sheep Lane was widened and renamed Market Street, and its vista closed at the top end by the colonnaded façade of the new Theatre Royal, itself replacing the decayed little building in the Lace Market. Within the space of a few years the main arteries of the town-centre were transformed, sometimes a new one (like Albert Street) being driven through the labyrinth. The destruction (some inevitable, some desirable, some neither) was followed by an efflorescence of ornate Victorian architecture in various styles, which changed forever the face of Long Row and the other shopping-thoroughfares. Especially individual and flamboyant was the work of Watson Fothergill, born in 1814 as Fothergill Watson, whose still extant offices in George Street give a fair sample of his ebullient taste. But there is no need to walk so far – his work can be seen in the new frontage he clapped onto the much older Black Boy Hotel, and in Jessop's store, and in the

Westminster Bank building which stands on the site of Thurland Hall.

Despite all this redevelopment the town was still full of old gabled houses. Anne Gilbert, in her *Recollections of Old Nottingham*, mentions a 'lovely specimen of mediæval architecture' in St Peter's Gate, 'an overhanging house whose plaster panels were adorned with an exquisitely beautiful design', which caused Ruskin to spend a night at the George Hotel 'in order to rise very early and make a sketch of it ere the world was stirring'.

The extension of the boundaries was quickly followed in the early eighteen eighties by the building of the 'boulevards', straight, wide and tree-lined, but without any of the pavement cafés or wicked continental gaieties which the name suggests. With the Mansfield Road as a fourth side the Gregory, Radford, Lenton and Castle boulevards almost completed a rough square. These new roads totalled three and a quarter miles, and represented, in the words of Chambers, 'a most interesting piece of town-planning, carried out by the officers of the Corporation in the teeth of opposition from wise-acres who thought a sixty-foot road a waste of valuable land'.

Heading these officers was a remarkable Town Clerk, Samuel George Johnson. From 1815 to 1870 the town had been well enough served by the Enfield family in a part-time capacity, but the growing complexity of local government demanded the exclusive attention of a first-class man. Johnson was brought in from outside Nottingham, but he gave the town brilliant and unstinted service. A strong character, he would stand up boldly against unwarranted interference from Whitehall, but he preferred the diplomatic method. Once, in a Council debate, an irate councillor accused him of being two-faced. 'Nay,' said Johnson with a smile, looking round the assembly he was trying to coax into the right decision, 'I am sixty-faced.' Although, or perhaps because, he was a lawyer, he knew when to ignore the letter of a regulation. Faced with a smallpox epidemic in the second year of his appointment, he sanctioned the vaccination of four thousand people without legal authority. 'We could not wait while the people were dying', he said, 'for the Board of Guardians to act.'

The expanding town created fresh transport needs and traffic problems. The Long Row cab rank that had sufficed in 1845 could not cope with the lengthening journeys and more numerous passengers. By 1853 there were horse-omnibuses to Arnold and Beeston. Horse-trams started in 1874 and, apart from the messy experiment with steam recalled by Laura Knight, continued until electrification began in 1901. This last development was bad luck for the short-lived Nottingham Suburban Railway Company, formed in 1886 to serve places like Mapperley, Sherwood and Daybrook, glimpses of whose already moribund cuttings and tunnels used to mystify me in the nineteen twenties.

Long-distance rail communications were improving. At the end of Victoria's reign the Great Central built a new main line through the city from north to south, providing another direct route to London to compete with the Midland one so belatedly inaugurated in 1880. The Central line offered quite a challenge to the engineers. Long tunnels and cuttings had to be cut through the sandstone hills from New Basford to beyond the Lace Market. In the old parts of the town the excavators found themselves so close to the foundations of the buildings that some had to be underpinned with timber. Once the men found themselves in the basement of a bank in Victoria Street, close to the safe. On another occasion they emerged into the rock cellars of the Old Cross Keys in Byard Lane, pausing to refresh themselves liberally before reporting their arrival. At the Dog and Partridge they were unlucky. There seemed to be only herb and ginger beers. Despite all these distractions the work was finished, the Victoria Station raised its proud clock-tower against the sky, and the London expresses roared through the new tunnels into the twentieth century. Who could have foreseen, on that day of celebrations, that long before the new century was over they would, in another sense, have reached the end of the line?

It was a hard-working, hard-playing town.

The factories had begun the practice of a Saturday half-day as early as about 1861. The shop-assistants had to wait another twenty years before early closing on Thursdays became the rule.

On Saturday night and Christmas Eve the Market Place did a brisk trade until a late hour. The masters kept at it no less than the men. It was their sons, perhaps, who were given a little more latitude – it is noticeable that what are now the professional football clubs, supported by the masses, were middle-class amateur organizations in their early days.

More and more, as time passed, the river and its immediate neighbourhood drew together the various sporting activities. The famous Trent Bridge cricket ground had been laid out as early as 1838 by a notable cricketer, William Clarke, who had married the landlady of the adjacent inn. Forest, after playing in various places, including two years on the said cricket ground, finally established themselves on their present site in 1898, the year in which they won the F.A. Cup for the first time. Notts. County, who themselves had carried off the Cup in 1894, did not go to their present ground at Meadow Lane, on the north side of the river, until 1910. When the horse-races on the Forest ceased after more than two centuries, a course was laid out at Colwick, just down-stream from Trent Bridge, in 1892. Other sports by their very nature developed round the river. Regattas began soon after the founding of the Nottingham Trent Aquatic Club in 1845. The various rowing-clubs whose names are familiar in pro-grammes all over the country were founded from 1862 onwards. The Nottingham Swimming Club was formed in 1880, though bathing in the Trent had been a traditional pleasure for centuries, and proper changing-rooms with a paid attendant had been provided in 1857. A sailing-club started in 1887. Nottingham was fortunate among industrial cities in keeping the riverside relatively unbuilt on and unspoilt: the lie of the land and the postponement of enclosures preserved the banks of the Trent until their amenities were appreciated. A stretch of those banks became a promenade for the citizens with the opening of the Victoria Embankment in 1901. A new Trent Bridge was opened in 1871, but even its forty-foot width had to be doubled in the nineteen twenties.

There was no less variety of indoor amusement in the town. There was the Theatre Royal, seating 2200 people, at whose opening night the future Dame Madge Kendal had led the audience in 'God Save the Queen', and in the nineties came the Grand Theatre, famous for its melodramas, at Hyson Green. There were several music-halls of robust Victorian style, in which none the less, we are assured, 'order and decorum' were 'most rigidly enforced'. At one time or another the people of Victorian Nottingham were able to see most of the great stage performers from Little Tich to Henry Irving, while at the Mechanics Institution they could hear Jenny Lind sing, Fanny Kemble read Shakespeare, and Dickens read Dickens.

CHAPTER EIGHTEEN

The Twentieth Century

RECENT history is notoriously hard to write.

There is too much material. Every omission affronts someone. The pediment of Nottingham's Council House is, to quote an official description, 'elaborately ornamented with figures in high relief, representing the activities of the Council', but such activities offer a writer only limited inspiration. Each century produces its own good stories and eccentric characters, but the nearer he gets to his own time the more careful he must be in using them. With relief he turns back to the authors and artists. They at least have left uninhibited records of themselves and the town they knew.

The Edwardian era found Harold and Laura Knight struggling to establish themselves as painters, Lawrence starting as a clerk at Haywood's surgical-appliance factory in Castle Gate, Roberts donning the maroon gold-circled cap of Mundella School, and John Drinkwater working as an insurance company's office-boy, so poor that he 'used to buy rotten fruit in the Market Place' to eke out his threepenny lunch.

Harold Knight's solid reputation as a portraitist has been overshadowed by his wife's more varied and popular work. He was at the High School when she was at Brincliffe on the other side of the playground wall, but they met first at the School of Art. In *The Magic of a Line* Dame Laura recaptured, seventy years later, the atmosphere of those days when ladies were barred from the life-class if a nude model was provided. Harold was the outstanding student, winning numerous national awards at South Kensington. 'Whenever possible,' she recalled, 'I fixed my easel close to his.' Their appreciation was mutual and not confined to each other's artistic talent.

When it came to earning a livelihood, they met the usual obstacles. Harold was first off the mark, getting a few portrait commissions from local worthies. In 1903 they married and 'converted a top office on the South Parade into a studio'. Though they had already fallen in love with the Yorkshire coast, they tried to form a connection in their own city, but without success. 'Harold and I left Nottingham for the last time with only fifteen pounds in our pockets. "Shaking the dust from our feet," we exclaimed.' It is hard to say how much better they would have fared had they been starting now. Certainly the Midland Group of Artists, with their headquarters across the street from the Playhouse, represent a lively and forward-looking movement, and the University, besides putting on regular shows in its own gallery, provides a fellowship for a practising artist. Whether there are any more commissions and sales, either to individuals or to institutions, is another matter.

No amount of early appreciation would ever have moulded Lawrence into the image of a respected 'local author'. Catherine Carswell wrote in *The Savage Pilgrimage*: 'Nobody who ever heard him describe the scenes and persons of his boyhood, or watched him recreate with uncanny mimicry the talk, the movements, and the eccentricities of the men and women among whom he grew up, can doubt, but that Lawrence, if he had liked, might have been a new kind of Dickens of the Midlands.' He did not like. And he cooked his goose, so far as Nottingham was concerned, on that spring day in 1912 when he ran away with Professor Weekley's wife.

His short spell of clerking had been followed by teaching and a course at the University College, leading in 1908 to a qualified post in Croydon. When he went south, 'he looked like a man under sentence of exile', recalled Jessie Chambers, the original of 'Miriam' in *Sons and Lovers*. She was his confidante in those days. They often went to the Theatre Royal, where Sarah Bernhardt's electrifying performance in *La Dame aux Camélias* so unnerved him that he rushed out, afraid, he wrote afterwards to the long-suffering Jessie, lest one day he might, like Armand in the play, 'become enslaved by a woman'.

The White Peacock, full of Nottingham references, came out in 1911. He had already written the first draft of *Sons and Lovers*. His teaching career ceased abruptly with his illness that November. Seeking lighter work, perhaps as a language instructor in a German university, he turned to his former French professor, Ernest Weekley, who had once himself held such a post and had married a German girl. Weekley, a kindly man later famous as an etymologist, invited him to lunch.

The Weekleys lived in Victoria Crescent, between Mapperley and Sherwood. In *The Intelligent Heart* Harry T. Moore has described the fateful meeting between the 'magnificent blonde tall animal, with high cheekbones and green "Tartar" eyes flecked with brown', and her husband's ex-student, whom she herself remembered afterwards as 'a long thin figure' with 'quick, straight legs' and 'light, sure movements'. They fascinated each other. Frieda practically ignored her husband's presence. Lawrence stayed till dusk, talking volubly, then started his eight-mile walk through the countryside to Eastwood. His subsequent letter was no conventional 'thank-you' for the lunch, but a declaration that she was the most wonderful woman in England.

In the next few weeks they met several times. There was a walk with two of her children in Derbyshire, there was a Sunday without her husband at Victoria Crescent. Lawrence declined her invitation to stay the night, but within a month of that first inflammatory encounter they were sitting, 'full of hope and agony', on the deck of a steamer bound for Germany. Weekley, abandoned with three young children, behaved with dignity. It was partly his English scholar-and-gentleman demeanour that had driven the 'magnificent blonde animal' to flight. Exactly forty years later he wrote a dry objective answer to Harry Moore's inquiries about his pupil. Lawrence, he said, 'was not a degree student at Nottingham and what work he did in French was of a fairly elementary kind'.

Cecil Roberts, with a genteeler background, knew more

poverty. In 1907, at fifteen, he became a Corporation clerk in the Markets and Fairs Department at eight shillings a week. He worked in a cubby-hole under the old Exchange, cut off from daylight and fresh air, with 'smells from the butchers' stalls in the bloody Shambles, from a penny public lavatory and also from the open stalls . . . of plucked poultry and cooped hens.' Twenty years later, when the whole insanitary rabbit-warren was swept away, he was a best-selling novelist, advancing with sure step to an armchair in the Athenaeum and a villa in Italy. And almost another forty years on, in 1965, I saw him receive the freedom of the city in the Council House built over the very spot where once he had been a 'preposterous office boy'. His delight in the coincidence was evident – and infectious.

Herein lies another problem of writing recent history. First-hand memories mingle with research. It becomes harder to distinguish the important from the personal. My own first dateable memory is of the visit of George V and Queen Mary in June 1914, seen from a high window in Lister Gate. But I recall only the splendour of the mounted policemen, and how my uncle, all too soon to be in France with the Royal Horse Artillery, injured his hand when firing the royal salute from the Castle. I did not feel I had really seen their Majesties until fourteen years later in Woodthorpe Park, when the bearded King, in grey frock-coat and buttonhole, proclaimed in his guttural voice that henceforth the Mayor of Nottingham would be a *Lord* Mayor.

Up to 1914, it has been said, English history was rather an extension of the Victorian era than the opening of a new one. This applies to Nottingham. There were superficial changes that caused a flutter at the time. The Midland Station rose in 1903 to rival the Great Central's Victoria, the new trams went jangling up and down more of the city's hills, taxis appeared in the Market Place to dismay the cabbies, and the first films began to flicker in the 'picture palaces'. Deeper changes might be coming – Labour won two council seats in 1908 and the Suffragettes burnt down the Boat Club in 1913 – but few even dimly foresaw the transformed society that was on its way. The High School governors seemed boldly original in choosing a scientist, Dr G. S. Turpin, to succeed Gow, an appointment for a long time almost unique among schools represented on the Headmasters' Conference.

Nottingham was still primarily the city of lace. At its 1911 peak, the trade employed about 22,000 people, full time, half the national total. The 1914 war struck that trade not, strictly speaking, a 'mortal' blow (since it is still alive and even healthy, employing about 5000) but one that toppled it for ever from its dominant position. Apart from the general dislocation of world markets affecting all business, there had been a revolution in public taste, a revulsion against fussy ornament in every form, the nineteen twenties' passion for the plain. Yet, wrote Professor F. A. Wells in 1966, 'it would be wrong to think of it as a depressed industry. On its reduced scale it is fairly prosperous and whenever fashion turns towards lace the limits of capacity are soon reached.' A research centre has been established, and Nottingham (which once strove vainly to prevent foreign rivals from getting hold of its wonderful machines) is now not too proud to study improvements devised abroad.

The city's experience of the First World War was much like any other town's. Men – and horses – departed, Belgian refugees arrived. Khaki was everywhere, then garish hospital blue. Zeppelins came in 1916. We used to file down to the candle-lit cellar and sit there till the 'All Clear'. The damage done by the Germans was nothing compared with that of the 1918 explosion at the Chilwell Ordnance Factory, when about a hundred and thirty munition-workers were killed. It was a fine evening. I was playing outside when I heard the crash four miles away behind the hill. I ran indoors to tell my mother there was going to be a thunderstorm.

In France and on other fronts the Nottingham men fought and died with the rest of their generation. They are commemorated by Wallis Gordon's 'belatedly classical triumphal arch', as Pevsner calls it, in the Victoria Embankment gardens. But it was a less formal riverside the men in the trenches remembered, one where some at least of the old wild flowers had survived into

Cecil Howitt's Council House, which replaced the dilapidated Georgian Exchange in 1929. His Times *obituary (1968) called it 'probably still the finest municipal building outside London' – but Pevsner disliked its 'neo-Baroque display'.*

Trent Bridge. Few industrial cities have treated their river so well. Nottingham's riverside is largely unbuilt on, a place where one can still stroll for pleasure or take a boat out.

Jesse Boot's dream of a Nottingham University began to take shape when this first building was opened by George V in 1928. A real 'campus university', rurally sited three miles from the city centre, it is also much used for conferences.

Peter Moro's Playhouse – an exciting and much admired piece of theatrical architecture – a place equally famous for artistic achievement and local controversy.

the twentieth century. One soldier in Flanders poured his nostalgia into verse:

> Out here the dogs of war run loose,
> Their whipper-in is Death;
> Across the spoilt and battered fields
> We hear their sobbing breath.
> The fields where grew the waving corn
> Are heavy with our dead;
> Yet still the fields at home are green
> And I have heard it said,
> > There are crocuses at Nottingham,
> > Wild crocuses at Nottingham,
> > Blue crocuses at Nottingham,
> > Though here the earth is red.

In the Castle grounds there is a statue of the local air-ace, Albert Ball. He shot down more than forty enemy pilots, but hated 'this beastly killing' and confessed to his father that he was 'beginning to feel like a murderer'. He was killed himself at twenty, and a V.C. was added to the glittering heap of Allied decorations already won.

The war ended. Nottingham shared the general boom and slump, but, not depending on a single industry, never knew the despair of Jarrow or the cotton-towns. The lace trade was halved and went on diminishing, despite publicity campaigns and protective tariffs, but there was a new demand for hosiery and ready-made clothes. Apart from the famous trio of drugs, bicycles and tobacco, there was a healthy diversification of manufactures. Today there are engineering firms producing totalizators, telephones, calculating-machines – everything from a heavy press to a precision instrument, including lace-making machinery. You may build your house with Nottingham bricks or Nottingham prefabricated units, and furnish it with Nottingham furniture. Your daughter's ballet tights and your son's cricket bat may both have been made in the city.

Between the wars, however, there was serious unemployment. When the High School wanted a new caretaker in 1935, there were 1475 applicants. In the nineteen twenties my mother's advertisement for a maid brought such a stream of girls that she had to interview some in one room while my aunt dealt simultaneously with the overflow in another.

These economic conditions were reflected in strikes and election-contests. If not quite Byron's 'political pandemonium', the town was lively enough in the era of Stanley Baldwin and Ramsay MacDonald. Meetings in the Market Place went on to a late hour, and, when the platforms and banners were folded away, a vociferous residue continued the debate indefinitely. As a schoolboy I was often one of them. I am glad to know that Nottingham's own version of 'Speakers' Corner' flourishes to this day.

In 1926 the General Strike brought back a whiff, however faint, of the old Chartist atmosphere. The locked-out miners crowded in from the collieries round the city's edge. There were only minor disorders, but the lack of newspapers magnified every rumour. We crouched with our headphones, twiddling the cat's-whisker of our crystal-sets to miss none of the interminable wireless bulletins. High drama alternated with low comedy. All rifle bolts were withdrawn from our school armoury, and we were told not to come in our cadet uniforms, lest we be mistaken for 'the military' and assaulted. Masters, armleted as special constables, took over traffic duty at complicated intersections like the approaches to Trent Bridge, where they were embarrassed by the unnecessary passing and repassing of their grinning pupils on bicycles. But the crisis passed, and the ten days had not shaken Nottingham, much less the world.

The Council in those years notched up a fair record of social progress, especially in housing. Its earliest estates, Professor K. C. Edwards told the British Association in 1966, 'set an example to other local authorities in lay-out and in the design and quality of dwellings.' The ideal then was the garden suburb. No one foresaw the day when gardening would have to compete with non-stop television, and when the Englishman, if outdoors at all, would prefer the endless tinkering and titivation of his car to the clipping of his privet.

One could still be prodigal with land. In 1924 the Corporation made a brilliant bargain, picking up Wollaton Hall and its deer-park for £200,000. The money was soon recovered by selling off a relatively small area for private building. The ratepayers gained, free of cost, a ninety-acre site for their own housing-estate, to-gether with the land needed to lay out Middleton Boulevard, Willoughby's Elizabethan mansion for a Natural History Museum, and a residue of several hundred acres over which deer and visitors could roam at will. Seven years afterwards, New-stead Abbey was bought and given to the city by Sir Julien Cahn. Lying further out, this estate was kept unaltered, the house becoming a Byron shrine full of manuscripts, pictures and relics, while the 'lucid lake', woods and cascades described in *Don Juan* can be appreciated by even the least literate.

Both before and after the Second World War there were boun-dary extensions. Today the population is well over three hundred thousand. The whole conurbation, with adjacent areas such as West Bridgford, makes up what is effectively one community of half-a-million. In its housing-programmes the city has learnt the hard truth that one sometimes has to run fast even to stay where one is. Populations grow, standards rise, and as new estates blossom on the outskirts the central areas decay. For half-a-century the councillors have been preoccupied with the problem. They must often have felt as if they were pouring water into a colander.

There was slum-clearance in late Victorian days, when the unspeakable 'Rookeries' were demolished in the Parliament Street area. There was extensive clearance between the wars. But all the time many of the houses so joyfully spawned in the eighteen fifties were degenerating into the slums of the nineteen fifties.

Such was St Ann's Ward. James I had ridden through green fields to drink the water, and a good deal else, at St Ann's Well. Now, according to a study group whose report was published by the University in 1967, the district was a grey depressing zone of cobbled streets, collapsing walls and tottering chimney-stacks. Barely half the houses had hot water, only one in ten an indoor lavatory. Many children came to school without breakfast, dirty and badly clothed. This neighbourhood had a large proportion of the city's coloured immigrants and was the scene, in 1958, of an alarming but isolated outbreak of racial violence. In general Nottingham has a good record for integration. The study group reported that 'the coloured children, particularly the Jamaicans, were often as well if not better dressed and clothed, and as clean if not cleaner, than their English counterparts'.

Girding at councillors is a favourite British sport, equalled only by that of satirizing 'do-gooders', as if nowadays to do good had somehow become reprehensible. It is a pity that more of the cynics have not walked the mean streets, taught in the schools, and sat round committee-tables discovering just how intractable the problems are. On one occasion at least, when the Nottingham councillors tried to accelerate the removal of this notorious St Ann's slum by cutting the red tape, their initiative was frustrated by Whitehall's insistence that all the usual procedures must be observed.

While the estates of the nineteen twenties spread through the suburbs, in the centre the Council was planning its own new House and arousing fevered controversy.

For two centuries the Exchange had presented its plain early Georgian frontage to the Market Place. Its architectural qualities were not much appreciated, its practical convenience was slight. Behind and beneath it, the stinking Shambles required a hot-water supply to keep them even tolerably clean, and that hot water cost almost as much as the rent the butchers paid.

One thing led to another. It was agreed, the Shambles must go. In that case, why not a wholesale redevelopment, with a worthy town hall backed by high-class shops and offices? And, if the Shambles were unacceptable, what of the foodstuffs exposed to flies and dust in the open market? And if the stalls went elsewhere, under cover, and an ornamental square was substituted, how could Goose Fair continue on its ancient site?

Thus the town centre was to lose, at one blow, its hitherto little-regarded Georgian Exchange, its picturesque market and its immemorial carnival. Once more Nottingham rang with protest, but sentiment fought a losing battle against considerations of hygiene and traffic circulation. After 1927 the Fair moved out to its present site on the Forest, where it no longer paralysed the normal life of the city. The rows of stalls vanished from the cobbled Market Place, which was transformed with grass and trees and flower-beds, subterranean lavatories and a processional way leading up to the new Council House, opened by the then Prince of Wales on 22 May 1929.

This building was to some eyes impressive, to others pretentious. 'Neo-Baroque display,' Pevsner called it. Yet in 1968 the *Times* obituary of its architect, the Nottingham-born Cecil Howitt, thought it 'probably still the finest municipal building outside London'. The Corporation certainly did not ignore local talent: the figures on the front were modelled by Joseph Else, the art-school principal, and various former students were responsible for the statues at the base of the dome, while Denholm Davis painted the historical frescoes in the shopping-arcade. The site was awkward for so symmetrical a building – it was impossible to align the processional approach with it, and from some aspects the high dome on its Ionic columns gives the illusion of being off-centre.

Even while this controversial construction was in progress, the nucleus of the present university was rising on a grassy ridge above the lake at Highfields. That estate, once the home of the cultivated Lowes, had been bought by Sir Jesse Boot with the idea of laying out a model industrial town like Port Sunlight. Then he thought of making it a public park. Meanwhile, he had become interested in the campaign to develop the University College. 'From all I hear,' he wrote, 'the university extension movement seems to be making but little progress. I do not like to think that my native city should fall in any way short of other large towns.' He sent £50,000, then a still larger cheque and the offer of the riverside site where now the War Memorial stands. Finally, on one of his periodical visits from his retirement in the Channel Islands, the crippled millionaire took a drive to view Highfields again. Someone remarked, what a good site for the university. With characteristic decisiveness, Boot began practical discussions that same afternoon. Morley Horder's simple grey building with its slender tower was opened by George V in 1928. But charters were not then handed out as liberally as in more recent times, and it took the College another twenty years to earn independent university status. Many additional blocks and halls of residence have since risen on what is truly, in the American sense, a campus. Appropriately enough, the institution Boot endowed includes a widely known pharmacy department, and one of the latest developments is a medical school, to be linked with the first new teaching hospital planned in Britain for a generation.

During this period the High School has also seen vast changes. Its Victorian battlements still stand out against the northern sky, but a long process of expansion started in 1932 when the school found its own benefactor in another local manufacturer, J. D. Player, an Old Boy and a governor. After the interruption of the war, a second building-programme was financed by a special appeal to mark the 450th anniversary in 1963. The simple T-shaped building of my youth is now a complex of quadrangles, archways and corridors, bewildering to an Old Boy forty years on, especially when revisiting the place on a festive occasion.

Much of this transformation was accomplished during the long régime of C. L. Reynolds, from 1925 to 1953. Shy, stern, awkward but essentially kindly, he came from teaching at Dartmouth and Rugby, which many feared was not the best experience for running a day school. He had a horror of what he termed 'calf-love' and 'pavement love-making', though the phenomena referred to were innocent enough. A boy, he decreed, must not walk up Waverley Street with a pupil of the adjacent Girls' High School, even though she were his sister: the censorious world could not *know* she was his sister. Yet Reynolds could mellow and move with the times. Twenty years later he was permitting and indeed encouraging inter-school activities, and when he retired the numerous presentations included one from the girls whose predecessors he had once eyed with such apprehension.

Since 1917 the school had received a direct grant from Whitehall. By 1945, though the comprehensive-versus-grammar controversy had not started, serious problems loomed ahead. The governers had to make a quick decision. Should they keep the grant and sacrifice future freedom, or renounce public money and 'go independent', relying on fees and endowments to cover the formidable cost of modern education? With only one dissentient they voted for the second course, and Nottingham acquired one of the very few independent day public schools in the country. It was a gamble, so far justified. In many minds 'public school' is equated with 'boarding school', and parents had to pay substantial fees without getting a coveted social label for their sons in return. Such a school could only survive by demonstrating that its education was worth the money. Fortunately, its academic standing was high and went on rising under the next headmaster, K. R. Imeson. 'Nottingham H. S. surges to the top,' proclaimed a *Times* headline in 1968, when the 'league table', based on the ratio between Sixth Form numbers and open awards at Oxford and Cambridge, showed the High School first in England, leading Christ's Hospital and St Paul's.

Agnes Mellers' foundation was not the only one to progress. Both the Bluecoat School and its one-time denominational rival, High Pavement, developed out of recognition. For eight dynamic years, from 1920, High Pavement was built up by Dr H. J. Spenser, a former High School boy and Cambridge Double First, who had returned to Nottingham after being Rector of Glasgow High School and head of University College School. His successor, G. J. R. Potter, a scientist from Oundle, completed High Pavement's transformation into a grammar school with a nation-wide reputation. In 1931 the girls were hived off to form the Manning School.

Mundella meantime achieved grammar-school status and at Bulwell, in 1929, the County established the Henry Mellish, also now well known in the academic world. Just outside the southern boundary, but essentially part of 'Greater' Nottingham, the West Bridgford Grammar School acquired a thrustful neighbour in the Becket School, which in the aforementioned 'league table' was placed fifth-equal, with an Oxbridge success-ratio ahead of Dulwich and Winchester. The city itself built new grammar schools, soon after the Second World War, at Forest Fields, Bilborough and Clifton Hall.

The educational development of widest interest, though, after the University itself, was the creation of the College of Technology, whose towering mass in Burton Street is a landmark no one can miss. It started in 1945 with nearly two thousand students, taking over the technical classes long provided in Shakespeare Street near by, and the first instalment of the present massive buildings was opened by Princess Alexandra in 1958. Within a few more years the numbers had risen to seven thousand, many students coming from far outside the region and a good proportion working for university degrees.

On the opposite street-corner from where the College of Technology now rises there stood in my childhood a shabby little cinema known as Pringle's Picture House. Here in 1948 the Playhouse was started by a band of enthusiasts.

There had always been the Theatre Royal, a plush-and-gilt staging-post for the Number One tours in the golden age when no star was too bright to shine upon the provinces. In the nineteen twenties it would be packed for Martin Harvey, Frank Benson, Matheson Lang, Godfrey Tearle, Esmé Percy (with a different Shaw each night and the full version of *Man and Superman* on Friday) and anything musical from *Rose Marie* to the Carl Rosa in *The Valkyrie*. But attempts to establish a repertory theatre met with poor support. For three happy years, 1921 to 1923, I used to trudge over the hill to Hyson Green, where, in the tatty old Grand Theatre, Fay Compton's mother with her other two daughters, Viola and Ellen, made a gallant effort to do for Nottingham what 'Queen Horniman' had done for Dublin and Manchester. In vain. Little did I know, as I went out into the night starry-eyed and elated, that no theatre could survive on a schoolboy's rapture. The money Edward Compton had left lasted just those three years. Then the curtain came down and never rose again.

Yet it was not all waste. That premature pioneering must have sown seeds, contributed something to create the public of the future. Nottingham developed an amateur movement with good technical standards. The Co-operative Society provided a theatre at its arts centre in George Street. After the Second World War the time seemed ripe for a fresh attempt at establishing professional repertory, and, despite rebuffs from some quarters, the original Playhouse was opened under the direction of André van Gyseghem. He and his successors proved that good drama could also be good box-office. In the face of virulent opposition, and at one critical point only by the casting vote of the Lord Mayor, the Council was persuaded to build the present Playhouse in Wellington Circus, appropriately next door to Nottingham's own Albert Hall, where symphony concerts are held.

The designer was Peter Moro, associate architect of the Festival Hall. Inside and out, from the powerful concrete drum of the auditorium roof to the peacock-blue stalls, and from the superb backstage equipment to the lively foyers and coffee-bars glimpsed through its plate-glass front, the place is a delight. Harold Hobson, after a life-long experience of the world's theatres, judged it 'easily the best I have seen architecturally and as a functioning playhouse'. In the *Observer* Penelope Gilliatt called it 'the most exciting and hospitable piece of theatrical architecture we have'. Both the building and its productions, however, while winning national acclaim, continue to excite violent counter-emotions locally. Opening it in 1963, on behalf of Princess Margaret who was unwell, Lord Snowdon wished the Playhouse 'not only many artistic and commercial triumphs but many fierce arguments'. In the years that followed, especially the John Neville period, all those wishes were fulfilled.

Fortunately Nottingham can laugh at itself. This was nowhere better demonstrated than in the revue, *'Owd Yer Tight*, written by a local journalist, Emrys Bryson, and staged at the 1965 Arts Festival, when it was enjoyed by a first-night audience including the Lord Mayor, Jennie Lee, Minister for the Arts, and the chairman of the Arts Council. This revue set out to satirize with Aristophanic irreverence the very community that was paying for it to be put on. The script is a gallimaufry of gleanings, contrasting recent public utterances with echoes from the town's ancient records. Every aspect of local life came under disrespectful scrutiny, especially the pretensions of authority, and no controversy, even those raging round the theatre itself, was avoided as too tricky to be spot-lit on the public stage.

Here the tradition of Nottingham protest was seen to be alive and kicking, though with no heads broken and no need to call out the Dragoons. Along with protest there was pure good-humour, and the swinging lyrics showed that a people's inborn gaiety can survive even the Industrial Revolution. One number ran:

> I met him at the Goosefair when autumn mist did cling.
> He took me on the roundabouts, he took me on a swing,
> He said he would be true to me.
> Oh, it was all so new to me!
> He stroked my hair and bought for me a monkey on a string.
>> He was working on the Goosefair,
>> The Goosefair, the Goosefair.
>> He was working on the Goosefair
>> In Nottingham that day.

The couple try the dodgem cars, the helter-skelter, the ghost train and the mighty wheel, and the girl is given gingerbread, chips and peas, a sugar mouse, a chocolate cat and a stick of candy floss, after which the song concludes convincingly:

> I met him at the Goosefair when autumn mist lay thick.
> He held my hand, he hugged me tight, and then he kissed me
>> quick.
> And as the lights were growing dim,
> He begged of me to marry him
> And ride upon Love's Roundabout for ever. I WAS SICK.

The same brand of unsentimental high spirits enlivened Gilbert Macklam's 'Ballad of Nottingham', the refrain hammering home the title of the whole revue:

> I'll sing you a song of Nottingham, a city of great renown,
> Famed far and near for the many pretty girls who wander
>> round the town.
> But perchance you meet in a city street a beauty in blue jeans
>> clad,
> Have a care, young sir, and beware of her –
> She may be a long-haired lad . . .
>> Oh, 'owd yer tight in the middle of the night, is what the
>> busmen say.

Later verses traverse the Market Square, the boating-lake at Highfields, and the Trent Bridge cricket ground. The ballad ends:

I'll sing you a song of Nottingham, a city of great renown,
Famed far and near for the many thirsty girls who wander
  round the town.
So perchance you meet in a city street a girl who says she's
  lost her key,
Then invite her in and fill her up with gin –
Ten to one she'll be me . . .
  Oh, 'owd yer tight in the middle of the night, is what the
    busmen say.

It is all rather different from the Robin Hood ballads, but it carries the authentic tang of twentieth-century Nottingham. I think it would have gone down very well with those lusty outlaws, huddled round their camp-fires long ago.

CHAPTER NINETEEN

Today – and Tomorrow

THIS book began with some nostalgic wanderings round the city I knew as a boy. Now, after many months of research and writing, after countless conversations and questions and systematic visits to look at this and that, I must try to see the place unsentimentally as it is today, and to guess, with whatever forebodings, what it may be like by the end of the century.

I ended that first chapter standing pensively at the foot of Feargus O'Connor's statue in the Arboretum. Looking round that eminently Victorian park and the houses bordering it, I could not see much obvious change after fifty years. Where was that visionary transformation of the whole surrounding area, the Civic Centre projected by the Reconstruction Committee as long ago as 1943, much to the disgust of my mother, who thought the war bad enough, without any additional nonsense? She need not have worried. There is no sign yet, nor likely to be for a few years longer, I am told, of the new roads, public hall, health centre, library, museum and other amenities planned to replace the quiet little world she knew. Only the towering College of Technology to the south, and the demolition of some villas near by, show that the plans have not been shelved. The College is reaching out to meet the College of Art and Design, next to the park gates, and their union will produce one of the giant national polytechnics, covering thirty acres. That, incidentally, is just two-and-a-half times the area of the Arboretum itself, which seemed in childhood large enough for every kind of exploration and adventure.

The old Chartist firebrand who in life looked to the future now faces in the wrong direction. There are other high points in the park and from these I could see plenty of changes on the skyline. It is a platitude now to say that the towns of Britain, and the world, become daily more alike. Similar cranes are silhouetted menacingly against every sky, and when they go they leave behind them much the same standardized hunks of prestigious modern architecture. 'For its size,' the *Times* property correspondent assures me, 'few places can match the redevelopment activity of Nottingham. . . . Nottingham sets the pace.' Should we cheer, or groan?

Nevertheless, walking its streets, I find many of the buildings I remember and, though perhaps a shop-front has been redesigned, a familiar name in new lettering. But it does not take long to discover that, even behind an unaltered façade of Victorian individuality, a stealthy transformation has been at work. 'Of course, you know they've been taken over by So-and-so's in London, now?' In the heart of the town I believe only one department store remains under local ownership, though the main bookseller and a wine merchant preserve their independence. They are not typical. And as with shops, so it has been with industry. The big concerns mostly get sucked into bigger, nation-wide combines. Luckily, in a town of such multifarious trades, there is still scope for the man with ideas. But in time the dilemma arises: if he does not expand his business he cannot survive, and if he does he becomes worth taking over. The age of the local tycoon, whether tyrant or philanthropist, has passed, and with it one of the ingredients that gave nineteenth-century towns their distinctive flavour.

My eye lights on a name-plate. 'The East Midlands Regional Board' for something or other. I realize how much worse this process is for the life of the smaller places. What London has done to Nottingham, Nottingham has done in some respects to neighbouring towns, absorbing and amalgamating, streamlining and computerizing, concentrating responsibility and initiative. This is the centripetal modern society we are creating everywhere. Nottingham, by sheer size and geographical position, is an inevitable choice for a regional centre, and until all England is

engulfed by London suburbia these major provincial cities are
sure to count for something. But this sort or relative importance
is a poor exchange for the authentic personality such towns used
to have.

Is there much local pride today?

I asked numerous people. I found a general feeling that it did
still exist, especially in sport, but it was otherwise weak among
the young. Perhaps, it was suggested, we had been too smug in
the past. Half-a-century ago we boasted that our city was 'Queen
of the Midlands'. Now, when it is much closer to becoming a
kind of regional capital, at least for the East Midlands, the phrase
is less used.

Today's mobility of labour blights the growth of civic
patriotism. One famous national group of stores says of its young
future managers: 'A typical trainee could expect to move his
home six times in the ten years normally looked on as the training
period.' Few young people consciously want to stay where they
were born and grew up, even fewer give thought to where they
will finally settle. In the event, many do stay in Nottingham
because there are plenty of varied jobs and technical training
available. The region is prosperous now and likely to remain so.
'If ever', proclaimed a *Sunday Times* pundit recently, 'an area
were destined geographically and commercially to boom, it was
the East Midlands, centred on the golden triangle of Nottingham,
Leicester and Derby.' I hope he is right, and that at least it will
never be unemployment that impels young people to get out of
Nottingham.

But with the ambitious and above-average intelligent minority
it is a different matter, and they after all are the ones who down
the ages have given cities their distinctive development. Looking
at old school photographs brings home to me how things have
changed. Of my contemporaries only a few went to a university.
In practice that meant Oxford or Cambridge. One or two contented themselves with Redbrick, but if you could not get to
Oxford, Cambridge or at a pinch Durham, there seemed little
point in going further than the University College in Shakespeare

Street. So, yearly, this handful of bright boys went off, became schoolmasters, parsons, civil servants, industrial chemists, and so forth, and except for holidays most of them never came back: a doctor's son might return and join his father in practice, but in general, as nowadays, a graduate was lost to the community that had produced him. A brain-drain of that modest volume did not matter. It was offset by the fertilizing influx of other young professional men who settled in the city and came to feel that it was their own. Meantime, scores of equally bright or even brighter boys never considered a university. They were articled to solicitors or accountants in the town, they entered the family business, they found 'openings' (as we used to say) with the big industrial concerns, or they went into local government, meaning the government of their native city. And mostly they married local girls, and a cynic would say, 'That was the end of that, how dreary!' but in fact it was not necessarily the end of anything, but rather the beginning of a new cycle in the life of the community, no more unhealthy or monotonous than the reappearance of green leaves in spring.

Today it is all quite different and, we are assured, much better.

There are far more bright boys, but far fewer bright fathers owning a business to bequeath. Every boy and girl above a certain (fairly modest) level of ability is hounded on by his teachers to compete for a university place. Faced with a bewildering list of names, the groves of Academe having now proliferated into a jungle of Amazonian proportions, any self-respecting candidate starts by eliminating the university lovingly endowed by his forefathers for his benefit and for the intellectual enrichment of the neighbourhood. The grants system offers scant temptation to save other people's money by attending his local foundation and living at home. Some homes, it must be admitted in fairness, do not offer much temptation either. And the temptations in the other direction are overpowering. So the would-be student applies to a seat of learning as far from his parents as possible. This, the educationists tell us, guarantees him the chance to study without interruption and to develop a sense of responsibility.

It may well be so. I am not concerned here to argue about

university education, only to state the effects of the system, as I see them, upon a local community. In a community like Nottingham, which itself possesses a university, they seem to be two-fold.

From each generation of boys and girls the cream is scooped off and spread through universities all over the country. After graduating, few return to work in their native city. This was always so, and natural, but in earlier days plenty of cream was never taken away.

Conversely, the local university, built up not only by millionaires but by less opulent idealists whose efforts meant personal sacrifice, may now be a finer academic institution than they dared to foresee, but its roots in the community may be shallower than they intended. Of course, the existence of a university *as* an institution and of its staff as a cultural leaven in the region are of undeniable, probably incalculable, value. Highfields is an important centre for conferences and activities of many kinds. Concerts, plays and art exhibitions are put on there from time to time which might find no place elsewhere in the area, and there are evening lectures with free transport provided from the middle of the city. Both collectively and individually, too, the academic colony makes its contribution and involves itself in the wider world outside the campus. To give only one instance: the early struggles of the Playhouse attracted the keen personal support of the then Vice-Chancellor. But it is the students we are concerned with at the moment.

I talk to a young man from the other side of England. How often does he go into the town? Roughly once a week. Some of his friends go less often. Does he know any students whose homes are in Nottingham? One or two – but of course they live in hall. I form the impression of thousands of young people, swarming to Highfields from distant places, inhabiting the hilltop for a few years, and then dispersing, with virtually no effect upon themselves or upon the city from this purely geographical connection. Was this in Jesse Boot's mind when he revisited the site and dreamed his dream? If not, does it matter? To the life of the city I believe it may.

More and more the country, we are continually told, is going to be run by graduates, its commerce, industries and public services no less than the old learned professions. Nottingham will presumably attract the graduates it needs. But I can see no reason to hope that more than a tiny proportion will be either natives, returning with fruitful experience outside, of Nottingham graduates, who have spent formative student years in the city, learned to like it, and chosen it as their future home. Far more probably, the managerial and professional posts will be filled by their contemporaries from elsewhere, who have never clapped eyes on Nottingham before the day of the interview – always supposing that the interview is held in Nottingham at all. Now it is perfectly true that a person of any age *can* fall in love with a new place, identify himself with it, and make a rich contribution to its life. There have been many examples in the history of this and other towns. I think at once of Deering in the eighteenth century and the foreign lace merchants of the nineteenth. It would be over-optimistic to expect this as a rule. More typically, the young newcomer will have parents at one end of England, in-laws at the other, and his deepest friendships anywhere. All these influences will draw his interest away from the locality in which he earns his living. The result could be a managerial and professional class which literally 'has no time' for local politics and cultural enterprises. Yet in days gone by the leadership and participation of this class were indispensable, even though some of the initiative and pressure came from the sturdy self-educated working men. And today that second category has gone with the wind of social progress: the modern equivalent of the Chartist or frame-workers' leader has been absorbed among the graduates and is as thoroughly uprooted as the rest of them.

This is the age not only of the computer but of the commuter. 'It doesn't matter where you live,' people say, 'so long as the roads are right.' They comb the countryside for redundant rectories and paired cottages that can be knocked into one. Towards the end of the working-day their thoughts turn increasingly to the beating of the rush-hour jam at Trent Bridge and, if it is winter, to the possibility of one of those bleak, acrid mists that come wreathing up from the river and make Nottingham the foggiest town in Britain. Once snugly home at Bingham or Edwalton, Keyworth or Cotgrave, or even at Southwell or Newark, which is twenty miles away, few will return gladly to participate in the activities of the city. Who can blame them? This, on a smaller scale, is the pattern of life established by London and the Home Counties, and reflected in conurbations everywhere.

Nottingham is still fortunate, however, in that not everyone needs to commute from a distance in order to live in an agreeable setting. There is the leafy valley of the Park, within minutes of the Market Place. There are houses along the Trent embankments. There are the estates bordering the deer park at Wollaton and other green spaces such as Woodthorpe. None of these is more than two or three miles from the city-centre, and in years to come there is a good chance that the centre itself will come to life again as a partly residential area. Along with the inevitable new shops and offices, multi-storey car-parks, bus-stations and the like, there will be hundreds of flats, certainly on the old Victoria Station site and perhaps elsewhere. The unhappily notorious St Ann's Ward begins only a few minutes' walk beyond the Victoria site. Its final clearance is confidently expected by the end of 1976 and it will be a poor tale if, after all the outcry, the new homes that replace its slums are not designed to create a pleasant neighbourhood, housing twelve or thirteen thousand instead of the present twenty thousand.

In such schemes I can see some hope that a healthy life will be kept going in the city, and that its historic centre will not ossify each evening, when Little John strikes six, into silent blocks of shops and offices.

A little way from O'Connor's statue I could see, through the leafless branches fringing the park, the corner of Portland Road where I grew up and my mother lived for thirty years. Our old house was bought by a Pole and turned into flats.

There have been a lot of Poles in Nottingham since the Second World War. There are about a thousand Ukrainians too, and enough Latvians and Lithuanians to maintain their distinctive social organizations. The Ukrainians have their own youth club and a group of dancers who are much in demand. These people are probably more settled in Nottingham now than many English arrivals from other districts. They have, after all, less choice. There is a church where an Italian priest says Mass each week, but the Italians in the town, like the Spaniards, are more likely to be temporary residents, working in the hotels and restaurants. There is a strong Irish section, some more permanently settled than others. They have a club near the Roman Catholic cathedral.

But of course it is the coloured immigrants who catch the eye – the Indian taxi-driver who runs me up to Sherwood from the Market Place, the courteous Jamaican bus-conductor who momentarily shocks me by charging for my grip. I cannot recall ever paying even for the biggest suitcase shoved under the stairs. Then I reflect that it is probably laid down somewhere in the small-print regulations. The chirpy local-born conductors know which rules to enforce and which to forget about. If you come from Jamaica, you cannot afford to put a foot wrong.

There are about ten thousand West Indians, five thousand Indians and Pakistanis. That means roughly one coloured person for every twenty in the city, and presumably a higher proportion among the children and the age-groups at work. There is a Sikh temple in the Meadows, there are Indian films on Sunday mornings at a cinema in Derby Road, and the enterprising Chinese, not content with running their own national restaurants, have entered the fish-and-chip trade. Some hairdressing-salons now specialize in the technical problems presented by the kinky coiffure. Ordinary little corner-shops find it worth while to carry new lines in Oriental foodstuffs as well as continental delicatessen. There is no clearly demarcated coloured quarter, though some areas, like St Ann's, have many more West Indians and Asians than others.

They are seen mainly in transport jobs, hospital work, and manual occupations, not many yet in the big shops and offices, though some have their own small shops and restaurants, and in time no doubt they will appear as stall-holders in the Central

Market. The first generation have to fight prejudice and also to surmount more reasonable obstacles. Thus, a Sikh teacher arrived some years ago, whose professional qualifications were held, not unfairly, to be insufficient for a post in an English school. Undeterred, Mr J. S. Dosanjh became a bus-driver, then acquired a taxi, and proceeded to take a Nottingham B.A. and thereafter an M.Ed., submitting a highly relevant thesis on the adjustment problems of Punjabi children in the town. At the time of writing, he is teaching in a Nottingham school and thinking about a Ph.D. Such a case may be rare but it is real.

The city's racial structure has clearly altered radically in recent years, but the quality of its life has not necessarily declined. There is talk of 'threatened standards'. It would be odd if some of those standards came in fact to be reinforced by, for example, Asians bringing back that respect for parental authority and the family unit which has become so unfashionable among the English-born. And the Jamaicans, it is worth remembering, scored not too badly in the survey of St Ann's.

Perhaps this admixture of widely varied stocks, with mother-tongues ranging from Urdu to Ukrainian, will be seen in time to have given the old city a much-needed transfusion of vitality, offsetting those other tendencies that threaten it with an anaemic uniformity.

If new arrivals, whether from another continent or even the next county, are to become citizens in every sense and not just reluctant ratepayers, they must somehow be made to feel that they belong, and that is not easy as the manageable communities of the past swell into conurbations. I used to smile when my mother laid down the paper after a fruitless perusal of the Births, Marriages and Deaths, complaining that Nottingham was getting too big and she did not know people as once she did. The population being then about a quarter of a million, I thought her complaint somewhat belated, but I see now that there was something in it. We are mostly agreed that there are too many people in the world and in Britain – and that goes for Nottingham too.

'The paper', to my parents, was the *Nottingham Guardian*, a staid Conservative morning paper combining national with local news, thus enabling the solid burgesses, if they wished, to dispense with the more sensational sheets published in the metropolis. There was a rival daily, the Liberal *Nottingham Journal*, and each had an evening paper as running-mate, while a weekly, the *Nottinghamshire Guardian*, enabled the news to be summarized in one issue, with some more leisurely literary features, and due emphasis on county matters, with an eye to busy country readers and nostalgic emigrants in Sydney or Saskatoon. Now the rivals are amalgamated into one morning and one evening paper, and the weekly has ceased. It is something of an achievement to retain even one morning paper against the competition of the London giants, who themselves from time to time devour their weaker brethren. The *Guardian Journal* is now one of a mere handful of provincial organs of this type and its circulation is modest, though perhaps influential. Fortunately it is buttressed by the *Nottingham Evening Post and News* with an immense readership: it really does seem to go into almost every home in the city and to be bought in the small towns over a wide area. If the ordinary citizen declares that he has 'seen it in the paper', this is now the paper he means. Neither radio nor television news bulletins threaten its popularity, nor the fact that London is near enough by fast train to bombard the city, if it seemed worth while, with bundles of its own evening papers, as it does many other provincial towns. This at least is a healthy sign. So popular a medium offers great opportunities for giving a region coherence and its people a sense of identity. I have heard it complained that these opportunities could sometimes be seized more boldly, and that the local press should not be content so often merely to report controversies but should offer a lead.

What in earlier days might have seemed a dangerous monopoly is now broken by television and radio services. On a regional basis Nottingham has been unfortunate. Neither the B.B.C. nor I.T.V. recognizes the meaninglessness of the term. 'the Midlands', with the result that under both authorities the big eastern cities, Nottingham and Leicester, have been poor relations in a disunited family dominated by Birmingham. They thus receive precisely the same 'Midland' news and features as I do myself, living within sight of the Welsh mountains. As a sop to Nottingham's dignity, it possesses a small television studio from which East Midland speakers can broadcast without travelling to Birmingham, but this does not increase the city's share of programme time. The whole future of regional radio is now in grave doubt.

Radio Nottingham, on the other hand, with its pleasant jingly call-sign and perky local voices, was one of the first stations established to serve really small areas. It is too early yet to judge the experiment. Such stations operate on a shoe-string, which makes it hard to avoid an amateurish flavour in some of the material and those who broadcast it. There are manifest possibilities in a regular programme such as 'What are they up to now?' devoted to the shortcomings of officialdom and other grievances, heartening evidence that the citizens have not lost their traditional love of protest. No less encouraging, but in a quite different way, was the response to talks giving personal reminiscences of the town, 'If I remember right', and a series on local history, with excellently illustrated accompanying booklets, which indicated that the man in the street *can* take an interest in his street, especially if it is an old one. Radio stations like these, serving a single community, could do a lot to bind that community together and strengthen an awareness of itself as a social organism.

I suppose this is what we want? At all events, when we plan new homes, we pay lip-service to the idea – and money too, for centres and whole-time organizers – in an attempt to synthesize a community spirit out of thin air. If we cannot keep it alive in the old towns where it has flourished naturally for a thousand years, I would not give much for our chances in the new.

What will Nottingham be like by the end of the century? Its external appearance is not too difficult to imagine, if present plans are carried out. Even the massive recent buildings, the high-rise developments at Balloon Wood and Hyson Green and elsewhere, will not disguise the immemorial undulations of the land. The Castle (unless Arthur Seaton gets under it with his explosives) will remain a conspicuous landmark on its rock. The Trent, a cleaner Trent, will still trace its curly course around the southern edge. It will have to be cleaner, because soon the citizens will be drinking it as well as the clear water from the Derbyshire moors which used to meet our needs. New crossings will relieve the existing bottle-necks at Trent Bridge and Clifton—or such is the pious hope: there might, of course, be new traffic as well, creating new bottle-necks. But at least the City Engineer has done his best, producing a plan for the whole network of primary roads likely to be needed in the early years of the twenty-first century, if our descendants are not to be demented. There will be urban motorways and multi-level junctions, swirling and convoluting, but also, we are promised, pedestrian precincts where it should be possible to stroll with an insouciance unknown since the first stage-coach came lurching over the cobbles. Down-stream, in the lee of Colwick's bosky hump, where the race-course runs, there will be a vast sports and amusement centre, facing another, now projected by the county at Holme Pierrepont, on the opposite side of the river.

I find it a not unpleasant vision. I only wish I could see more clearly the shadowy figures moving against the architectural background so confidently sketched in.

It is certainly going to be a big city. Can it be a great one? I believe that, with an effort, it could be. But those are the people, not I, who will need to believe – and to act on their belief.

Select Bibliography

J. Bramley, *Short History of Plumptre Hospital* (Nottingham, 1946)

Emrys Bryson, *'Owd Yer Tight* (Nottingham, 1967)

J. D. Chambers, *Modern Nottingham in the Making* (Nottingham, 1945)

—, *Nottinghamshire in the Eighteenth Century* (Nottingham, 1932)

J. D. Chambers et al., *A Century of Nottingham History, 1851–1951* (Nottingham, 1952)

Roy A. Church, *Economic and Social Change in a Midland Town: Victorian Nottingham 1815–1900* (1966)

City of Nottingham Official Handbook, ed. J. Burrow (n.d.)

Ken Coates and Richard Silburn, *St Ann's: Poverty, Deprivation and Morals in a Nottingham Community* (Nottingham, 1967)

Guy Denison, *This Is Your Nottingham* (3rd ed., Nottingham, n.d.)

East Midlands Economic Planning Council, *The East Midlands Study* (1966)

K. C. Edwards, *Nottingham and Its Region* (1966)

A. Gilbert, *Recollections of Old Nottingham* (Nottingham, 1904)

Duncan Gray, *Nottingham, Settlement to City* (Nottingham, 1953)

—, *Nottingham through 500 Years: a Short History of Town Government* (Nottingham, 1949)

Alice Stopford Green, *Town Life in the Fifteenth Century* (1894)

T. C. Hine, *Nottingham, Its Castle, etc.* (Nottingham, 1876)

Historic Towns, Maps and Plans, Earliest Times to 1800, ed. M. D. Lobel (1969)

Lucy Hutchinson, *Memoirs of Colonel Hutchinson* (1806)

The Journeys of Celia Fiennes, ed. Christopher Morris (1947)

Maurice Keen, *The Outlaws of Medieval Legend* (1961)

Laura Knight, *The Magic of a Line* (1965)

—, *Oil Paint and Grease Paint* (1936)

Robert Mellors, *Old Nottingham Suburbs: Then and Now* (Nottingham, 1914)

Harry T. Moore, *The Intelligent Heart: the Story of D. H. Lawrence* (1955)

Nikolaus Pevsner, *The Buildings of England: Nottinghamshire* (Harmondsworth, 1951)

Stanley Pigott, *Hollins: a Study of Industry 1784–1949* (Nottingham, 1949)

Cecil Roberts, *The Growing Boy* (1967)

—, *The Years of Promise* (1968)

A. W. Thomas, *A History of Nottingham High School* (Nottingham, 1957)

Malcolm I. Thomis, *Old Nottingham* (Newton Abbot, 1968)

A. C. Wood, *A History of Nottinghamshire* (Nottingham, 1947)

—, *A History of the University College, Nottingham* (Oxford, 1953)

Map-minded readers may like to know that the $2\frac{1}{2}$ inch (1:25,000) Ordnance Survey map covers Nottingham on sheets SK 43–4, 53–4, 63–4.

Index